LSE ON
EQUALITY

LSE ON
EQUALITY

EDITED BY MEGHNAD DESAI

LSE
BOOKS

First published 1995
in LSE Books
by the Academic Publications Committee
The London School of Economics & Political Science
Houghton Street, London WC2A 2AE

British Library Cataloguing in Publication Data
A catalogue record for this book is available from the British Library

Phototypeset and printed in the UK by Intype
Wimbledon Park
London SW19 8DR

Cover design by Andrew Holmes
Typography by Sarah Dyson

ISBN 0 7530 1045 3

Contents

Meghnad Desai

Introduction

This book, written on the occasion of the centenary of the LSE, is a collection by writers associated with the LSE over the last hundred years and concerns the broad theme of equality. There are few direct debates in it, but over the years a debate went on inside the LSE which was very much a reflection of, and a pacesetter for, the debate about equality going on in the wider society. There is no set LSE line on equality: there were as many people for it as against it and within each 'camp' as many variants of definition of equality as there were writers.

The criterion for inclusion, apart from the quality of the thought expressed, is that the writer must have been a teacher or in some other way associated with the LSE for a long enough period to be identified with the LSE. I have not tried to achieve complete coverage by way of departments, and many important pieces on the subject written by people who were not at the LSE, or did not write their seminal pieces while at LSE, have been left out. I have also not tried to revisit some of the issues covered – for example, measurement of inequality in Dalton's piece – by including the more recent work. Much of this work is highly technical and, except for one piece by Dalton, I have tried also to make the collection as accessible as possible.

There are, of course, the classics. Tawney on equality, from which I have taken two essays. The first Professor of Economics at the LSE was Edwin Cannan who, as will be seen from Dalton's piece included here, was very influential in making people think about inequality seriously. But he tried to understand inequality in a strictly economic theoretic framework, as will be seen from the extract I have included on equality between the sexes, surely one of the early discussions in economics. Then there is the seminal work of Lionel Robbins, with its attack on utilitarianism, which was supposed to provide an economic theoretic rationale for equalising redistribution of incomes. Contemporary with

Tawney and Cannan is the raw and biting diatribe from the Webbs, 'The Decay of Capitalist Civilisation'.

LSE also has a pioneering tradition in the statistical and quantitative treatment of social issues. It is in this spirit that the piece by Hugh Dalton on measurement of equality is included. It is a mathematical piece, but it was also central in the new developments in the area, when interest in equality revived in the 1960s and 1970s.[1]

There was always a strong *anti-egalitarian* philosophical tendency at the LSE. Robbins and Hayek in the Economics department, and Oakshott in the Government department were its exemplars. There is thus a batch of writings against equality in a book of readings of that name edited by William Letwin who was at the LSE for many years in the Government department. This collection includes a piece by the economist Lord Bauer as well as by John Charvet, who has been at the LSE for much of his career, and by Letwin himself.

But besides the economists, the political theorists and the socialists, LSE also has other social sciences. The Malinowski Lecture by James Woodburn, reproduced here, shows the possibility of egalitarian arrangements in 'simple' societies. By going into the necessary details of how the egalitarian arrangements are asserted and sustained, Woodburn perhaps illustrates, by negation as it were, how difficult the notion of equality can be to define, much less assert and achieve in modern societies.

Tawney, whose piece appears at the beginning, is of course one of the most gifted writers in the English language, and his moral outrage against the privileged society that he saw around him in the 1920s is almost palpable. The period is interesting because although the LSE started in 1895 and the Fabians were socialists, much of the debate on equality seems to have erupted after the First World War. In Tawney's writing the feudal aristocratic world of Edwardian England is still very much alive. In those days 1 per cent of the adult population owned 60 per cent of the personal wealth of Great Britain and 10 per cent owned more than 90 per cent.[2] It had always been thus. Indeed, reconstructing the wealth data as far as they would go back, Peter Lindert, whose work is quoted by Charles Feinstein in the piece already cited, has found that between 1670 and 1925 the share of the top 5 per cent stayed between 80 and 90 per cent with very little change.

Of course, numbers are never simple. Definitions and measurements are very tricky in this highly sensitive area, and some of the later essays deal with such problems.[3] But it is remarkable that starting soon after the first edition of *Equality*, which appeared in 1931, wealth distribution began to get less unequal. Thus the share of the top 1 per cent in total personal wealth (excluding pension rights) fell from 61 per cent in 1923 to 18 per cent in 1989. Much of this wealth only went, however, to the next 9 or 19 per cent. Thus the top 10 per cent share shrank from 89 per cent to only 53 per cent. But of course the 1989 figure was a reversal from the steady downward trend up to 1976 when it had dropped to 50 per cent.

It is this trend downwards and indeed its reversal during the years when Mrs Thatcher was Prime Minister that forms the background to this collection. Egalitarianism was taken for granted as a crusading philosophy at the time Tawney was writing and for fifty years later. Those who did not agree with egalitarian distribution were on the defensive and even when their arguments were incisive (for example, as in the case of Lionel Robbins) their impact on policy or political debate was limited. Those who were against egalitarianism were *conservative*. It was only in the 1960s and 1970s that a *radical* defence of inequality emerged and William Letwin's long piece, which appeared as an introduction to his collection *Against Equality*, illustrates this reversal. Mrs Thatcher had intellectual ammunition prepared for her in the many libertarian and radical right think tanks.

Tawney and Letwin represent the two ends of the debate. One is a moral argument against inequality and the other is a philosophical defence of it. One may almost say that the 'Religion of Inequality' which Tawney excoriates reappears sixty years later as the 'Philosophy of Inequality'. On the one hand, the argument is that inequality is socially created and tolerated but is harmful to the poor and corrupting to the rich. The inegalitarians regard incomes as the outcome of an unintended economic process which in the course of production generates an income outcome that reflects initial endowments of wealth and personal capabilities and which, if interfered with, will adversely affect total income and may indeed also compromise liberty and the quality of life. Indeed the inegalitarians come close to regarding the income outcome as *natural*, not in the biological or genetic sense – as they have been much misunderstood to have done – but in the sense in which economists since Knut Wicksell have used the word; as an equilibrium outcome of the decentralised decisions of thousands of individuals. This is the sense in which the term 'Natural Rate of Unemployment' has been used in recent days.[4]

But even economists in those early days were arguing for an egalitarian distribution. Alfred Marshall and A. C. Pigou, the two Cambridge economists who no doubt influenced Hugh Dalton, had argued for a redistributive policy on the basis of the Law of Diminishing Marginal Utility. This law said that the more one has of anything, less is an extra addition worth in terms of utility. This doctrine is explained in non-technical terms in the first of the two contributions by Hugh Dalton included here. Dalton rehearses the arguments for lesser inequality, recognising full well that complete equality may cause more harm than good. The notion of equality of outcomes is suitably distinguished from the equality of opportunity and the conflict between efficiency and equity is also discussed. This conflict is not one that can be *resolved*, but it can be clearly debated. Dalton also introduces considerations of fairness and justice, never far away from the debates on equality; and once we speak of fairness, any hope of unanimity or 'scientific' agreement disappears.

This is seen in John Charvet's piece, where he criticises the work of Rawls which had not then appeared in the form of the book *A Theory of Justice*, which became justly famous and influential in the 1970s, but of an earlier article in which the essence of the Rawlsian position was captured.[5] Charvet makes the cogent point that to treat people as equal *a priori* requires the removal of all the social relationships within which (unequal) societies are embedded. The 'State of Nature' device (here we go again with the intrusion of *nature*, this time on the side of the egalitarians) is, according to Charvet, a means of desocialising individuals to make it easier to argue for equality. But if equality requires desocialising the context then, Charvet argues, the argument cannot be used to govern social relations or social policy.

The Webbs will have none of this. In their contribution, it is eloquently argued that inequality of income and wealth vitiates the economic, social and political freedoms that people are supposed to enjoy in modern societies. They take the argument beyond the normal economic ones by questioning the legitimacy of authority, say of managers, and argue for an industrial democracy in the workplace. The title of the book from which this extract is taken, *The Decay of Capitalist Civilisation*, reflects the pessimism and the anger which the Webbs must have felt by the end of the First World War. Liberalism had failed in their views, since it only cared about freedom of property, that is, the propertied. The time had come to move on to equality, which was for the rest, that is, the bottom 90 per cent who owned 10 per cent of personal wealth. In modern parlance the Webbs make the point that in order to have equal outcomes, it is not enough to have formal equality, say as before the law, but it may require unequal allocations and positive discriminations if we start from the initial premise of endowments of wealth being unequal. Sen has recently made this point very forcefully.[6]

By the time Peter Bauer comes to write of *The Grail of Equality*, much has changed. Indeed, citing Tocqueville, he argues that equality matters so much precisely because there is so much of it about. The smaller the differences the more people fuss about them. Whether the fact that the top 10 per cent owned 50 per cent by 1976 is too little inequality or too much is obviously a matter of political philosophy if not of taste. Bauer not only argues that income outcomes are determined by economic rationality but advances the criticism that the New Right fashioned of the welfare state: that its tax/transfer mechanism was *unequalising*. This attack on the welfare state as the outdoor relief for the middle classes became very powerful and considerably unhinged the traditional left in its unswerving support of the welfare state. Thus the naturalness of the unequal outcomes and the perversity of attempts to interfere with any such natural arrangement – the twin pillars of the inegalitarian critique – become clear here.

But inequality could lie in the eyes of the beholder, not just because of philosophical preferences but perhaps because it has been badly defined and measured. What does it mean to say that situation A is more unequal than situation B? Hugh Dalton's second contribution is justly famous since much of the new literature on the measurement of inequality[7] starts from Dalton's article. The piece is technical (perhaps the most technical of any written by anyone who later became the Chancellor of the Exchequer!) but it clarifies a number of problems. The essence of the argument, however, appears in fairly easy prose at the outset. Let me quote it fully:

Let us assume, as is reasonable in a preliminary discussion, that the economic welfare of different persons is additive, that the relation of income to economic welfare is the same for all members of the community, and that, for each individual, marginal economic welfare diminishes as income increases. Then, if a given income is to be distributed among a number of persons, it is evident that economic welfare will be a maximum when all incomes are equal.[8]

There you have the essential economic argument for an egalitarian redistributive policy. The rest of Dalton is a hard slog through some interesting issues on the measurement of income inequality. Now, though much more work has been done on the properties of such measures, and so on, the assumptions stated so clearly by Dalton have not been much relaxed.

This is precisely where Lionel Robbins makes his classic attack on the utilitarian argument for greater equality. People's utilities or welfare are *not additive* unless you assume them to be so. Nothing in economic theory justifies such an assumption, so that to make it is not a scientific or objective exercise but a normative judgment by the economist making it, with which other economists, who may well accept utility theory, may disagree. While each of us has a diminishing marginal utility from income, the levels of utility obtained by us are not comparable and hence not commensurable and certainly not additive. This attack on the *interpersonal comparability of utility* became the cause of a lot of writing in what was then called new welfare economies. Robbins for ever removed the idea that economic *experts* could decide on distributional issues on the basis of objective scientific theories. Egalitarianism is a political doctrine, a philosophical one, but not a matter of science.

The devastating effect of the Robbins's critique on the redistributive programme of old welfare economics is difficult to exaggerate. Solutions proposed by Kaldor and Scitovsky, who were also at the LSE in the 1930s, proposed criteria for evaluating aggregate gains and losses from any proposed policy change, for example, the repeal of corn laws or, say, the reform of the Common Agricultural Policy. But this ignored Robbins's basic objection about interpersonal comparisons and substituted the implicit notion that similarly affected people – gainers or losers

– could be bunched together and a money comparison could be made as between the magnitudes of the gain and the loss. In some cases a policy move could be justified on the 'political utilitarian' grounds that the majority favoured such a move. But within twenty years of Robbins's critique, Arrow's work on social choice showed, much to the dismay of political majoritarians, that majority rule failed to satisfy a minimal set of rationality conditions.[9] The revival of interest in the measurement of inequality which was pioneered by Tony Atkinson, Amartya Sen and others, proceeds in my view by adopting Dalton's assumptions, albeit in a better mathematical language but also by ignoring the Robbins critique.

The point is not that redistributive policies cannot be pursued but after Robbins the authority of the science of economics could not be claimed for such policies. Robbins put the arguments for and against equality back to where they belong in the realm of value judgments. In this way the arguments for inegalitarianism which aim for scientific certainty are no less false than those for equality. It is an area in which one may clarify and highlight the disagreements but one cannot resolve all differences. Thus there is no scientific argument either way that egalitarian policies will harm growth or well-being. Research can be cited on either side. Nor is it valid to argue as some 'naturalists' have done, that economic/market outcomes being unintended are somehow beyond correction.

It is in this light that the last two essays should be read. James Woodburn, as an anthropologist, shows how egalitarian societies not only can exist but do. These are simple hunter-gatherer societies. But not all hunter-gatherer societies are egalitarian. So it is possible to ask what set of institutions and economic arrangements are required to reinforce egalitarian tendencies of a society. These are simple societies but they are not *poor* societies. The levels of well-being are quite high, and they are self-sustaining. Woodburn is also quite right to warn that he is not putting forward some technologically deterministic rule that immediate-return societies can be egalitarian and that delayed-return societies cannot be. It is just that establishing and maintaining and reinforcing equality is a complex dynamic process which requires a lot of social co-operation and cannot be left to chance or a once for all 'revolution'.

The beauty of Cannan's piece on inequality between the sexes is that the emphasis is on understanding the forces that sustain the inequality (i.e., make it an equilibrium outcome which is repeated). As one can see from the references Dalton makes to Cannan, he was interested in pursuing the equality question because, in some sense, he was an egalitarian rather than not, as compared, for example, to Robbins. So while Cannan invokes a productivity argument to explain the unequal wages of men and women he also notes the structural barriers of access to certain occupations, to education, and so on. But he also emphasises that consumer action such as boycotts can change economic outcomes. The influence of *opinion* as he calls it, or bias as we might call it today, is frequently ignored; indeed, in some work, such as that of Gary Becker, it is the person discriminating who suffers and not the one discriminated against.[10] Cannan does not take bias as given but as manipulable. He also says how spending more money on the health and nutrition of girls could have a positive effect on wage inequality. Cannan is no slave either to economic theory or to arguments about the naturalness of economic outcomes. The knowledge of science is pursued to improve the reality, not to accept it uncritically.

Notes

1. A. B. Atkinson, *The Economics of Inequality*, Oxford: Clarendon Press, 1995; A. Sen, *On Economic Inequality*. Oxford: Clarendon Press, 1975 contain detailed references to the author's own work as well as that of others.
2. C. Feinstein, 1975, 'The Equalising of Wealth'. Nuffield College, Oxford, unpublished.
3. J. Wedgwood, *The Economics of Inheritance*, London, Routledge, 1929.
4. For a recent update on the natural rate, see R. Cross (ed.), *The Natural Rate of Unemployment: Reflections on 25 Years of the Hypothesis*, London, Cambridge University Press, 1995.
5. J. Rawls, *A Theory of Justice*. Oxford: OUP, 1972.
6. A. Sen, *Reconsidering Inequality*. Oxford: Clarendon Press, 1994.
7. A. B. Atkinson, 'On The Measurement of Inequality', *Journal of Economic Theory*, Vol. 2 is justly credited for initiating this new literature.
8. H. Dalton, 'The Measurement of Inequality of Incomes', *Economic Journal*, September, 1920, pp. 348–363; H. Dalton, *Some Aspects of the Inequality of Incomes in Modern Communities*, Essay 1, 2 & 3. London: George Routledge & Sons Ltd, 1929, pp. 3–29.

9. K. J. Arrow, *Social Choice and Individual Values*, New York: John Wiley, 1951.
10. Gary Becker, *The Economics of Discrimination*, Chicago: University of Chicago Press, 1957.

R. H. Tawney

The Religion of Inequality

Discoursing some sixty years ago on the text, 'Choose equality and flee greed', Matthew Arnold observed that in England inequality is almost a religion. He remarked on the incompatibility of that attitude with the spirit of humanity, and sense of the dignity of man as man, which are the marks of a truly civilised society. 'On the one side, in fact, inequality harms by pampering; on the other by vulgarising and depressing. A system founded on it is against nature, and, in the long run, breaks down.'[1]

Much has changed since Arnold wrote, and not least what he called the Religion of Inequality. The temper which evoked his criticism, the temper which regarded violent contrasts between the circumstances and opportunities of different classes with respectful enthusiasm, as a phenomenon, not merely inevitable, but admirable and exhilarating, if by no means extinct, is no longer vociferous. Few politicians today would dwell, with Mr Lowe, on the English tradition of inequality as a pearl beyond price, to be jealously guarded against the profane. Few educationalists would seek, with Thring, the founder of the Headmasters' Conference and one of the most influential figures in the educational world of his day, to assuage the apprehension felt by the rich at the extension of education by arguing that 'the law of labour' compels the majority of children to work for wages at the age of ten, and that 'it is not possible that a class which is compelled to leave off training at ten years of age can oust, by superior intelligence, a class which is able to spend four years more in acquiring skill'. Few political thinkers would find, with Bagehot, the secret of English political institutions in the fact that they have been created by a 'deferential people'; or write, as Erskine May wrote in his *Democracy in Europe*, of the demoralisation of French society, and the paralysis of the French intellect, by the attachment of France to the bloodstained chimera of social equality; or declare, with the melancholy assurance of Lecky, that liberty and equality are irreconcilable enemies, of which the latter can triumph only at the expense of the former. When Taine published his *Notes sur l'Angleterre* in 1872, he could describe it, by contrast with France, as still haunted by the ghost of the feudal spirit, a country governed by 100,000 to 120,000 families with an income of £1,000 a year and upwards, in which 'the lord provides for the needs of his dependent, and the dependent is proud of his lord'. It is improbable that, if he analysed the English scene today, even the relentless exigencies of historical antithesis would lead him to regard it as gilded with quite the same halo of haughty benevolence and submissive gratitude.[2]

Institutions which have died as creeds sometimes continue, nevertheless, to survive as habits. If the cult of inequality as a principle and an ideal has declined with the decline of the aristocratic society of which it was the accompaniment, it is less certain, perhaps, that the loss of its sentimental credentials has so far impaired its practical influence as to empty Arnold's words of all their significance. It is true, no doubt, that, were he writing today, his emphasis and illustrations would be different. No doubt he would be less impressed by inequality as a source of torpor and stagnation, and more by inequality as a cause of active irritation, inefficiency and confusion. No doubt he would say less of great landed estates, and more of finance; less of the territorial aristocracy and the social system represented by it, and more of fortunes which, however interesting their origin, are not associated with historic names; less of the effects of entail and settlement in preventing the wider distribution of property in land, and more of the economic forces, in his day unforseen, which have led to a progressive concentration of the control of capital; less of the English reverence for birth, and more of the English worship of money and economic power. But, if he could be induced to study the statistical evidence accumulated since he wrote, it is probable that he would hail it as an unanticipated confirmation of conclusions to which, unaided by the apparatus of science, he had found his way, and, while noting with interest the inequalities which had fallen, would feel even greater astonishment at those which had survived. Observing the heightened tension between political democracy and a social system marked by sharp disparities of circumstance and education, and of the opportunities which circumstance and education confer, he would find, it may be suspected, in the history of the two generations since his essay appeared a more impressive proof of the justice of his diagnosis than it falls to the lot of most prophets to receive. 'A system founded on inequality is against nature, and, in the long run, breaks down.'

Men are rarely conscious of the quality of the air they breathe. It is natural that a later generation of Englishmen, if they admit that such criticisms may not have been without significance for the age to which they were addressed, should deny, nevertheless, that they are relevant to their own. On a question of the kind, where the sentiments of all of us are involved, we are none of us reliable witnesses. The course of wisdom, therefore, is to consult observers belonging to other nations, who are accustomed to a social climate and tradition different from our own, and who are less practised, perhaps, in the art of not letting the left side of their brain know what the right side thinks.

Anthropologists who study the institutions of primitive peoples are accustomed to devote some part of their work to a description of the curious ritual, by which, among such peoples, the gradations of the social hierarchy are preserved and emphasised. They draw a picture of the ceremonial distinctions which shelter the chiefs and their families from contact with the common herd of inferior men; of the *karakia*, the spells and incantations, by which they call down prosperity and provide employment for their followers; of the *mana*, the prerogatives of sovereignty and jurisdiction, whose infringement will cause pestilence or famine to smite the community; of the *tapus* which are designed, therefore, to protect the *mana* from being outraged by the profane. The centre of the system, they inform us, is the sanctity of class, which has a significance at once economic and religious, and the conviction that prosperity will be blighted and morality undermined if that sanctity is impaired. And this system, it seems, is so venerable and all-pervading, so hallowed by tradition and permeated with pious emotion, that not only does it seem inconceivable to its adherents that any other system should exist, but, until attention is called to it by the irreverent curiosity of strangers, they are often not even conscious of the fact of its existence.

Not all communities are so fortunate as to become the subject of sociological investigation. The world is large and anthropologists are few, and the problems of Melanesia and Malaya are so absorbing, that it is natural that science should not yet have found time to turn the full blaze of its searchlight upon Europe. But, though visitors to England do not pretend to have explored the mysteries of *mana* and *karakia*, they sometimes use expressions whose meaning appears to be not wholly remote from that attaching to those formidable words.

They are interested in education, and comment, with Professor Clarke, now Principal of the Institute of Education in London, on the 'class-saturated thinking' which persists in calling a certain kind of secondary school elementary, and deplore 'the deep and historical social cleavage that runs right through English education to this day', and ask with dismay: 'Is English education to escape from the toils of religious sectarianism only to find itself involved in a much more pervasive and far-reaching conflict of social sectarianism?' They inquire into English industrial conditions, and express bewilderment, with an American investigator, at the survival into the opening years of the present century of the doctrine that a certain wage is 'enough for a workman', a doctrine now, doubtless, less powerful than it was, but to which even recent comparisons of the economic outlook of America and England still continue to draw attention. They analyse the historical elements in English cultural life, and argue, with Herr Dibelius, that it has been impoverished because the tradition of a single group – *das Gentlemanideal* – has imposed itself on the rest as a national ideal, so that 'England alone, of all modern peoples, has allowed its ethical outlook to be prescribed by a single type of human being', and that 'the Englishman's social ethic is less deep and exacting than that of other civilised nations because it deliberately includes only a fraction of the common human ideal'. They discuss the psychology of contemporary politics, and find, like Herr Wertheimer, that it is marked, 'more than in any other country, by a strong element of what might be called proletarian snobbery', which inspires the British working class with a 'tenderly wistful interest in the vacuous doings of the upper ten thousand'. They attempt, like M. André Siegfried, a synthetic study of modern England, and are surprised to notice that even in the army, where it might be supposed that personal qualities were all-important, the English tradition, like that of pre-war Germany, and unlike that of France and the British Dominions, still prefers that the commissioned ranks should be recruited from what is sometimes described as 'the officer class', as though the capacity for leadership were an attribute, not of individual human beings, but of some particular social stratum. They return, like visitors from Australia and New Zealand, to renew association with their spiritual ancestry, and complain that England is not one nation, but two, and that, if they are at home in the one, they have little opportunity of mixing with the other, because, except in the world of public affairs, the circles are still largely self-contained and rarely intersect.[3]

Such observers contrast what seems to them, rightly or wrongly, the element of stratification in English social arrangements with the tradition of equality which is the glory of France, where the spirit of an age when the word 'aristocrat' was a term of abuse is not wholly forgotten, or with the easy-going democracy of the younger British communities, which have no aristocracy to remember. They come to the conclusion that Englishmen are born with *la mentalité hiérarchique*, and that England, though politically a democracy, is still liable to be plagued, in her social and economic life, by the mischievous ghost of an obsolete tradition of class superiority and class subordination. They find in the sharpness of English social divisions, and in the habit of mind which regards them as natural and inevitable, a quality which strikes them, according to their varying temperaments, as amusing or barbarous, or grotesque.

Here are these people, they say, who, more than any other nation, need a common culture, for, more than any other, they depend on an economic system which at every turn involves mutual understanding and continuous co-operation, and who, more than any other, possess, as a result of their history, the materials by which such a common culture might be inspired. Yet, so far from desiring it, there is nothing, it seems, which they desire less. They spend their energies in making it impossible, in behaving like the public schoolboys of the universe. *Das Gentlemanideal* has them by the throat; they frisk politely into obsolescence on the playing-fields of Eton. It is all very characteristic, and traditional, and picturesque. But it is neither good business nor good manners. It is out of tune with the realities of today. What a magnificent past Great Britain has had!

It is mainly, of course, though by no means exclusively, of the strata which till recently set the tone of social life and national policy that such critics are thinking. Nor, though everyone will sympathise with their dissent from the diagnosis, is it easy for them to dissent from it convincingly; for, if the picture is a caricature, it is a caricature which, in their unguarded moments, they draw of themselves. One of the regrettable, if diverting, effects of extreme inequality is its tendency to weaken the capacity for impartial judgment. It pads the lives of its beneficiaries with a soft down of consideration, while relieving them of the vulgar necessity of justifying their pretensions, and secures that, if they fall, they fall on cushions. It disposes them, on the one hand, to take for granted themselves and their own advantages, as though there were nothing in the latter which could possibly need explanation, and, on the other hand, to be critical of claims to similar advantages advanced by their neighbours who do not yet possess them. It causes them, in short, to apply different standards to different sections of the community, as if it were uncertain whether all of them are human in the same sense as themselves.

Mr H. G. Wells writes that what is called the class war is an old habit of the governing classes.[4] The temper which he describes, though no longer so aggressive and self-confident as in the past, is by no means extinct. It continues to find expression in an attitude which deplores in one breath the recurrence of class struggles, and the danger to prosperity caused by class agitation and the intrusion of class interests into politics, and defends in the next, in all innocence and good faith, arrangements such as those involving, for example, educational inequality, which, whatever their merits, are certainly themselves a cause of class divisions. It seems natural to those who slip into that mood of tranquil inhumanity that working-class children should go to the mill at an age when the children of the well-to-do are just beginning the serious business of education; and that employers, as the history of coal reveals, should be the sole judges of the manner of conducting an industry on which the welfare of several hundred thousand families depends; and that, while property-owners are paid compensation for disturbance, workmen should be dismissed without appeal on the word of a foreman; and that different sections of the community should be distinguished, not merely by differences of income, but by different standards of security, of culture, and even of health. When they are considering the provision to be made for unemployed wage-earners, they are apt to think it shocking that some men should be able to live without work, even though they have worked all their lives and are anxious to continue working. But, when they are repelling attacks upon property, they sometimes seem to think it monstrous that other men should not, even though they may never have worked seriously at all. Without any consciousness of inconsistency they will write to *The Times*, deploring in the first sentence the wickedness of some sections of the community in pressing for increased expenditure upon the social services which benefit them and their children, and urging in the next the importance of so reducing taxation that other sections may have more to spend on themselves. As long as they are sure that they are masters of the situation and will hold what they have, they are all kindness and condescension. Only question their credentials, however, and the lamb becomes a lion, which bares its teeth, and lashes its tail, and roars in every accent of grief and indignation, and will gobble up a whole bench of bishops, with the Archbishop of Canterbury at their head, if it imagines, as it imagined during the crisis of 1926, that the bishops are a party to laying hands upon its bone.

Swift remarks that mankind may judge what Heaven thinks of riches by observing those upon whom it has been pleased to bestow them. Those who apply that maxim will be disposed, perhaps, to agree with Arnold's contention that great inequalities, whatever other advantages they may possess, are likely, at all events, to be injurious to the rich. But the temper which regards such inequalities with indulgence is not at all confined to the rich, and the belief that it is confined to them, as though all that is needed, for a different spirit to prevail, were some external change in the machinery of society, is the politician's illusion.

Clearly, such a change is required, and, clearly, it is coming. Everyone who is not blind realises, indeed, that, if the issue between individualism and socialism is merely a matter of the structure and mechanism of industry, then it has, in large measure, already been decided. Everyone sees that the characteristic of the phase on which the economic system is now entering will, as far as the larger and more essential undertakings are concerned, be some form of unified direction under public control. But then, if that is all that the issue means, though technically interesting, it is not of any great moment, except to specialists. Organisation is important, but it is important as a means, not as an end in itself; and, while the means are debated with much zeal and ingenuity, the end, unfortunately, sometimes seems to be forgotten. So the question which is fundamental, the question whether the new organisation, whatever its form and title, will be more favourable than the old to a spirit of humanity and freedom in social relations, and deserves, therefore, that efforts should be made to establish it, is the object of less general concern and less serious consideration than the secondary, though important problem, which relates to the procedure of its establishment and the technique of its administration.

It is rarely considered, and more rarely finds overt expression in the world of public affairs. The reason is simple. An indifference to inequality, as the foreign observers remark, is less the mark of particular classes than a national characteristic. It is not a political question dividing parties, but a common temper and habit of mind which throws a bridge between them. Hence even those groups which are committed by their creed to measures for mitigating its more repulsive consequences rarely push their dislike of it to the point of affirming that the abolition of needless inequalities is their primary objective, by the approach to which their success is to be judged, and to the attainment of which other interests are to be subordinated. When the press assails them with the sparkling epigram that they desire, not merely to make the poor richer, but to make the rich poorer, instead of replying, as they should, that, being sensible men, they desire both, since the extremes both of riches and poverty are degrading and anti-social, they are apt to take refuge in gestures of deprecation. They make war on destitution, but they sometimes turn, it seems, a blind eye on privilege.

The truth is that, in this matter, judged by Arnold's standard, we are all barbarians, and that no section or class is in a position to throw stones at another. Certainly a professional man, like the writer of these pages, is not.

> High Heaven rejects the lore
> Of nicely calculated less and more:

and how, when he accepts an income five times as large as that of the average working-class family, can he cavil at his neighbours merely because their consciences allow them to accept one twenty, or thirty, or fifty times as large? Certainly the mass of the wage-earners themselves, in spite of the immense advance which they have achieved since Arnold wrote, are but little better entitled to adopt a pose of righteous indignation.

What the working-class movement stands for is obviously the ideal of social justice and solidarity, as a corrective to the exaggerated emphasis on individual advancement through the acquisition of wealth. It is a faith in the possibility of a society in which a higher value will be set on human beings, and a lower value on money and economic power, when money and power do not serve human ends. But that movement is liable, like all of us, to fall at times below itself, and to forget its mission. When it does so, what it is apt to desire is not a social order of a different kind, in which money and economic power will no longer be the criterion of achievement, but a social order of the same kind, in which money and economic power will be somewhat differently distributed.

Its characteristic fault is not, as is sometimes alleged, that the spirit behind it is one of querulous discontent. It is, on the contrary, that a considerable number among those to whom it appeals are too easily contented – too ready to forget fundamental issues and to allow themselves to be bought off with an advance in wages, too willing to accept the moral premises of their masters, even when they dispute the economic conclusions which their masters draw from them, too distrustful of themselves and too much disposed to believe that the minority which has exercised authority in the past possesses a *mana*, a mysterious wisdom, and can wield a *karakia*, a magical influence bringing prosperity or misfortune.[5] Their sentiment is just, but their action is timid, because it lacks a strong root of independent conviction to nourish and sustain it. If leaders, their bearing not infrequently recalls, less the tribune, than the courtier: they pay salaams of exaggerated amplitude to established proprieties, as though delighted and overawed by the privilege of saluting them. If followers, they are liable, with more excuse, to behave on occasion in a manner at once docile and irritable, as men who alternately touch their hats and grumble at the wickedness of those to whom they touch them.

Heaven takes, to paraphrase Homer, half the virtue from a man, when, if he behaves like a man, he may lose his job; and it is not for one who has not experienced the wage-earners' insecurity to be critical of the wage-earners' patience. But it would be better, nevertheless, both for them and for the nation as a whole, if they were more continuously alive, not only to their economic interests, but to their dignity as human beings. As it is, though they resent poverty and unemployment, and the physical miseries of a proletariat, they do not always resent, as they should, the moral humiliation which gross contrasts of wealth and economic power necessarily produce. While they will starve for a year to resist a reduction in wages, they still often accept quite tamely an organisation of industry under which a dozen gentlemen, who are not conspicuously wiser than their neighbours, determine the conditions of life and work for several thousand families; and an organisation of finance which enables a handful of bankers to raise and lower the economic temperature of a whole community; and an organisation of justice which makes it difficult, as Sir Edward Parry has shown,[6] for a poor man to face the cost of obtaining it; and an organisation of education which still makes higher education inaccessible to the great majority of working-class children, as though such children had, like anthropoid apes, fewer convolutions in their brains than the children of the well-to-do.

They denounce, and rightly, the injustices of capitalism; but they do not always realise that capitalism is maintained, not only by capitalists, but by those who, like some of themselves, would be capitalists if they could, and that the injustices survive, not merely because the rich exploit the poor, but because, in their hearts, too many of the poor admire the rich. They know and complain that they are tyrannised over by the power of money. But they do not yet see that what makes money the tyrant of society is largely their own reverence for it. They do not sufficiently realise that, if they were as determined to maintain their dignity as they are, quite rightly, to maintain their wages, they would produce a world in which their material miseries would become less unmanageable, since they would no longer be under a kind of nervous tutelage on the part of the minority, and the determination of their economic destinies would rest in their own hands.

Thus inequality, as Arnold remarked, does not only result in pampering one class; it results also in depressing another. But what does all this mean except that the tradition of inequality is, so to say, a complex – a cluster of ideas at the back of men's minds, whose influence they do not like to admit, but which, nevertheless, determines all the time their outlook on society, and their practical conduct, and the direction of their policy? And what can their denial of that influence convey except that the particular forms of inequality which are general and respectable, and the particular arrangement of classes to which they are accustomed, so far from being an unimportant detail, like the wigs of judges or the uniform of postmen and privy councillors, seem to them so obviously something which all right-thinking people should accept as inevitable that, until the question is raised, they are hardly conscious of them? And what can the result of such an attitude be except to inflame and aggravate occasions of friction which are, on other grounds, already numerous enough, and, since class divisions are evidently far-reaching in their effects, to cause it to be believed that class struggles, instead of being, what they are, a barbarous reality, which can be ended, and ended only, by abolishing its economic causes, are permanent, inevitable or even exhilarating.

The foreign critics, therefore, can console themselves with the reflection that they have not, after all, aimed so wide of the mark. But to those who cannot regard the fate of their fellow-countrymen with the detachment of foreigners, these proofs of their predilection for worshipping images are less consoling. They will observe that the ritual of the cult is even more surprising than the albs and chasubles and aumbries, which so shocked the late Lord Brentford and the House of Commons a few years ago. They will note that its own devotees do not seem to find in it a source of unmixed gratification, since it keeps them in a condition of morbid irritation with each other, so that, however urgent the need for decisive action may be, such action is impossible, because, as has repeatedly been seen in the twenty years since 1918, defence and attack neutralise each other, as in trench warfare, and the balance of forces produces a state of paralysis. They will reflect that such a paralysis, which is the natural result of a divided will, is less noticeable in nations where classes are less sharply divided, and that, since a united will can no longer today be secured, as it was secured in the past, by restricting political power to the classes endowed with social power and opportunity, the time may have come, perhaps, to increase the degree in which the latter, as well as the former, are a common possession. They will ask, in short, whether one condition of grappling more effectively with the economic difficulties of the nation

– not to mention its intellectual and moral deficiencies – may not be, in the words of Arnold, to 'choose equality'.

Psychologists tell us that the way to overcome a complex is not to suppress it, but to treat it frankly, and uncover its foundations. What a community requires, as the word itself suggests, is a common culture, because, without it, it is not a community at all. And evidently it requires it in a special degree at a moment like the present, when circumstances confront it with the necessity of giving a new orientation to its economic life, because it is in such circumstances that the need for co-operation, and for the mutual confidence and tolerance upon which co-operation depends, is particularly pressing. But a common culture cannot be created merely by desiring it. It must rest upon practical foundations of social organisation. It is incompatible with the existence of sharp contrasts between the economic standards and educational opportunities of different classes, for such contrasts have as their result, not a common culture, but servility or resentment, on the one hand, and patronage or arrogance, on the other. It involves, in short, a large measure of economic equality – not necessarily in the sense of an identical level of pecuniary incomes, but of equality of environment, of access to education and the means of civilisation, of security and independence, and of the social consideration which equality in these matters usually carries with it.

And who does not know that to approach the question of economic equality is to enter a region haunted, not, indeed, 'by hobgoblins, satyrs, and dragons of the pit', yet by a host of hardly less formidable terrors – 'doleful voices and rushings to and fro', and the giant with a grim and surly voice, who shows pilgrims the skulls of those whom he has already despatched, and threatens to tear them also in pieces, and who, unlike Bunyan's giant, does not even fall into fits on sunshiny days, since in his territory the sun does not shine, and, even if it did, he would be protected against the weaknesses that beset mere theological ogres by the inflexible iron of his economic principles? Who does not recognise, when the words are mentioned, that there is an immediate stiffening against them in the minds of the great mass of his fellow-countrymen, and that, while in France and Scandinavia, and even in parts of the United States, there is, at least, an initial sympathy for the conception, and a disposition to be proud of such economic equality as exists, in

England the instinctive feeling is one, not of sympathy, but of apprehension and repulsion, as though economic equality were a matter upon which it were not in good taste to touch? And who does not feel that, as a consequence of this attitude, Englishmen approach the subject with minds that are rarely more than half open? They do not welcome the idea, and then consider whether, and by what means, the difficulties in the way of its realisation, which are serious enough, can be overcome. They recite the difficulties with melancholy, and sometimes with exultant, satisfaction, because on quite other grounds – grounds of history, and social nervousness, and a traditional belief that advantages which are shared cease to be advantages at all, as though, when everybody is somebody, nobody will be anybody – they are determined to reject the idea.

So, when the question is raised whether some attempt to establish greater economic equality may not be desirable, there is a sound of what Bunyan called 'doleful voices and rushings to and fro'. They rear, and snort, and paw the air, and affirm with one accord that the suggestion is at once wicked and impracticable. Lord Birkenhead, for example, declared that the idea that men are equal is 'a poisonous doctrine', and wrung his hands at the thought of the 'glittering prizes' of life being diminished in value; and Mr Garvin, with his eye for the dangers of the moment, and the temptations to which his fellow-countrymen are most prone to succumb, warns us against the spirit that seeks the dead level and ignores the inequality of human endowments; and Sir Ernest Benn writes that economic equality is 'a scientific impossibility', because Professor Pareto has shown, he says, that 'if the logarithms of income sizes be charted on a horizontal scale, and the logarithms of the number of persons having an income of a particular size or over be charted on a vertical scale, then the resulting observational points will lie approximately along a straight line', and that, if only this were more generally known, the poor, like the wicked, would cease from troubling. A great industrialist, like Sir Herbert Austin, and a distinguished minister of religion, like Dean Inge, rehearse, in their different ways, the same lesson. The former implores us to 'cease teaching that all men are equal and entitled to an equal share of the common wealth', and 'enrich the men who make sacrifices justifying enrichment', and 'leave the others in their contentment, rather than try to mould material that was never intended to withstand the fires of refinement'. The latter complains, in an address at Oxford – with a view, perhaps, to mitigating the class feeling which he rightly deplores – that 'the government is taking the pick of the working classes and educating them at the expense of the rate-payers to enable them to take the bread out of the mouths of the sons of professional men'. This deplorable procedure, he argues, cannot fail to be injurious to the nation as a whole, since it injures 'the upper middle classes', who are 'the cream of the community'.[7]

When he hears this comminatory chorus directed against the idea of equality by men of such eminence, the first impulse of the layman is to exclaim with Moses, 'Would God that all the Lord's people were prophets!' He wishes that he himself, and all his fellow-countrymen, were capable of charting logarithms on horizontal and vertical scales in the manner of Sir Ernest Benn, and of escaping with confidence the dead-level of mediocrity so justly deprecated by Mr Garvin, and of being moved by the righteous indignation which fills Dean Inge when he contemplates those vessels of wrath, the working classes. But he knows, to his dismay, that these gifts have been denied to ordinary men, and that it would, indeed, be a kind of presumption for ordinary men to desire them, for to do so would be to aspire to an impious and unattainable equality with their betters. So he is bewildered and confounded by the perversity of the universe; he is oppressed by the weight of all this unintelligible world. If only the mass of mankind were more intelligent, they would realise how unintelligent their pretensions are. But they are condemned, it seems, to be unaware of their inferiority by the very fact of their inferiority itself.

When an argument leads to an *impasse*, it is advisable to re-examine the premises from which it started. It is possible that the dilemma is not, after all, quite so hopeless as at first sight it appears to be. Rightly understood, Pareto's law is a suggestive generalisation; and the biological differences between different individuals are a phenomenon of great interest and significance and Dean Inge is, doubtless, more than justified in thinking that the working classes, like all other classes, are no better than they should be, and in telling them so with the apostolic fervour which he so abundantly commands. It is the natural disposition

23

of clever and learned people to attack the difficult and recondite aspects of topics which are under discussion, because to such people the other aspects seem too obvious and elementary to deserve attention. The more difficult aspects of human relations, however, though doubtless the most interesting to nimble minds, are not always the most important. There are other ways than that of the eagle in the air and the serpent on the rock, which baffled the author of the Book of Proverbs. There are other sides of the truth about mankind and its behaviour than those which are revealed by biological investigation, or expressed in the logarithms which delight the leisure of Sir Ernest Benn.

It is these simpler and more elementary considerations that have been in the minds of those who have thought that a society was most likely to enjoy happiness and good will, and to turn both its human and material resources to the best account, if it cultivated as far as possible an equalitarian temper, and sought by its institutions to increase equality. It is obvious, indeed, that, as things are today, no redistribution of wealth would bring general affluence and that statisticians are within their rights in making merry with the idea that the equalisation of incomes would make everyone rich. But, though riches are a good, they are not, nevertheless, the only good; and because greater production, which is concerned with the commodities to be consumed, is clearly important, it does not follow that greater equality, which is concerned with the relations between the human beings who consume them, is not important also. It is obvious, again, that the word 'Equality' possesses more than one meaning, and that the controversies surrounding it arise partly, at least, because the same term is employed with different connotations. Thus it may either purport to state a fact, or convey the expression of an ethical judgment. On the one hand, it may affirm that men are, on the whole, very similar in their natural endowments of character and intelligence. On the other hand, it may assert that, while they differ profoundly as individuals in capacity and character, they are equally entitled as human beings to consideration and respect, and that the well-being of a society is likely to be increased if it so plans its organisation that, whether their powers are great or small, all its members may be equally enabled to make the best of such powers as they possess.

If made in the first sense, the assertion of human equality is clearly untenable. It is a piece of mythology against which irresistible evidence has been accumulated by biologists and psychologists. In the light of the data presented – to mention only two recent examples – in such works as Dr Burt's admirable studies of the distribution of educational abilities among school-children, or the Report of the Mental Deficiency Committee,[8] the fact that, quite apart from differences of environment and opportunity, individuals differ widely in their natural endowments, and in their capacity to develop them by education, is not open to question. There is some reason for holding, for instance, that, while 80 per cent of children at the age of ten fall within a range of about three mental years, the most backward may have a mental age of five, while the most gifted may have one of as much as fifteen.

The acceptance of that conclusion, nevertheless, makes a smaller breach in equalitarian doctrines than is sometimes supposed, for such doctrines have rarely been based on a denial of it. It is true, of course, that the psychological and political theory of the age between 1750 and 1850 – the theory, for example, of thinkers so different as Helvétius and Adam Smith at the beginning of the period, and Mill and Proudhon at the end of it – greatly underestimated the significance of inherited qualities, and greatly overestimated the plasticity of human nature. It may be doubted, however, whether it was quite that order of ideas which inspired the historical affirmations of human equality, even in the age when such ideas were still in fashion.

It is difficult for even the most sanguine of assemblies to retain for more than one meeting the belief that Providence has bestowed an equal measure of intelligence upon all its members. When the Americans declared it to be a self-evident truth that all men are created equal, they were thinking less of the admirable racial qualities of the inhabitants of the New World than of their political and economic relations with the Old, and would have remained unconvinced that those relations should continue even in the face of proofs of biological inferiority. When the French, who a century and a half ago preached the equalitarian idea with the same fervent conviction as is shown today by the rulers of Russia in denouncing it, set that idea side by side with liberty and fraternity as the motto of a new world, they did not mean that all men are equally intelligent or equally virtuous, any more than that they are equally tall or equally fat, but that the unity of their national life should no longer be torn to pieces by obsolete property rights and meaningless juristic distinctions. When Arnold, who was an inspector of schools as well as a poet, and who, whatever his failings, was not prone to demagogy, wrote 'choose equality', he did not suggest, it may be suspected, that all children appeared to him to be equally clever, but that a nation acts unwisely in stressing heavily distinctions based on birth or money.

Few men have been more acutely sensitive than Mill to the importance of encouraging the widest possible diversities of mind and taste. In arguing that 'the best state for human nature is that in which, while no one is poor, no one desires to be richer', and urging that social policy should be directed to increasing equality, he did not intend to convey that it should suppress varieties or individual genius and character, but that it was only in a society marked by a large measure of economic equality that such varieties were likely to find their full expression and due need of appreciation.[9] Theologians have not, as a rule, been disposed to ignore the fact that there are diversities of gifts and degree above degree. When they tell us that all men are equal in the eyes of God, what they mean, it is to be presumed, is what Jeremy Taylor meant, when he wrote, in a book today too little read, that 'if a man be exalted by reason of any excellence in his soul, he may please to remember that all souls are equal, and their differing operations are because their instrument is in better tune, their body is more healthful or better tempered; which is no more praise to him than it is that he was born in Italy'. It is the truth expressed in the parable of the prodigal son – the truth that it is absurd and degrading for men to make much of their intellectual and moral superiority to each other, and still more of their superiority in the arts which bring wealth and power, because, judged by their place in any universal scheme, they are all infinitely great or infinitely small. And, when observers from the Dominions, or from foreign countries, are struck by inequality as one of the special and outstanding characteristics of English social life, they do not mean that in other countries differences of personal quality are less important than in England. They mean, on the contrary, that they are more important, and that in England they tend to be obscured or obliterated behind differences of property and income, and the whole elaborate façade of a society that, compared with their own, seems stratified and heirarchical.

The equality which all these thinkers emphasise as desirable is not equality of capacity or attainment, but of circumstances, institutions, and manner of life. The inequality which they deplore is not inequality of personal gifts, but of the social and economic environment. They are concerned, not with a biological phenomenon, but with a spiritual relation and the conduct to be based on it. Their view, in short, is that, because men are men, social institutions – property rights, and the organisation of industry, and the system of public health and education – should be planned, as far as is possible, to emphasise and strengthen, not the class differences which divide, but the common humanity which unites, them.

Such a view of the life which is proper to human beings may, of course, be criticised, as it often has been. But to suppose that it can be criticised effectively by pointing to the width of the intellectual and moral differences which distinguish individuals from each other is a solecism, an *ignoratio elenchi*. It is true, of course, that such differences are important, and that the advance of psychology has enabled them to be measured with a new precision, with results which are valuable in making possible both a closer adaptation of educational methods to individual needs and a more intelligent selection of varying aptitudes for different tasks. But to recognise a specific difference is one thing; to pass a general judgment of superiority or inferiority, still more to favour the first and neglect the second, is quite another.[10] The nightingale, it has been remarked, was placed in the fourth class at the fowl show. Which of a number of varying individuals is to be judged superior to the rest depends upon the criterion which is applied, and the criterion is a matter of ethical judgment. That judgment will, if it is prudent, be tentative and provisional, since men's estimates of the relative desirability of initiative, decision, common sense, imagination, humility and sympathy appear, unfortunately, to differ, and the failures and fools – the Socrates and St Francis – of one age are the sages and saints of another. Society would not be the worse, perhaps, if idiots like Dostoevsky's were somewhat less uncommon, and the condemnation passed on those who offend one of these little ones was not limited to offenders against children whose mental ratio is in excess of eighty-five.

It is true again, that human beings have, except for certain elementary, though still sadly neglected, matters of health and development, different requirements, and that these different requirements can be met satisfactorily only by varying forms of provision. But equality of provision is not identity of provision. It is to be achieved, not by treating different needs in the same way, but by devoting equal care to ensuring that they are met in the different ways most appropriate to them, as is done by a doctor who prescribes different regimens for different constitutions, or a teacher who develops different types of intelligence by different curricula. The more anxiously, indeed, a society endeavours to secure equality of consideration for all its members, the greater will be the differentiation of treatment which, when once their common human needs have been met, it accords to the special needs of different groups and individuals among them.

It is true, finally, that some men are inferior to others in respect of their intellectual endowments, and it is possible – though the truth of the possibility has not yet been satisfactorily established – that the same is true of certain classes.[11] It does not, however, follow from this fact that such individuals or classes should receive less consideration than others, or should be treated as inferior in respect of such matters as legal status, or health, or economic arrangements, which are within the control of the community.

It may, of course, be deemed expedient so to treat them. It may be thought advisable, as Aristotle argued, to maintain the institution of slavery on the ground that some men are fit only to be living tools; or, as was customary in a comparatively recent past, to apply to the insane a severity not used towards the sane; or, as is sometimes urged today, to spend less liberally on the education of the slow than on that of the intelligent; or, in accordance with the practice of all ages, to show less respect for the poor than for the rich. But, in order to establish an inference, a major premise is necessary as well as a minor; and, if such discrimination on the part of society is desirable, its desirability must be shown by some other argument than the fact of inequality of intelligence and character. To convert a phenomenon, however interesting, into a principle, however respectable, is an error of logic. It is the confusion of a judgment of fact with a judgment of value – a confusion like that which was satirised by Montesquieu when he wrote, in his ironical defence of slavery: 'The creatures in question are black from head to foot, and their noses are so flat that it is almost impossible to pity them. It is not to be supposed that God, an all-wise Being, can have lodged a soul – still less a good soul – in a body completely black.'

Everyone recognises the absurdity of such an argument when it is applied to matters within his personal knowledge and professional competence. Everyone realises that, in order to justify inequalities of circumstance or opportunity by reference to differences of personal quality, it is necessary, as Professor Ginsberg observes, to show that the differences in question are relevant to the inequalities.[12] Everyone now sees, for example, that it is not a valid argument against women's suffrage to urge, as used to be urged not so long ago, that women are physically weaker than men, since physical strength is not relevant to the question of the ability to exercise the franchise, or a valid argument in favour of slavery that some men are less intelligent than others, since it is not certain that slavery is the most suitable penalty for lack of intelligence.

Not everyone, however, is so quick to detect the fallacy when it is expressed in general terms. It is still possible, for example, for one eminent statesman to ridicule the demand for a diminution of economic inequalities on the ground that every mother knows that her children are not equal, without reflecting whether it is the habit of mothers to lavish care on the strong and neglect the delicate; and for another to dismiss the suggestion that greater economic equality is desirable, for the reason, apparently, that men are naturally unequal. It is probable, however, that the first does not think that the fact that some children are born with good digestions, and others with bad, is a reason for supplying good food to the former and bad food to the latter, rather than for giving to both food which is equal in quality but different in kind, and that the second does not suppose that the natural inequality of men makes legal equality a contemptible principle. On the contrary, when ministers of the Crown responsible for the administration of justice to the nation, they both took for granted the desirability and existence at any rate on paper of legal equality. Yet in the eighteenth century statesmen of equal eminence in France and Germany and in the nineteenth century influential thinkers in Russia and the United States and, indeed, the ruling classes of Europe almost everywhere at a not very distant period, all were disposed to think that, since men are naturally unequal, the admission of a general equality of legal status would be the end of civilisation.

Our modern statesmen do not agree with that view, for, thanks to the struggles of the past, they have inherited a tradition of legal equality, and, fortified by that tradition, they see that the fact that men are naturally unequal is not relevant to the question whether they should or should not be treated as equal before the law. But they have not inherited a tradition of economic equality, for that tradition has still to be created. Hence they do not see that the existence of differences of personal capacity and attainment is as irrelevant to the question whether it is desirable that the social environment and economic organisation should be made more conducive to equality as it is to the question of equality before the law, which itself, as we have said, seemed just as monstrous a doctrine to conservative thinkers in the past as the suggestion of greater economic equality seems to them today.

And Sir Ernest Benn, who says that economic equality is a scientific impossibility, is quite unconscious, apparently, of the ambiguities of his doctrine. He ignores the obvious fact that, in some economic matters of the first importance – protection by the police against violence and theft, and the use of the roads, and the supply of water, and the provision of sewers, and access to a minimum of education and medical attendance, all of which were once dependent on the ability of individuals to pay for them – all members of civilised communities are now secured equality irrespective of their personal attainments and individual economic resources. He fails to see that the only question is whether that movement shall be carried forward, or rather, since in fact it is carried forward year by year, how quickly society will decide to establish complete environmental equality in respect of the external conditions of health, and education, and economic security. So he behaves like the countryman who, on being for the first time introduced to a giraffe at a circus, exclaimed indignantly, 'There ain't no such animal.' He says that equality is a scientific impossibility, and draws a sharp line between the natural and, as he thinks, the healthy state of things, under which each individual provides all his requirements for himself, and the unnatural and morbid condition, under which the community, consisting of himself and his fellows, provides some of them for him.

Such a line, however, is quite arbitrary, quite fanciful and artificial. Many services are supplied by collective effort today which in the recent past were supplied by individual effort or not supplied at all, and many more, it may be suspected, will be so supplied in the future. At any moment there are some needs which almost everyone is agreed should be satisfied on equalitarian principles, and others which they are agreed should be met by individuals who purchase what their incomes enable them to pay for, and others, again, about the most suitable provision for which opinions differ. Society has not been prevented from seeking to establish equality in respect of the first by the fear that in so doing it may be perpetrating a scientific impossibility. Nor ought it to be prevented from moving towards equality in respect of the second and third, if experience suggests that greater equality in these matters also would contribute to greater efficiency and to more general happiness.

'But,' it will be said, 'you are forgetting Pareto's law, and the logarithms, and the observational points. These are hard realities. No ingenious sophistry will enable you to make light of *them*.' It is wrong, as we all know, to speak disrespectfully of the equator; and if the equator, which is a simple idea, deserves to be approached in a spirit of deference, how much more is such deference incumbent on those who venture within the awful ambit of economic law? There is, however, as St Paul says, one glory of the sun and another glory of the moon; there are powers celestial and powers terrestrial; there are laws and laws. There are scientific laws which state the invariable relations between phenomena, and there are juristic laws which state how men should conduct themselves, and there are laws which are neither juristic nor, in the full sense, scientific, though they belong, no doubt, to the same category as the latter. Such laws neither state invariable relations nor prescribe conduct, but describe how, on the whole, under given historical and legal conditions, and when influenced by particular conventions and ideas, particular groups of men do, as a rule, tend to behave.

It is evident that, as economists have often reminded us, many economic laws are of the third class, not of the first or second. They indicate the manner in which, given certain historical conditions, and a certain form of social organisation, and certain juristic institutions, production tends to be conducted and wealth to be distributed. They are not the less instructive and useful on that account, to those, at least, who know how to interpret them. But those who, though successful and rich, are not fully alive to the pitfalls which yawn for the unwary, and who are delighted when they hear of a law which jumps, as it seems to them, with their own instinctive preference for success and riches, sometimes find in economic laws a source of intellectual confusion, which it is distressing to all persons of humanity, and in particular, it may be suspected, to economists to contemplate. They snatch at elaborate formulae in order to demonstrate that the particular social arrangements that they have been accustomed to admire are the product of uncontrollable forces, with which society can tamper only at its peril. They run to the fashionable nostrum of the moment, in order to shuffle off their responsibilities upon some economic automaton. Like a drunkard who pleads an alcoholic diathesis as an excuse for drinking, they appeal to economic laws, the majority of which are merely a description of the manner in which, in a certain environment and in given circumstances, men tend to behave, as a proof that it is impossible for them to alter their behaviour.

How men in given circumstances tend to behave, and how, as a consequence, wealth tends in such circumstances to be distributed, are subjects about which valuable and illuminating, if necessarily tentative, generalisations have been produced by economists. But their behaviour, as economists have often told us, is relative to their circumstances; and the distribution of wealth depends, not wholly, indeed, but largely, on their institutions; and the character of their institutions is determined, not by immutable economic laws, but by the values, preferences, interests and ideals which rule at any moment in a given society.

These values and preferences are not something fixed and unalterable. On the contrary, they have changed repeatedly in the past, and are changing today; and the distribution of wealth has changed, and is changing, with them. It was of one kind in France and of the old régime, where a large part of the wealth produced was absorbed by the privileged orders, and quite another in France after the Revolution, where wealth previously paid in taxation and feudal dues was retained by the peasantry. It is of one kind in Denmark today and of another kind in England. Thanks largely to changes in fiscal policy and to the development of the social services, which Sir Ernest Benn finds so distasteful, it is different in the England of 1937 from what it was in the England of 1857, and, if experience may be trusted, it will be different again in the England of 1957. To suppose, as he supposes, that it must necessarily be wrong to aim at greater economic equality, because Pareto suggested that, under certain conditions, and leaving the effects of inheritance, fiscal policy, and social services out of account, the curve of distribution in several different countries and ages tended, as he thought, to conform to a certain shape, is a pardonable error, but an error none the less. It implies a misunderstanding of the nature of economic laws in general, and of Pareto's law in particular, at which no one, it is probable, would have been more amused than Pareto himself, and which, indeed, he expressly repudiated in a subsequent work.[13] It is to believe in economic Fundamentalism, with the New Testament left out, and the Books of Leviticus and Deuteronomy inflated to unconscionable proportions by the addition of new and appalling essays. It is to dance naked, and roll on the ground, and cut oneself with knives, in honour of the mysteries of Mumbo-Jumbo.

Mumbo-Jumbo is a great god, who, if he is given his head, is disposed to claim, not only economics, but the whole world, as his kingdom, and who is subtle enough to deceive even the elect; so that Sir Ernest Benn is to be pitied, rather than blamed, for yielding to his seductions, and for feeling the same kind of reverence for Mumbo-Jumboism as was inspired in Kant by the spectacle of the starry heavens and by the moral law. But the power of Mumbo-Jumbo, like that of some other spirits, depends on the presence of an initial will to believe in the minds of his votaries, and can, if only they are not terrified when he sends forth his thunders and his lightnings – the hail of his logarithms and the whirlwind of his economic laws – be overcome. If, when he tells them that a certain course will result in the heavens falling, they summon up the resolution to pursue it all the same, they will find that, in a surprising number of cases, though they may have succeeded in improving the earth, the heavens, nevertheless, remain much where they were. And, when his prophets are so much alarmed by the symptoms of increasing equality, and by the demand for its still further increase, that they declare that equality is a scientific impossibility, they ought not, indeed, to be treated unkindly, or hewn in pieces before the Lord, like the prophets of an earlier Mumbo-Jumbo; but they should be asked to undergo, for the sake both of themselves and of their neighbours, what to nimble minds, with a gift for quick and sweeping generalisation, is sometimes a hardly less painful discipline. They should be asked to study the facts. The facts, they will find, show that the distribution of wealth in a community depends partly, at least, upon its organisation and institutions – its system of property rights, its economic structure, its social and financial policy – and that it is possible for it to give these matters a bias either towards greater equality or towards greater inequality, because different communities, at different times, have done, in fact, both the one and the other.

Perhaps, therefore, the remote Victorian thinkers, like Arnold and Mill, who dealt lightly with Mumbo-Jumbo, and who commended equality to their fellow-countrymen as one source of peace and happiness, were not speaking so unadvisedly as at first sight might appear. They did not deny that men have unequal gifts, or suggest that all of them are capable of earning, as the author of *The Confessions of a Capitalist* tells us that he earns,[14] £10,000 a year, or of making a brilliant show when their natural endowments are rigorously sifted and appraised with exactitude. What they were concerned to emphasise is something more elementary and common-place. It is the fact that, in spite of their varying characters and capacities, men possess in their common humanity a quality which is worth cultivating, and that a community is most likely to make the most of that quality if it takes into account in planning its economic organisation and social institutions – if it stresses lightly differences of wealth and birth and social position, and establishes on firm foundations institutions which meet common needs, and are a source of common enlightenment and common enjoyment. The individual differences of which so much is made, they would have said, will always survive, and they are to be welcomed, not regretted. But their existence is no reason for not seeking to establish the largest possible measure of equality of environment, and circumstance, and opportunity. On the contrary, it is a reason for redoubling our efforts to establish it, in order to ensure that these diversities of gifts may come to fruition.

It is true, indeed, that even such equality, though the conditions on which it depends are largely within human control, will continue to elude us. The important thing, however, is not that it should be completely attained, but that it should be sincerely sought. What matters to the health of society is the objective towards which its face is set, and to suggest that it is immaterial in which direction it moves, because, whatever the direction, the goal must always elude it, is not scientific, but irrational. It is like using the impossibility of absolute cleanliness as a pretext for rolling in a manure heap, or denying the importance of honesty because no one can be wholly honest.

It may well be the case that capricious inequalities are in some measure inevitable, in the sense that, like crime and disease, they are a malady which the most rigorous precautions cannot wholly overcome. But, when crime is known as crime, and disease as disease, the ravages of both are circumscribed by the mere fact that they are recognised for what they are, and described by their proper names, not by flattering euphemisms. And a society which is convinced that inequality is an evil need not be alarmed because the evil is one which cannot wholly be subdued. In recognising the poison it will have armed itself with an antidote. It will have deprived inequality of its sting by stripping it of its esteem.

So to criticise inequality and to desire equality is not, as is sometimes suggested, to cherish the romantic illusion that men are equal in character and intelligence. It is to hold that, while their natural endowments differ profoundly, it is the mark of a civilised society to aim at eliminating such inequalities as have their source, not in individual differences, but in its own organisation, and that individual differences, which are a source of social energy, are more likely to ripen and find expression if social inequalities are, as far as practicable, diminished. And the obstacle to the progress of equality is something simpler and more potent than finds expression in the familiar truism that men vary in their mental and moral, as well as in their physical characteristics, important and valuable though that truism is as a reminder that different individuals require different types of provision. It is the habit of mind which thinks it, not regrettable, but natural and desirable, that different sections of a community should be distinguished from each other by sharp differences of economic status, of environment, of education and culture and habit of life. It is the temper which regards with approval the social institutions and economic arrangements by which such differences are emphasised and enhanced, and feels distrust and apprehension at all attempts to diminish them.

The institutions and policies in which that temper has found expression are infinite in number. At one time it has coloured the relations between the sexes; at another, those between religions; at a third, those between members of different races. But in communities no longer divided by religion or race, and in which men and women are treated as political and economic equals, the divisions which remain are, nevertheless, not insignificant. The practical form which they most commonly assume – the most conspicuous external symptom of difference of economic status and social position – is, of course, a graduated system of social classes, and it is by softening or obliterating, not individual differences, but class gradations, that the historical movements directed towards diminishing inequality have attempted to attain their objective. It is, therefore, by considering the class system that light upon the problem of inequality is, in the first place at least, to be sought, and it is by their attitude to the relations between classes that the equalitarian temper and philosophy are distinguished from their opposite.

A society which values equality will attach a high degree of significance to differences of character and intelligence between different individuals, and a low degree of significance to economic and social differences between different groups. It will endeavour, in shaping its policy and organisation, to encourage the former and to neutralise and suppress the latter, and will regard it as vulgar and childish to emphasise them when, unfortunately, they still exist. A society which is in love with inequality will take such differences seriously, and will allow them to overflow from the regions, such as economic life, where they have their origin, and from which it is difficult wholly to expel them, till they become a kind of morbid obsession, colouring the whole world of social relations.

The meaning of class

The idea of 'class', most candid observers will admit, is among the most powerful of social categories. Its significance is sometimes denied on the ground that, as Professor Carr-Saunders and Mr Caradog Jones remark in their valuable book, a group described as a class may 'upon many an issue be divided against itself.'[15] But this is to confuse the fact of class with the consciousness of class, which is a different phenomenon. The fact creates the consciousness, not the consciousness the fact. The former may exist without the latter, and a group may be marked by common characteristics, and occupy a distinctive position *vis-à-vis* other groups, without, except at moments of exceptional tension, being aware that it does so.

While, however, class is a powerful category, it is also an ambiguous one, and it is not surprising that there should be wide differences in the interpretations placed upon it both by sociologists and by laymen. War, the institution of private property, biological characteristics, the division of labour, have all been adduced to explain the facts of class formation and class differentiation. The diversity of doctrines is natural, since the facts themselves are diverse. Clearly, there are societies in which the position and relations of the groups composing them have been determined ultimately by the effect of conquest. Clearly, the rules under which property is held and transmitted have played a large part in fixing the conditions by which different groups are distinguished from each other. Clearly, there are circumstances in which the biological characteristics of different groups are a relevant consideration. Clearly, the emergence of new social groups is a natural accompaniment of the differentiation of economic functions – of the breaking up, for example, of a relatively simple and undifferentiated society into a multitude of specialised crafts and professions, each with its different economic *métier*, its different training and outlook and habit of life, which has been the most obvious consequence of the transition of large parts of Europe from the predominantly agricultural civilisation of two centuries ago to the predominantly industrial civilisation of today.

These different factors have, however, varying degrees of importance in different ages, different communities, and different connections. In Western Europe, for example, the imposition of one race upon another by military force was of great importance during some earlier periods of its history, but in recent centuries has played but little part in modifying its social structure. Certain groups are marked, it seems, by different biological characteristics. Such characteristics require, however, the lapse of considerable periods to produce their result, while marked alterations in social structure may take place in the course of a single lifetime.

It is difficult to suppose that the broad changes in social classification which have occurred in the immediate past – the profound
modification of class relations, for example, which was the result
of the French Revolution, or the rise of new types of class system
and the obliteration of the old, which has everywhere
accompanied the development of the great industry, or the more
recent growth of a *nouvelle couche sociale* of technicians, managers,
scientific experts, professional administrators, and public servants – are most appropriately interpreted as a biological
phenomenon.

Nor, important though economic forces have been, can the
gradations of classes be explained, as is sometimes suggested,
purely as a case of economic specialisation. It may be true,
indeed, that the most useful conception of a class is that which
regards it as a social group with a strong tinge of community of
economic interest. But, while classes are social groups, not all
social groups, even when they have common economic interests,
can be described as classes. 'Classes,' observed Lord Bryce, in
writing of the United States of a generation ago, 'are in America
by no means the same thing as in the greater nations of Europe.
One must not, for political purposes, divide them as upper and
lower, richer and poorer, but rather according to the occupations
they respectively follow.'[16] His distinction between occupational
and social divisions still retains its significance. Stockbrokers,
barristers and doctors, miners, railway-men and cotton-spinners
represent half a dozen professions; but they are not normally
regarded as constituting half a dozen classes. Postmen, brick-
layers and engineers pursue sharply contrasted occupations, and
often have divergent economic interests; but they are not distinguished from each other by the differences of economic status,
environment, education, and opportunity, which are associated
in common opinion with differences between classes. A community which is marked by a low degree of economic differentiation may yet possess a class system of which the lines are
sharply drawn and rigidly defined, as was the case, for example,
in many parts of the agricultural Europe of the eighteenth
century. It may be marked by a high degree of economic differentiation, and yet appear, when judged by English standards, to be
comparatively classless, as is the case, for example, with some
British Dominions.

The conception of class is, therefore, at once more fundamental and more elusive than that of the division between different types of occupation. It is elusive because it is comprehensive. It relates, not to this or that specific characteristic of a group, but to a totality of conditions by which several sides of life are affected. The classification will vary, no doubt, with the purpose for which it is made, and with the points which accordingly are selected for emphasis. Conventional usage, which is concerned, not with the details of the social structure, but with its broad outlines and salient features, makes a rough division of individuals according to their resources and manner of life, the amount of their income and the source from which it is derived, their ownership of property or their connection with those who own it, the security or insecurity of their economic position, the degree to which they belong by tradition, education and association to social strata which are accustomed, even on a humble scale, to exercise direction, or, on the other hand, to those whose normal lot is to be directed by others. It draws its class lines, in short, with reference partly to consumption, partly to production; partly by standards of expenditure, partly by the position which different individuals occupy in the economic system. Though its criteria change from generation to generation, and are obviously changing today with surprising rapidity, its general tendency is clear. It sets at one end of the scale those who can spend much, or who have what is called an independent income, because they are dependent for it on persons other than themselves, and at the other end those who can spend little and live by manual labour. It places at a point between the two those who can spend more than the second but less than the first, and who own a little property or stand near to those who own it.

Thus conventional usage has ignored, in its rough way, the details, and has emphasised the hinges, the nodal points, the main watersheds. And in so doing, it has come nearer, with all its crudity, to grasping certain significant sides of the reality than have those who would see in the idea of class merely the social expression of the division of labour between groups engaged in different types of economic activity. For, though differences of class and differences of occupation may often have sprung from a common source, they acquire, once established, a vitality and momentum of their own, and often flow in distinct, or even divergent, channels. The essence of the latter is difference of economic function: they are an organ of co-operation through the division of labour. The essence of the former is difference of status and power: they have normally been, in some measure at least, the expression of varying degrees of authority and subordination. Class systems, in fact, in the historical forms which they most commonly have assumed, have usually been associated – hence, indeed, the invidious suggestion which the word sometimes conveys – with differences, not merely of economic *métier*, but of social position, so that different groups have been distinguished from each other, not only, like different professions, by the nature of the service they render, but in status, in influence, and sometimes in consideration and respect. Even today, indeed, though somewhat less regularly than in the past, class tends to determine occupation rather than occupation class.

Public opinion has in all ages been struck by this feature in social organisation, and has used terms of varying degrees of appropriateness to distinguish the upper strata from the lower, describing them sometimes as the beautiful and good, sometimes as the fat men, sometimes as the twiceborn, or the sons of gods and heroes, sometimes merely, in nations attached to virtue rather than beauty, as the best people. Such expressions are not terms of precision, but they indicate a phenomenon which has attracted attention, and which has certainly deserved it. The note of most societies has been, in short, not merely vertical differentiation, as between partners with varying tasks in a common enterprise, but also what, for want of a better term, may be called horizontal stratification, as between those who occupy a position of special advantage and those who do not.

The degree to which such horizontal divisions obtain varies widely in the same community at different times, and in different communities at the same time. They are more marked in most parts of Europe than in America and the British Dominions, in the east of America than in the west, in England than in France; and they were obviously more marked in the England of half a century ago than they are in that of today. Being in constant motion, they are not easily photographed, and they are hardly described before the description is out of date. But such divisions exist to some extent, it will be agreed, in most societies, and, wherever they exist to a considerable extent, they are liable, it will also be agreed, to be a focus of irritation. Accepted in the past with placid indifference, they resemble, under modern political and economic conditions, a sensitive nerve which vibrates when touched, a tooth which, once it has started aching, must be soothed or extracted before it can be forgotten, and attention paid to the serious business of life. It is possible that they possess certain advantages; it is certain that they possess also certain grave disadvantages. The advantages – if such there are – are most likely to be enjoyed, and the disadvantages removed, if their main features, at any rate, are, in the first place, neither denounced, nor applauded, but understood.

The economic and social contours

Income, economists tell us, may be regarded from either of two points of view. It may be interpreted as a product or as a dividend, as a stream of goods in process of creation, or as a stream of goods in process of consumption. And classes, which rest upon economic foundations, have two different aspects, which correspond to these different aspects of the national income. They may be regarded, on the one hand, as composed of a series of economic groups, holding different positions in the productive system, and, as employer and employed, capitalist and wage-earner, landlord, farmer, and labourer, discharging different, if occasionally somewhat attenuated, functions within it. They may be regarded, on the other hand, as a series of social groups, distinguished from each other by different standards of expenditure and consumption, and varying in their income, their environment, their education, their social status and family connections, their leisure and their amusements.

When attention is turned upon the organisation of industry and the relations of the various interests engaged in it – their disputes, their agreements, their attempts to establish more effective co-operation or their failure to achieve it – it is naturally the first aspect of the class system which springs into prominence. Society is regarded as an economic mechanism, the main elements in whose structure correspond to different classes. In discussions of the traditions, habits and manner of life by which different classes are characterised – the social institutions which they have created, the types of schools which they attend, the varying environments in which they live – the feature which attracts attention is naturally the second. Society then presents itself, not as a productive machine, but as an organism composed of groups with varying standards of life and culture. The class system takes off its overalls or office coat, and wears the costume appropriate to hours of ease.

Before goods can be consumed goods must be produced. It is obvious that these two aspects of social organisation are closely connected, as obverse and reverse, or flower and root. The material fabric of civilisation is always crumbling and always being renewed; the wealth which renews it is hewn daily in the gloom of the mine and fashioned unceasingly in the glare of the forge. Both the hierarchy of the world of leisure, therefore, and the hierarchy of the world of productive effort, have their common foundation in the character and organisation of the economic system. But, while they have a common foundation, the lines of the one are not a mere replica of those of the other. They correspond, but they do not coincide; in England, indeed, they coincide less closely than in younger communities, such as the United States, where the action of economic forces on the structure of society encounters fewer breakwaters built by tradition, and is therefore more simple, immediate, and direct. The social fabric is stretched upon an economic framework, and its contours follow the outlines of the skeleton which supports it. But it is not strained so taut as to be free from superfluous folds and ornamental puckers. Moulded, as it was, on the different structure of the past, it has not always adjusted itself with nicety to the angles of the present. It contains elements, therefore, which, like the rudimentary organs of the human body, or the decorative appendages of the British Constitution, have survived after their function has disappeared and their meaning been forgotten.

England is peculiar in being marked to a greater degree than most other communities, not by a single set of class relations, but by two, of which one is the product of the last century of economic development, and the other, though transformed by that development and softened by the social policy of the democratic era, contains, nevertheless, a large infusion of elements which descend from the quite different type of society that existed before the rise of the great industry. It is the combination of both – the blend of a crude plutocratic reality with the sentimental aroma of an aristocratic legend – which gives the English class system its peculiar toughness and cohesion. It is at once as businesslike as Manchester and as gentlemanly as Eton; if its hands can be as rough as those of Esau, its voice is as mellifluous as that of Jacob. It is a god with two faces and a thousand tongues, and, while each supports its fellow, they speak in different accents and appeal to different emotions. Revolutionary logic, which is nothing if not rational, addresses its shattering syllogisms to the one, only to be answered in terms of polite evasion by the other. It appeals to obvious economic grievances, and is baffled by the complexities of a society in which the tumultuous impulses of economic self-interest are blunted and muffled by the sedate admonitions of social respectability.

Regarded as an economic engine, the structure of English society is simpler than that of some more primitive communities. In spite of the complexity of its detailed organisation, its main lines are drawn not by customary or juristic distinctions, which are often capricious, but by the economic logic of a system directed towards a single objective, the attainment of which, or the failure to attain it, can be tested by the arithmetical criterion of profit or loss. Its most obvious feature is also its most characteristic. It is the separation of the groups which organise, direct and own the material apparatus of industry from those which perform its routine work, and the consequent numerical preponderance of the wage-earning population over all other sections of the community.

Such a separation and such a preponderance, on the scale on which they exist at present, are a novel phenomenon. Till a comparatively recent period in the history of most European countries, while political power was far more highly centralised than it is today, a high degree of economic centralisation was, apart from certain peculiar undertakings, the exception. The legal and social cleavage which divided different classes, the noble from the *roturier*, the lord from the peasant, was often profound. But the control of the processes of economic life tended, of course with numerous exceptions, to be dispersed in the hands of large numbers of peasant farmers and small masters, who, subject to the discharge of their personal or financial obligations towards their superiors, conducted much of the humble routine of their economic affairs at their own discretion. Labour, property and enterprise were, to some considerable degree, not separated, but intertwined. Economic initiative and direction were fragmentary and decentralised. Conducted, not by mass attacks, but by individual skirmishes, the struggle with nature was ineffective because it was uncoordinated. The organisation of economic life, with its numerous tiny centres of energy, and its absence of staff-work and system, resembled that, not of an army, but of a guerilla band. In the picture drawn in the well-known estimate of Gregory King, or in the more reliable statistics of the Prussian Census, which even in 1843 showed only seventy-six workpeople to every hundred masters, pre-industrial society appears, compared with our own, like a collection of fishing-smacks beside a battle fleet.

Over the greater part of the world, such, or something like it, is still the normal type of economic structure. But the organisation and class relations of industrial societies are obviously different. Their note is the magnitude of the group dependent on wages, compared with those which are interested in the ownership of property and the direction of economic enterprise. Statisticians have attempted to measure the degree of 'Proletarianisation' in different countries. They have produced tables in which they are graded according to the percentage which the wage-earners and humbler salaried officials form of the total occupied population, from Russia, with 12 to 14 per cent of wage workers till a decade or so ago, Greece with 21, Bulgaria with 23, and France with 48, to the United States with 70 per cent, Australia with 71, Belgium and the Netherlands each with 73, and Great Britain with 78.[17] The materials for such investigations are defective, and accurate results are not to be expected. What is significant, however, is the broad difference of type in the economic structure of communities at the two ends of the scale. At the one extreme there are those in which the wage-earners form a minority scattered up and down the interstices of a society composed predominantly of small property-owners; at the other extreme there are those in which the wage-earners form half, two-thirds, or even three-quarters of the whole occupied population.

Of these two types of organisation it is obviously the second which is characteristic of England. Not only is she the country where the urban and industrial workers form the largest proportion of the total population, but its agricultural system itself, with its dependence on large numbers of landless agricultural labourers, approaches more closely to the industrial pattern than is the case in most other communities. The broad lines of her economic structure are revealed by the census, according to which 5.5 per cent of the occupied population were in 1931 employers or managers, 76.7 per cent employed, 11.8 per cent unemployed, and 6.0 per cent workers on their own account. Professor Bowley and Sir Josiah Stamp, adopting a different classification, estimated that, in 1924, 76 per cent of the occupied population were wage-earners, 14 per cent salaried, 6 per cent independent workers, and 4 per cent employers, farmers, or engaged in professions.[18] With the growing concentration of industry, the proportion of salaried workers tends, it is probable, to increase, and of employers to diminish; the independent producers are numerically insignificant; while the small master with two or three journeymen, who is still so conspicuous a figure in most continental countries, does not play a large part in most British industries, with the exception of agriculture, building, retail shopkeeping, and certain minor handicrafts.

In the striking predominance of the wage-working population the United Kingdom resembles the United States, Australia, and Belgium, and is sharply contrasted, not only with communities, like Denmark, where agriculture is overwhelmingly the largest occupation, but with the countries possessing important manufacturing industries, like France, and, to a less extent, Germany. Apart, indeed, from mining, metallurgy, and textiles, the economic structure of France is of a different pattern from that of England. For, while England has been the country of political stability and economic revolution, France is the classical land of political revolution and economic stability. It has known how to make the best both of the present and of the past. It has grafted the great industry on to its traditional social organisation, without, as yet, seriously undermining the latter.

Thus, in French agriculture, in 1921, the labourers and farmservants were actually fewer than the independent cultivators, the *chefs d'exploitation*, numbering 2,834,127 as against 5,219,464, while approximately three-quarters of the latter were peasant proprietors.[19] In French industry, when a census was taken in 1906, 20 per cent of the occupied population were independent producers – *travailleurs isolés* – neither working for others nor employing them, while 42 per cent of its workers in manufacturing industry were employed in establishments with not more than twenty employees, and only 22 per cent in establishments with more than a hundred. In England the proportion of farmland cultivated by occupying owners more than trebled between 1913 and 1927, rising from 10.7 per cent at the first date to over 36 per cent at the second. But it is still unique in the degree to which, not only its urban, but its rural population consists of wage-earners; and, whereas in France the small producer has held his own, not only in agriculture, but also in a considerable number of industries, in England, to an extent unknown elsewhere, he has lost his footing, not only in industry, but in agriculture. To a greater extent than is true of any other nation its happiness, its efficiency, its culture and civilisation, depend upon the condition of the wage-earning population.

This army of wage-earners, which forms over three-quarters of the nation, includes, of course, individuals of widely diverse incomes, economic positions, social conditions, personal interests and habits, types of culture, political opinions, and religious creeds. It is a class only when regarded from a limited economic angle, only in the sense that its members depend for their livelihood on the wage contract. But, though the economic side of life is not the only side, it has, nevertheless, an importance of its own, and the numerical preponderance of the wage-workers is obviously the first characteristic of the structure of English society, when it is regarded in its economic aspect, as an organisation for the production of wealth.

There is also, however, a second characteristic, which is not necessarily, indeed, associated with the first, but which, in England at least, accompanies it. It is the remarkable degree to which the wage-earning section of the population tends to be distinct from the section which owns property. The wage-earning class might, of course, be in receipt of income from sources other than wages. It might combine work for wages with the ownership of property, and supplement its earnings by interest in investments, as many professional workers in fact do, or as the peasant in certain countries supplements income from property by intermittent work for wages. And to some extent, indeed, this is the case. Weekly wage-earners own a considerable volume of property in the form of individual, and, still more, of collective, savings, such as savings bank deposits, shares in building societies, money to their account in health, unemployment and life insurance funds, and in the funds of trade unions, co-operative societies, and friendly societies.

In the aggregate, however, the amount thus owned, when set in relation to the number of adult wage-earners and to the property owned by other sections of the community, is impressive by its smallness rather than by its magnitude. To say that, except for their household goods and personal belongings, a large body of Englishmen are almost propertyless, and that an appreciable proportion of them – for example, the not inconsiderable number of miners who have been obliged to mortgage such property as they possess – probably do not own wealth to the value of the kit that they took into battle at Paschendaele or on the Somme, has a displeasing air of rhetorical exaggeration. But, when the evidence advanced by statisticians is considered, it is difficult to resist the conclusion that in England the ownership of property is, to say the least, somewhat highly concentrated.

Sir Josiah Stamp has given figures from which it appears that in 1919 about two-thirds of the aggregate wealth of the nation was held by just under 400,000 persons, or less than 1 per cent of the population, and one-third of it by as few as 36,000, or less than 1 per 1,000. According to Professor Clay, 64 per cent of the wealth was in 1920–1 in the hands of 1.6 per cent of the persons holding property, which means (since such persons form roughly one-half of the population) that rather less than two-thirds of the wealth was owned by 0.8 per cent of the population. The figures of estates subject to the death duties do not suggest that a tendency to the wider distribution of property has been operative since that date. In 1934–5, for example, 6.6 per cent of the owners of dutiable estates owned 66.3 per cent of the property, and 36.4 per cent of the property was actually owned by only 1 per cent of them. The figure which Professor Clay gave for the capital owned in 1920–1 by 13,500,000 persons with less than £100 was £912,000,000 or 7.6 of the aggregate wealth; while Professor Carr-Saunders and Mr Caradog Jones suggested £1,375,000,000 as a 'very rough estimate' of the accumulated savings of small investors in 1925. A more recent calculation puts such savings as £1,731,000,000 in 1934, inclusive of savings certificates, and £1,338,000,000 exclusive of them. International comparisons are full of pitfalls, but the figures adduced by Professor Clay, and by Mr Wedgwood in his admirable book, *The Economics of Inheritance*, suggest that the inequality in the distribution of property is somewhat greater in England than in France and Ireland, and considerably greater than in Australia.[20]

It is clear, therefore, that, even when allowance is made for deficiencies and ambiguities in the statistical evidence, the earnings of the three-quarters to four-fifths of the population who live by wages are only to a small extent supplemented by receipts from property. While the distribution of income is less unequal than that of wealth, this concentration of property gives a peculiar and distinctive stamp to the social structure of England, which differentiates it sharply from that of some other communities. Marriage, Mr Chesterton has somewhere observed, would not be regarded as a national institution if, while a small minority of the population were polygamous, the majority did not marry at all; and property can hardly be said to be a national institution in England, in the sense in which it was a national institution in some earlier ages, or as it is a national institution in some other countries today. Where conditions are such that two-thirds of the wealth is owned by approximately one per cent of the population, the ownership of the property is more properly regarded as the badge of a class than as the attribute of a society.

A famous theory has suggested that the progressive concentration of ownership in the hands of a diminishing number of owners is a tendency inherent in capitalist civilisation. The generalisation was prompted by the contrast between the distribution of property in England in the early days of the great industry and that obtaining in the contemporary peasant societies of the Continent, where the great industry had hardly as yet got on to its feet, and it has not been confirmed by the subsequent course of economic history. While the difference between the character and significance of property in these two types of community is not less impressive than it was, it is a difference between two phases of economic development, not, as Marx is usually understood to have suggested, between the earlier and later stages of the same phase. So far from diminishing, as he seems to have anticipated would be the case, the number of property-owners in England has tended, if anything, to increase in the course of the last half-century. Though still astonishingly small, it is probably larger today than at any time since he wrote.

But, of course, the distinction between the majority, who are mainly dependent on wages, and the minority, who are largely concerned with proprietary interests, is not the only significant line of division in the economic system. There is also the familiar division between the directed and the directors; between those who receive orders and those from whom orders proceed; between the privates and the non-commissioned officers of the industrial army and those who initiate its operations, determine its objective and methods, and are responsible for the strategy and tactics on which the economic destiny of the mass of mankind depends. Since the control of industrial enterprise belongs in law to the ordinary shareholder, and in practice to the entrepreneurs who command the use of his savings and act on his behalf, the proprietary classes, either personally or through their agents, take, as seems to them expedient, the decisions upon which the organisation and conduct of industry depend, and, within the limits prescribed by law or established by voluntary agreement, are responsible for their action to no superior authority. The wage-earners act under their direction; have access to the equipment, plant, and machinery, without which they cannot support themselves, on condition of complying with the rules laid down, subject to the intervention of the state and of trade unions, by their employers; and work – and not infrequently live – under conditions which, consciously or unconsciously, the latter have determined. Hence the third characteristic of the economic structure of industrial societies is the sharpness of the division between the upper and lower grades of the economic hierarchy. In the concentration of authority which springs from the separation of the functions of initiative and control on the hand, and of execution on the other, such societies resemble a pyramid with steeply sloping sides and an acute apex.

In the course of the last two generations that concentration of authority has passed into a new and more sensational stage. In the infancy of the great industry its significance was veiled by the multitude of small undertakings and the absence of combination between them, by the general belief that, with luck and perseverance, any able man could fight his way to the top, and by the fact that, since the employer was normally an individual, not a company, the relations between management and wage-earners, if often harsher than today, were also less remote and impersonal. In certain branches of industry and in certain communities such conditions still survive, but the current has obviously been flowing for two generations in the opposite direction. It is sometimes suggested that the growth of joint-stock enterprise, by increasing the number of small investors, has broadened the basis of industrial government. But, if joint-stock enterprise has done something to diffuse ownership, it has centralised control. The growth in the size of the business unit necessarily accelerates the process by which ever larger bodies of wage-earners are brigaded under the direction of a comparatively small staff of entrepreneurs. The movement towards combination and amalgamation, which is advancing so rapidly today in Great Britain, does the same. The emergence, side by side with questions of wages and working conditions, of questions of status and control is one symptom of the more definite horizontal cleavage which that centralisation of economic command has tended to produce.

So, when English society is considered as a series of groups engaged in production, the salient characteristic of its class structure is the division between the majority who work for wages, but who do not own or direct, and the minority who own the material apparatus of industry and determine industrial organisation and policy. Society is not merely, however, an economic mechanism in which different groups combine for the purpose of production; it is also a system of social groups with varying standards of expenditure and habits of life, and different positions, not only on an economic, but on a social scale. It has, therefore, a social as well as an economic, pattern. And, though the first is moulded upon the second, it has also a character and logic of its own, which finds expression in distinctive forms of organisation and give rise to separate and peculiar problems.

Regarded from the standpoint, not of the production of wealth, but of its use and consumption, the predominant characteristic of the English social system is simple. It is its hierarchical quality, and the connection of that quality with differences of wealth. All forms of social organisation are hierarchical, in the sense that they imply gradations of responsibility and power, which vary from individual to individual according to his place in the system. But these gradations may be based on differences of function and office, may relate only to those aspects of life which are relevant to such differences, and may be compatible with the easy movement of individuals, according to their capacity, from one point on the scale to another. Or they may have their source in differences of birth, or wealth, or social position, may embrace all sides of life, including the satisfaction of the elementary human needs which are common to men as men, and may correspond to distinctions, not of capacity, but of circumstance and opportunity.

It is possible to conceive a community in which the necessary diversity of economic functions existed side by side with a large measure of economic and social equality. In such a community, while the occupations and incomes of individuals varied, they would live, nevertheless, in much the same environment, would enjoy similar standards of health and education, would find different positions, according to their varying abilities, equally accessible to them, would intermarry freely with each other, would be equally immune from the more degrading forms of poverty, and equally secure against economic oppression. But the historical structure and spirit of English society are of a different character. It has inherited and preserved a tradition of differentiation, not merely by economic function, but by wealth and status, and that tradition, though obviously weakened during the last two generations, has left a deep imprint both on its practical organisation and on its temper and habits of thought. Thus not only is it, like all social systems, a pyramid, but it is a pyramid the successive tiers of which tend to correspond only to a small degree with differences of character and ability, and to a high degree with differences of social class. Not only is it a hierarchy, but it is a hierarchy whose gradations embrace those aspects of life where discrimination is inappropriate, because it ignores the common element in human requirements, as well as those where, because it is related to varying levels of human capacity, it is appropriate and necessary. It is marked, in short, by sharp differences, not only of economic status and economic power, but of pecuniary income, of circumstances, and of opportunity.

The distribution of pecuniary income in Great Britain has often been analysed. Professor Bowley has estimated that, in 1910, just over 1 per cent of the population took 30 per cent, and 5.5 per cent took 44 per cent, of the national income, leaving 70 per cent of the income to 98.9 per cent of the population, and 56 per cent of the income to 94.5 per cent of the population. Sir Josiah Stamp has stated that in 1919 'one-twelfth of the gross total income was received by about one-480th of the people and one-half by approximately one-ninth to one-tenth of the people'. Later investigations show much the same result. 'Speaking of the years 1929 or 1935,' writes Mr Colin Clark, 'we can say that one-tenth of the whole working population, with incomes over £250, took 42 per cent of the whole total of personal incomes, or just over one-half if we allow for the fact that the greater part of the non-personal incomes, in the form of undistributed company profits and such, accrued for the benefit of the rich. A small class, comprising $1\frac{1}{2}$ per cent of the population, with 'four-figure incomes and upwards, took 23 per cent of the whole total of personal incomes.'[21] The average income per person in the richest class, with incomes of over £10,000 each, was actually over 220 times that per person in the poorest class, embracing 11,800 receivers of incomes of under £125.

Income, it will be noted, is somewhat less unequally distributed than capital; but the steepness of the slope which such figures reveal is, it will be agreed, extraordinary. Pecuniary income, however, is not the only factor which requires to be taken into account in considering the gradations of the class system. For the distribution of income, as set out by the statisticians, may be subsequently altered by taxation and by expenditure on social services, and thus a high degree of inequality of pecuniary income may co-exist, as far, at least, as certain sides of life are concerned, with a considerable measure of practical equality. Such practical equality – though, thanks to such measures, slightly less remote than it was – is still very far, nevertheless, from having been approached. Hence, not only are there the oft-cited disparities of financial resources, which are susceptible of statistical measurement, but, what is more fundamental, education, health, the opportunities for personal culture and even decency, and sometimes, it would seem, life itself, tend to be meted out on a graduated scale. The destiny of the individual is decided, to an extent which is somewhat less, indeed, than in the past, but which remains revolting, not by his personal quality, but by his place in the social system, by his position as a member of this stratum or of that.

These contrasts of circumstances are more powerful as an instrument of social stratification even than the difference of income of which they are the consequence. Most infants, high medical authorities inform us, are born healthy, but of the children – predominantly, of course, the children of wage-earners – who enter the elementary schools at the age of five, no less than one-fifth are found to be suffering from physical defects which cripple their development and sow the seeds of illness in later years. When their formal education begins, they find in the elementary schools, with all the immense improvement that has taken place in those schools in the course of the last generation, conditions of accommodation, equipment and staffing which would not be tolerated for an instant in the schools attended by the well-to-do, and which are excluded, indeed, from grant-aided secondary schools by the regulations of the Board of Education. While the provision for the earlier stages of education is defective in quality, the provision for the later stages is defective in quantity. Educational considerations – considerations of the conditions most likely to promote the growth of human beings in physique and intelligence – dictate, as has often been pointed out, that all normal children shall pass from primary education to some form of secondary education. But the proportion of children leaving the elementary schools who enter what have hitherto been known as secondary schools is, in England and Wales as a whole, less than one-seventh, and in some areas less than one-tenth, while some three-quarters of them have hitherto entered full-time wage-earning employment at the age of fourteen.

Thus, even in childhood, different strata of the population are distinguished by sharp contrasts of environment, of health, and of physical well-being. A small minority enjoy conditions which are favourable to health, and receive prolonged and careful nurture, and are encouraged to regard themselves as belonging to a social group which will exercise responsibility and direction. The great majority are exposed to conditions in which health, if not impossible, is necessarily precarious, and end their education just at the age when their powers are beginning to develop, and are still sometimes encouraged to believe that the qualities most desirable in common men are docility, and a respect for their betters, and a habit of submission. As the rising generation steps year by year into industry, it enters a world where these social contrasts are reinforced by economic contrasts – by the differences of security and economic power which distinguish those who own property and control the industrial machine from those who are dependent on their daily labour and execute the routine work of the economic system. But the social contrasts continue, and are, indeed, intensified. In spite of the poets, there are no such inveterate respecters of persons as disease and death, and the disparities find expression in the difference between the liability to disease and death of impoverished and well-to-do areas – in the fact, for example, that in the less densely populated parts of Manchester the death-rate a decade ago was 10.5 per 1,000, and in the more densely populated parts, 16, and that in a poor district of Glasgow it was approximately twice what it was where poverty was less. More recent investigations underline the same point. It has been shown – to quote only one example – that in Stockton-on-Tees the standardised death-rate during the years 1931–4 was 11.5 per 1,000 for the better-off families, and more than twice as much – 26 per 1,000 – for the poorest.[22] The poor, it seems, are beloved by the gods, if not by their fellow-mortals. They are awarded exceptional opportunities of dying young.

A stratified class system appears, therefore, to have as its second characteristic the contrast described in the familiar phrase of Disraeli, the contrast not only between different levels of pecuniary income, but between different standards of physical well-being and different opportunities for mental development and civilisation. And it has, in addition, a third symptom, which is little less significant than these, and which is more conspicuous, perhaps, in England than in some other countries, for example the United States, where inequality of income is hardly less pronounced. It is the general, and, till recently, the almost unquestioning, acceptance of habits and institutions, which vest in particular classes a special degree of public influence and an exceptional measure of economic opportunity.

The association of political leadership with birth and wealth is a commonplace of English history; but it is not always realised how little that association was weakened after the advent of what is usually regarded as the age of democracy. Professor Laski, in his instructive analysis of the personnel of British Cabinets between 1801 and 1924, has shown that, for nearly two generations after the Act of 1867 had enfranchised the urban working classes, the greater part of the business of government continued, nevertheless, to be conducted by a small group of owners of great properties, who were enabled by their economic advantages and social connections to step into the exercise of political power with a facility impossible to ordinary men. Of 69 Ministers who held office between 1885 and 1905, 40 were the sons of nobility, 52 were educated at Oxford and Cambridge, and 46 were educated at public schools; while even between 1906 and 1916, 25 out of 51 Ministers were sons of nobility.[23] To turn from these figures to the prognostications of catastrophic social changes advanced in 1832 and 1867 is to receive a lesson in the vanity of political prophecies. Of all the institutions changed by the advent of political democracy, the traditional system of government by a small knot of rich families was for half a century that which changed the least. They heard the rumblings of the democratic tumbril, but, like the patient East,

> They let the legions thunder past,
> And plunged in thought again,

or, if not in thought, in whatever substitute for it they found more congenial.

The political phenomenon described by Professor Laski is today no longer so conspicuous as it was. But the forces which for long made political leadership so largely dependent upon the peculiar opportunities opened by birth and wealth have left their mark, as was to be expected, upon other departments of English life. They have tended to produce, in them also, a similar, though somewhat less noticeable, restriction of leadership to particular classes, with special opportunities and connections, which is only gradually being undermined by the wider educational provision that has been made since 1902.

'If one could not be Eton and Oxford,' writes Mr Algernon Cecil of the middle of last century, 'one did well in those days to be Harrow and Cambridge.' The evidence presented by Mr Nightingale, who has made a statistical analysis of the social antecedents of the personnel of the Foreign Office and Diplomatic Service between 1851 and 1929, suggests that his statement is true of a more recent period. Sixty per cent of it, he shows, has been drawn from the eleven most exclusive public schools while, of the remaining 40 per cent, well over one-half attended the lesser public schools, received a military or naval education, or were educated privately or abroad. 'The unchallengeable conclusion that emerges ... is that the British Foreign Office and Diplomatic Service has been a preserve for the sons of the aristocratic, *rentier* and professional classes ... The general influence which follows from a study of the effects of the various reforms in the examination regulations is that they have been substantial but not profound.' Professor Ginsberg, who has recently investigated the antecedents of 1,268 British subjects admitted to Lincoln's Inn at different periods between 1886 and 1927, reaches a somewhat similar conclusion with regard to the recruitment of one section of the legal profession. Over 75 per cent of them belonged, he finds, to the group classified by the census as 'upper and middle', while in no period did the sons of wage-earners amount to 1 per cent of the total admissions, except in the years 1923–7, when they formed 1.8 per cent of them.[24]

No adequate statistics are available of the classes from which other professions are recruited, and conclusions must necessarily, therefore, be tentative and provisional. But some indirect light is thrown upon the subject by an examination of the educational careers of those by whom positions of eminence in the professional world are at present occupied. In the year 1926, 71 out of 80 bishops and deans for whom information is available, 139 out of 181 members of the judicial profession, 152 out of 210 highly placed members of public departments, 63 out of 88 members of the Indian Civil Service and Governors of Dominions, and 99 out of 132 directors of banks and railways, had been educated at public schools. The more select 'public' schools appear to have a special attraction for the clergy and for directors of companies. Of the 80 deans and bishops, 51, and, of the 142 directors of banks and railways, 85, were educated at the fourteen most celebrated among them, while, of the whole 691, the number so educated was 330, or 47 per cent.[25] Even if it be assumed that all those for whom information is not available were educated at schools of other kinds, the high proportion educated at public schools remains striking. It will be realised, of course, that, since persons now eminent were educated between twenty-five and fifty years ago, such figures reflect the conditions prevailing in the last two decades of the nineteenth century rather than those of today. It is significant, however, that, even from 1924 to 1929, 64 per cent of the successful candidates for the administrative grade of the Civil Service still came, according to the evidence submitted to the Royal Commission, from 150 schools belonging to the Headmasters' Conference.[26]

'The philosophy of the boarding-school,' writes Mr R. F. Cholmeley, 'is, on the whole, a philosophy of the well-to-do,' who 'look out upon life from a fortress,' and another distinguished headmaster, contrasting the English educational dualism with the arrangements of France and Germany, where 'rich and poor are educated side by side', has observed that 'the public school is a school for the well-to-do'.[27] There are, no doubt, certain public schools, for example Christ's Hospital, which are attended by a considerable number of boys from elementary schools. But it is true, nevertheless, to say that the public schools, and, in particular, the most celebrated among them, are traditionally connected with the middle and upper classes, and, with certain conspicuous exceptions, are but rarely attended by the children of wage-earners. Drawing their pupils mainly, not from the public primary schools, but from the so-called preparatory schools, and catering for the requirements of the wealthier sections of the community, they form virtually a closed educational system of their own, side by side with the system of public education which has as its foundation the elementary school. They are even disposed, it seems, not to deny their isolation, but to be proud of it, and to suppose, as was recently explained by the governors of one of them, which had the misfortune, till the error was corrected, to be attended by an unusually large number of boys from elementary schools, that their character as public schools will somehow be impaired, if too many of such children are admitted to them. A public school, in short, is not a school that is easily accessible to the public, but a school that the great majority of the public are precluded from entering.

Equality and culture

Since life is a swallow, and theory a snail, it is not surprising that varieties of class organisation should be but inadequately represented in the terminology of political science. But the absence of a word to describe the type of society which combines the forms of political democracy with sharp economic and social divisions is, none the less, unfortunate, since it obscures the practical realities which it is essential to grasp. The conventional classification of communities by the character of their constitutional arrangements had its utility in an age when the principal objective of effort and speculation was the extension of political rights. It is economic and social forces, however, which are most influential in determining the practical operation of political institutions, and it is economic and social relations that create the most urgent of the internal problems confronting industrial communities. The most significant differences distinguishing different societies from each other are, in short, not different forms of constitution and government, but different types of economic and social structure.

Of such distinctions the most fundamental is that which divides communities where economic initiative is widely diffused, and class differences small in dimensions and trivial in their effects, from those where the conditions obtaining are the opposite – where the mass of mankind exercise little influence on the direction of economic enterprise, and where economic and cultural gradations descend precipitately from one stratum of the population to another. Both types may possess representative institutions, a wide franchise, and responsible government; and both, therefore, may properly be described as democracies. But to regard them as, on that account, resembling each other – to ignore the profound differences of spirit and quality between a democracy in which class divisions play a comparatively unimportant part in the life of society, and a democracy where the influence of such differences is all-pervasive – is to do violence to realities. It is like supposing that all mammals have the same anatomical structure, or that the scenery of England resembles that of Switzerland because both countries lie in the temperate zone. Such varieties should be treated by political scientists as separate species, and should be given distinctive names. The former contain large elements, not merely of political, but of social, democracy. The latter are political democracies, but social oligarchies.

Social oligarchies have existed under widely divergent material circumstances, and in the most sharply contrasted conditions of economic civilisation. In the past they were specially associated with the feudal organisation of agricultural societies, so that, in the infancy of the modern economic world, the expansion of commerce and manufacture was hailed, by some with delight, by others with apprehension, as the acid which would dissolve them. Today, since in most parts of Europe the peasant farmer has come to his own, it is highly industrialised communities that are their favourite stronghold. Though it is in countries such as England and Germany, where the great industry flowed into the moulds prepared by an aristocratic tradition, that they attain their full efflorescence, they do not only conform to an old tradition of aristocracy, they also themselves create a new tradition. They appear to be the form of social organisation which, in the absence of counteracting measures, the great industry itself tends spontaneously to produce, when its first outburst of juvenile energy is over, when its individualistic, levelling and destructive phase has given place to that of system and organisation.

The most instructive illustration of that tendency is given by the history of industrial America, because it is in America that its operation has been at once swiftest and least anticipated. The United States started on its dazzling career as nearly in a state of innocence as a society can. It had no medieval past to bury. It was free from the complicated iniquities of feudal land-law and the European class system. It began, at least in the north, as a society of small farmers, merchants, and master-craftsmen, without either a large wage-earning proletariat or the remnants of serfdom which lingered in Europe till a century ago. It believed that all men have an equal right to life, liberty, and the pursuit of happiness. The confident hope that it would be unsullied by the disparities of power and wealth which corrupted Europe was the inspiration of those who, like Jefferson, saw in the Revolution, not merely the birth of a new state, but the dawn of a happier society.

It is the general, if partial, realisation of that hope, in certain parts, at least, of America, which has made it for a century the magnet of Europe, and which still gives to American life much of its charm. It is marked, indeed, by much economic inequality; but it is also marked by much social equality, which is the legacy from an earlier phase of its economic civilisation – though how long it will survive in the conditions of today is a different question, on which Americans themselves sometimes speak with apprehension. But evidently it is not in the America of which Englishmen hear most, but in that of which they hear least, not in the America of Wall Street and Pittsburg and the United States Steel Corporation and Mr Morgan and Mr Ford, but in the America of the farmer and the country town and the Middle West, that this charm is today most likely to be found. And evidently the equality of manners and freedom from certain conventional restraints, to which, partly at least, it is due, exist, not because of the industrial expansion of America, but in spite of it.

Nearly a century ago, De Tocqueville, who wrote on the first page of his *De la Démocratie en Amérique* that the general equality of conditions in America was the fundamental fact from which all others seemed to be derived, gave to one of his later essays the significant title, 'How aristocracy may be engendered by manufactures.' 'If ever,' he wrote, 'a permanent inequality of conditions and aristocracy again penetrate into the world, it may be predicted that this is the gate by which they will enter.'[28]

Americans have led the world in the frequency and fullness of their official inquiries into economic organisation, and, if the results of such inquiries may be trusted, that prophecy, as far as industrial America is concerned, is today not far from fulfilment. And what is true of the great industry in the United States is not less true of other industrial communities. Their natural tendency, it seems, except in so far as it is qualified and held in check by other forces, is to produce the concentration of economic power, and the inequalities of circumstance and condition, which De Tocqueville noted as the mark of an aristocratic social order.

A right to the pursuit of happiness is not identical with the right to attain it, and to state the fact is not to pronounce a judgment upon it. To see in economic concentration and social stratification the mystery of iniquity and the mark of the beast, to regard as the result of a deliberate and sinister conspiracy qualities which are the result partly of a failure to control impersonal forces, partly, not of a subtle and unscrupulous intelligence, but of its opposite – of a crude appetite for money and power among the few, and a reverence for success in obtaining them among the many – would, no doubt, be naïve. Yes, but how irrational also to suppose, as in England it is much commoner to suppose, that such characteristics are anything but a misfortune which an intelligent community will do all in its power to remove! How absurd to regard them as inevitable and admirable, to invest them with a halo of respectful admiration, and to deplore, whenever their economic foundations are threatened, the crumbling of civilisation and the Goth at the gate! A nation is not civilised because a handful of its members are successful in acquiring large sums of money and in persuading their fellows that a catastrophe will occur if they do not acquire it, any more than Dahomey was civilised because its king had a golden stool and an army of slaves, or Judea because Solomon possessed a thousand wives and imported apes and peacocks, and surrounded the worship of Moloch and Ashtaroth with an impressive ritual.

What matters to a society is less what it owns than what it is and how it uses its possessions. It is civilised in so far as its conduct is guided by a just appreciation of spiritual ends, in so far as it uses its material resources to promote the dignity and refinement of the individual human beings who compose it. Violent contrasts of wealth and power, and an indiscriminating

devotion to institutions by which such contrasts are maintained
and heightened, do not promote the attainment of such ends,
but thwart it. They are therefore, a mark, not of civilisation, but
of barbarism, like the gold rings in the noses of savage monarchs,
or the diamonds on their wives and the chains on their slaves.
Since it is obviously such contrasts which determine the grounds
upon which social struggles take place, and marshal the comba-
tants who engage in them, they are a malady to be cured and a
problem which demands solution.

But are they a malady? Granted, it is sometimes retorted, that
sharp economic distinctions, with the complacency and callousness which such distinctions produce, are in themselves nauseous, are they not, nevertheless, the safeguard for virtues that
would perish without them? Is not even the attachment of Englishmen to the idea of class, vulgar and repulsive as are many
of its manifestations, the lantern which shelters a spark that, but
for its protection, would be extinguished or dimmed?

The characteristics of a civilised society, Mr Bell has argued in
his entertaining book,[29] are reasonableness and a sense of values,
and these qualities were made possible in the ages in which,
by general consent, they found their supreme and imperishable
expression, because they had as their vehicle an élite – an élite
which was released for the life of the spirit by the patient labour
of slaves and peasants. What was true of the Athens of Pericles,
and the Italy of the Renaissance, and the France of Voltaire, is
true, in a humbler measure, of every society which is sufficiently
mature to understand that freedom and intellectual energy are
more vital to its welfare than the mechanical satisfaction of its
material requirements. If it is to possess, not merely the comforts,
but the graces, of existence, it must be enamoured of excellence.
It must erect a standard of perfection, and preserve it inviolate
against the clamour for the commonplace which is the appetite
of the natural man, and of his eager hierophant, the practical
reformer. But a standard of perfection, it is urged, is the achievement of a minority, and inequality is the hedge which protects
it. It is the sacred grove which guards the shrine against the
hooves of the multitude. Like an oasis which few can inhabit,
but the very thought of which brings refreshment and hope to
the sand-weary traveller, inequality, it is argued, protects the

graces of life from being submerged beneath the dust of its daily necessities. It perpetuates a tradition of culture, by ensuring the survival of a class which is its visible embodiment, and which maintains that tradition in maintaining itself.

Compared with the formidable host which understands by civilisation the elaboration of the apparatus and machinery of existence, as though Athens, or Florence, or Elizabethan England were objects of respectful pity when set side by side with modern London or New York, those who press such considerations are clearly on the side of light. If the Kingdom of Heaven is not eating and drinking, but righteousness and peace, neither is civilisation the multiplication of motor-cars and cinemas, or of any other of the innumerable devices by which men accumulate means of ever-increasing intricacy to the attainment of ends which are not worth attaining. It is true that the mark of civilisation is respect for excellence in the things of the spirit, and a readiness to incur sacrifice for the sake of fostering it. It is true that excellence is impossible in the absence of severe and exacting standards of attainment and appreciation which check the taste for cheap success and shoddy achievement by cultivating a temper which discriminates ruthlessly between the admirable and the second-rate. It is true that such a temper has no more persistent or insidious foe than the perversion of values, which confuses the ends of life with the means, and elevates material prosperity, whether the interpretation put upon it is the accumulation of wealth or the diffusion of comfort, from the position of secondary and instrumental importance that properly belongs to it, into the grand and over-mastering object of individual effort and public approval.

In order, however, to escape from one illusion, it ought not to be necessary to embrace another. If civilisation is not the product of the kitchen garden, neither is it an exotic to be grown in a hot-house. Its flowers may be delicate, but its trunk must be robust, and the height to which it grows depends on the hold of its roots on the surrounding soil. Culture may be fastidious, but fastidiousness is not culture; and, though vulgarity is an enemy to 'reasonableness and a sense of values', it is less deadly an enemy than gentility and complacency. A cloistered and secluded refinement, intolerant of the heat and dust of creative effort, is the note, not of civilisation, but of the epochs which have despaired of it – which have seen, in one form or another, the triumph of the barbarian, and have sought compensation for defeat in writing cultured footnotes to the masterpieces they are incapable of producing. Its achievements may be admirable, but they are those of a silver age, not of a golden. The spiritual home of its votaries is not the Athens of Sophocles; it is the Alexandria of the scholiasts and the Rome of Claudian.

Clever men, it has been remarked, are impressed by their difference from their fellows; wise men are conscious of their resemblance to them. It would be ungracious to suggest that such an attitude is a mark rather of cleverness than of wisdom, but it is not wholly free from the spirit of the sect. When those who adopt it fall below themselves, when they relapse into glorifying what Bacon calls the *idola specus*, they are liable to rhapsodise over civilisation in the tone of a Muggletonian dispensing damnation to all but Muggletonians, as though its secret consisted in the fact that only a select minority is capable of enjoying it, as though it were a species of private entertainment to which a coterie of the right people had received an exclusive invitation.

What their error is they could learn from the great ages which they rightly admire. Neither of them, indeed, was quite the epicure's banquet which they are sometimes thought to have been. Athens, in its greatest days, like Florence in the fourteenth and fifteenth centuries, was a bustling commercial city, with an almost arrogant patriotism and a zest for politics which often found expression in crude and violent action. It was a city whose special boast was that it touched with its magic, not only, like its great rival, an élite, but common men. Its policy of progressive taxation and liberal expenditure upon communal services roused the fury of the rich. Its poets and philosophers took public affairs with tragic seriousness. Its children of light had an incurable habit of discussing questions of art in terms of morality, quite like that *bête noire* of the select, the unregenerate Ruskin.

In no age was the contact between men of letters and men of affairs closer than in the France of the eighteenth century; in no age was the stimulus to speculation more practical, or the influence of speculation upon policy more intimate and direct. The note of a substantial part, not only of its avowedly polemical writing, but of its literature and philosophy, was a belief in the possibility of an almost infinite improvement in the lot of mankind by the advancement of knowledge and the exercise of thought. It was the conviction that Reason is never so much herself as when she turns the weapons sharpened in solitude against the institutions which perpetuate darkness and the offenders whose eminence is maintained at the cost of the degradation of the mass of mankind.

For there is one characteristic, not mentioned by the author of *Civilisation*, which is common to the thought both of Athens and of eighteenth-century France, and which is not the least among the sources of the spell which they have laid on posterity. It is the quality which finds its noblest expression in the famous speech that Thucydides puts into the mouth of Pericles, and of which Voltaire, who lays aside his work as a man of letters to denounce the remnants of serfdom on the Church estates, and to expose the judicial murders of Calas and La Barre, is the grand example. It is – to use a word that at the moment is sadly misused – their humanism, their superb sense of the dignity of man. They speak a language of permanent persuasiveness, because it is not that of a party or a clique, but as universal as reason.

Humanism has many meanings, for human nature has many sides, and the attempt to appropriate it as the label of a sect is not felicitous. There is the humanism of the age which the word is most commonly used to describe, the humanism of the Renaissance, with its rediscovery of human achievement in art and letters. And there is the humanism of the eighteenth century, with its confidence in the new era to be opened to mankind by the triumphs of science, and its hatred of the leaden obscurantism which impeded its progress. There is the humanism which contrasts man with God, or, at least, with the God of some theologies; and there is the humanism which contrasts man with the brutes, and affirms that he is a little lower than the angels. These different senses of the word have often been at war: history is scarred, indeed, with the contentions between them. It ought not to be difficult, nevertheless, for the apostles of the one to understand the other; for indignant though some of them would be at the suggestion, they are using different dialects of a common language. If 'What a piece of work is man! how noble is reason! how infinite in faculty!' is the voice of humanism, so also is 'The sabbath was made for man, not man for the sabbath,' and 'The Kingdom of Heaven is within you.' Shelley's lines

> The loathsome mask has fall'n, the man remains
> Sceptreless, free, uncircumscribed, but man,

> Equal, unclass'd, tribeless, and nationless,
> Exempt from awe, worship, degree, the king
> Over himself! just, gentle, wise, but man,

are one expression of the humanist spirit. Dante's 'Consider your origin; ye were not formed to live like brutes, but to follow virtue and knowledge' is another.

Thus humanism is not the exclusive possession either of those who reject some particular body of religious doctrine or of those who accept it. It is, or it can be, the possession of both. It is not, as the fashion of the moment is disposed to suggest, the special mark of a generation which has lost its sense of the supernatural and is groping for a substitute. For, in order to be at home in this world, it is not sufficient, unfortunately, to disbelieve in another; and, in its intellectual interests, and order of life, and economic relations, such a generation is liable, in the mere innocent exuberance of its self-satisfaction, to display some traits, at least, which are not conspicuously humane. Humanism is the antithesis, not of theism or of Christianity – for how can the humanist spirit be one of indifference to issues that have been, for two thousand years, the principal concern and inspiration of a considerable part of humanity, or to a creed whose central doctrine is that God became man? – but of materialism. Its essence is simple. It is the attitude which judges the externals of life by their effect in assisting or hindering the life of the spirit. It is the belief that the machinery of existence – property and material wealth and industrial organisation, and the whole fabric and mechanism of social institutions – is to be regarded as means to an end, and that this end is the growth towards perfection of individual human beings.

The humanist spirit, like the religious spirit, is not, indeed, indifferent to these things, which, on their own plane, are obviously important; but it resists their encroachment upon spheres which do not belong to them. It insists that they are not the objects of life, but its instruments, which are to be maintained when they are serviceable, and changed when they are not. Its aim is to liberate and cultivate the powers which make for energy and refinement; and it is critical, therefore, of all forms of organisation which sacrifice spontaneity to mechanism, or which seek, whether in the name of economic efficiency or of social equality, to reduce the variety of individual character and genius to a drab and monotonous uniformity. But it desires to cultivate these powers in all men, not only in a few. Resting, as it does, on the faith that the differences between men are less important and fundamental than their common humanity, it is the enemy of arbitrary and capricious divisions between different members of the human family, which are based, not upon what men, given suitable conditions, are capable of becoming, but on external distinctions between them, such as those created by birth or wealth.

Sharp contrasts of opportunity and circumstance, which deprive some classes of the means of development deemed essential for others, are sometimes defended on the ground that the result of abolishing them must be to produce, in the conventional phrase, a dead-level of mediocrity. Mediocrity, whether found in the valleys of society or, as not infrequently happens, among the peaks and enimences, is always to be deprecated, though it is hardly curable, perhaps, as sometimes seems to be supposed, by so simple a process as the application to conspicuous portions of the social system of sporadic dabs of varnish and gilt. But not all the ghosts which clothe themselves in metaphors are equally substantial, and whether a level is regrettable or not depends, after all, upon what is levelled.

Those who dread a dead-level of income or wealth, which is not at the moment a very pressing danger in England, do not dread, it seems, a dead-level of law and order, and of security for life and property. They do not complain that persons endowed by nature with unusual qualities of strength, audacity or cunning are artificially prevented from breaking into houses, or terrorising their neighbours, or forging cheques. On the contrary, they maintain a system of police in order to ensure that powers of this kind are, as far as may be, reduced to impotence. They insist on establishing a dead-level in these matters, because they know that, by preventing the strong from using their strength to oppress the weak, and the unscrupulous from profiting by their cleverness to cheat the simple, they are not crippling the development of personality, but assisting it. They do not ignore the importance of maintaining a high standard of effort and achievement. On the contrary, they deprive certain kinds of achievements of their fruits, in order to encourage the pursuit of others more compatible with the improvement of individual character, and more conducive to the good of society.

Violence and cunning are not the only forces, however, which hamper the individual in the exercise of his powers, or which cause false standards of achievement to be substituted for true. They are also, in most societies, the special advantages conferred by wealth and property, and by the social institutions which favour them. At one time there has been the aristocratic spirit, which in England is now dead, with its emphasis on subordination and the respect which is due from the lower orders to the higher, irrespective of whether the higher deserve or not to be respected. At another time there has been the plutocratic or commercial spirit, which is very much alive, with its insistence on the right of every individual to acquire wealth, and to hold what he acquires, and by means of it to obtain consideration for himself and power over his fellows, without regard to the services – if any – by which he acquires it or the use which he makes of it.

Both have some virtues, which may have been in certain periods more important than their vices. But the tendency of both, when unchecked by other influences, is the same. It is to pervert the sense of values. It is to cause men, in the language of the Old Testament, 'to go a-whoring after strange gods', which means, in the circumstances of today, staring upwards, eyes goggling and mouths agape, at the antics of a third-rate Elysium, and tormenting their unhappy souls, or what, in such conditions, is left of them, with the hope of wriggling into it. It is to hold up to public admiration sham criteria of eminence, the result of accepting which is, in the one case, snobbery, or a mean respect for shoddy and unreal distinction, and, in the other case, materialism, or a belief that the only real forms of distinction are money and the advantages which money can buy.

Progress depends, indeed, on a willingness on the part of the mass of mankind – and we all, in nine-tenths of our nature, belong to the mass – to recognise genuine superiority, and to submit themselves to its influence. But the condition of recognising genuine superiority is a contempt for unfounded pretensions to it. Where the treasure is, there will the heart be also, and, if men are to respect each other for what they are, they must cease to respect each other for what they own. They must abolish, in short, the reverence for riches, which is the *lues Anglicana*, the hereditary disease of the English nation. And, human nature being what it is, in order to abolish the reverence for riches, they must make impossible the existence of a class which is important merely because it is rich.

It is not surprising, therefore, that the ages which were permeated most deeply with the sense of the dignity of man as a rational being were also ages which appear to have felt a somewhat slender respect for capricious distinctions of birth and fortune. It is not surprising that the temper which had as one of its manifestations humanism, of the perfecting of the individual, should have had as another manifestation an outlook on society which sympathised with the attempt to bring the means of a good life within the reach of all, and regarded the subordination of class to class, and the arrogance and servility which such subordination naturally produces, as barbarian or gothic, as the mark of peoples which were incompletely civilised. It is in that spirit that Herodotus, speaking of the Athenians, who were regarded, in comparison with the Spartans, as dreadfully ungentlemanly, remarks that 'it is evident, not in one thing alone, but on all sides of life, how excellent a thing is equality among men'. It is in that spirit that the French writers of the eighteenth century, whose pernicious influence was denounced by Burke in the famous essay which George III said every gentleman should read, declared that equality, as well as liberty, must be the aim of the reformer.

It is true, of course, that institutions, as always, fell short of the ideal. It is true that the economic basis of Athenian society was slavery, and that one result of the victory of the liberal idea in France was the soulless commercialism which came to its own in 1830. But, compared with the practice of the world around them, compared with Persia, or even with most parts of Greece in the fifth century, or with England and Germany in the eighteenth, the influence of Athens and France was felt to make for humanism in life and manners, as well as in literature and art, and against the harshness and brutality of traditional systems of social petrification. They not only generated light, but diffused it. Within the limits set by their history and environment, it was their glory to stand for the general development of qualities which were prized, not as the monopoly of any class or profession of men, but as the attribute of man himself.

Thus the testimony of history is not so wholly on one side as is often suggested. Whether it is practicable or not to attain a large measure of equality may fairly be disputed; but it is not necessary, it seems, to be afraid of seeking it, on the ground that it is the enemy of culture and enlightenment. It is not necessary to shrink from lowering barriers of circumstance and opportunity, for fear that the quality of civilisation will suffer as the radius of its influence is extended. It is true that civilisation requires that there shall be free scope for activities which, judged by the conventional standards of the practical world, are useless or even pernicious, and which are significant precisely because they are not inspired by utilitarian motives, but spring, like the labour of the artist or student, from the disinterested passion for beauty or truth, or merely from the possession of powers the exercise of which is its own reward. Experience does not suggest, however, that in modern England the plutocracy, with its devotion to the maxim *Privatim opulentia, publice egestas*, is, in any special sense, the guardian of such activities, or that, to speak with moderation, it is noticeably more eager than the mass of the population to spend liberally on art, or education, or the things of the spirit.

Nor, if the maintenance, by the institutions of property and inheritance, of a class of whose leisure these activities are the occasional by-product is one method of sheltering them, is it necessarily either the only method, or that which is most likely to encourage in society a temper that is keenly alive to their importance and disposed to make sacrifices for the sake of providing opportunities for their further development. Culture is not an assortment of aesthetic sugar-plums for fastidious palates, but an energy of the soul. It can win no victories if it risks no defeats. When it feeds on itself, instead of drawing nourishment from the common life of mankind, it ceases to grow, and, when it ceases to grow, it ceases to live. In order that it may be, not merely an interesting museum specimen, but an active principle of intelligence and refinement, by which vulgarities are checked and crudities corrected, it is necessary, not only to preserve intact existing standards of excellence, and to diffuse their influence, but to broaden and enrich them by contact with an ever-widening range of emotional experiences and intellectual interest. The association of culture with a limited class, which is enabled by its wealth to carry the art of living to a high level of perfection, may achieve the first, but it cannot, by itself, achieve the second. It may refine, or appear to refine, some sections of a community, but it coarsens others, and smites, in the end, with a blight of sterility even refinement itself. It may preserve culture, but it cannot extend it; and, in the long run, it is only by its extension that, in the conditions of today, it is likely to be preserved.

Thus a class system which is marked by sharp horizontal divisions between different social strata is neither, as is sometimes suggested, an indispensable condition of civilisation nor an edifying feature of it. It may, as some hold, be inevitable, like other misfortunes to which mankind is heir, but it is not lovable or admirable. It is the raw material out of which civilisation has to be made, by bringing the blind economic forces under rational control and sifting the gold of past history from its sand and sediment. The task of the spirit, whatever the name most appropriate to describe it, which seeks to permeate, not merely this fragment of society or that, but the whole community, with reason and mutual understanding, is not to flatter the natural impulses which have their origin in the fact of class, but to purify and educate them. It is to foster the growth of a classless society by speaking frankly of the perversions to which the class system gives rise and of the dangers which accompany them.

The forms which such perversions assume are, of course, innumerable, but the most fundamental of them are two. They are privilege and tyranny. The first is the insistence by certain groups on the enjoyment of special advantages which are convenient to themselves, but injurious to their neighbours. The second is the exercise of power, not for the common benefit, but in order that these special advantages may be strengthened and consolidated.

It is the nature of privilege and tyranny to be unconscious of themselves, and to protest, when challenged, that their horns and hooves are not dangerous, as in the past, but useful and handsome decorations, which no self-respecting society would dream of dispensing with. But they are the enemies, nevertheless, both of individual culture and of social amenity. They create a spirit of domination and servility, which produces callousness in those who profit by them, and resentment in those who do not, and suspicion and contention in both. A civilised community will endeavour to exorcise that spirit by removing its causes. It will insist that one condition, at least, of its deserving the name is that its members shall treat each other, not as means, but as ends, and that institutions which stunt the faculties of some among them for the advantage of others shall be generally recognised to be barbarous and odious. It will aim at making power, not arbitrary, but responsible, and, when it finds an element of privilege in social institutions, it will seek to purge it.

Notes

1. Matthew Arnold, Lecture on 'Equality' in *Mixed Essays*, 1903 edn, pp. ix, 48–97.
2. Arnold, p. 51; E. Thring, *Education and School*, 1864, pp. 4–5; Bagehot, *The English Constitution*, 1867, pp. 50–4; Erskine May, *Democracy in Europe*, 1877, vol. ii, p. 333; Lecky, *Democracy and Liberty*, 1899, vol. i, pp. 256–7; Taine, *Notes sur l'Angleterre*, 1872, p. 189, and *Histoire de la Littérature anglaise*, 1863, vol. iii, p. 650.
3. F. Clarke, 'An Elementary-Secondary School,' in *Hibbert Journal*, October 1927, p. 145, and *A Dominion View of English Education*, An Address delivered to the College of Perceptors, 14 February, 1929, Reported at length in *Cape Times*, 3 and 4 May, 1929; USA, *Special Report of Commissioner of Labour on Regulation and Restriction of Output*, 1904, pp. 810–11, and B. Austin and W. F. Lloyd, *The Secret of High Wages*, 1926, introduction (by W. T. Layton) and pp. 43, 75, 102, 107; W. Dibelius, *England*, 1929, pp. 205–7; E. Wertheimer, *Portrait of the Labour Party*, 1929, pp. 138, 139; A. Siefried, *L'Angleterre d'aujourd'hui*, 1924, p. 251. See also E. Banks, *School for John and Mary*, 1924.
4. H. G. Wells, *The Open Conspiracy*, 1928, p. 77.
5. See the remarks of H. de Man, *Au delà du Marxisme*, 1927, p. 89.
6. Sir E. A. Parry, *The Law and the Poor*, 1914.
7. Lork Birkenhead, reported in *The Times*, 30 September 1927, and 17 November 1928; J. L. Garvin, article in the *Observer*, 1 July 1928; E. J. P. Benn, *The Confessions of a Capitalist*, 1926, pp. 188, 189; Sir Herbert Austin, in *Daily Herald*, 13 May 1930; Dean Inge, reported in *Evening Standard*, 8 May 1928.
8. Cyril Burt, *The Distribution and Relations of Educational Abilities*, L.C.C., 1917; *Report of the Mental Deficiency Committee*, HMSO, Stationers, 1929.
9. Mill, *Principles of Political Economy*, 1865 edn, bk. iv. chap. vi, and *Autobiography*, 1909 edn, p. 133.
10. See the *Report of Consultative Committee of Bd. of Educ. on Psychological Tests of Educable Capacity*, 1924, p. 71; 'All our witnesses are agreed that intelligence does not cover temperament or character, and that, therefore, the important personal qualities of will, feeling and emotion are not dealt with by tests of intelligence.'
11. For a valuable discussion of recent work on the subject, see M. Ginsberg, 'The Inheritance of Mental Characters', in *The Rationalist Annual*, 1930, pp. 47–54.

12. M. Ginsberg, *The Problem of Colour in relation to the idea of Equality* (*Journal of Philosophical Studies*, Suppt. to vol. i, no. 2), 1926, p. 14.

13. See the discussion of Pareto's Law in Pigou, *Economics of Welfare*, ed. 1929, pp. 645–53, and the passages in Pareto's *Manuele di economia politica* there quoted.

14. Benn, p. 237.

15. A. M. Carr-Saunders and D. Caradog Jones, *A Surveyor of the Social Structure of England and Wales*, 1927, p. 71.

16. Bryce, *The American Commonwealth*, 1917, vol. ii, p. 297.

17. W. Woytinsky, *Die Welt in Zahlen*, 1926, bk. ii, pp. 46–7.

18. Bowley and Stamp, *The National Income*, 1927, p. 12; Carr-Saunders and Jones, *op. cit.*, pp. 61–3.

19. *Report on Economic Conditions in France in 1928*, by J. R. Cahill, HMSO, 1928, p. 225. For the English figures of occupying ownership, see Clapham, *An Economic History of Modern Britain*, Vol. III, p. 534.

20. For the statistics in this paragraph, see J. Stamp, *Wealth and Taxable Capacity*, 1922, pp. 101–2; H. Clay, 'The Distribution of Capital in England and Wales,' in *Manchester Statistical Soc. Trans.*, 1924–6, p. 73; Carr-Saunders and Jones, pp. 113–16, 165–7; G. D. H. and M. I. Cole, *The Condition of Britain*, 1937, pp. 77–9; J. Wedgwood, *The Economics of Inheritance*, 1929.

21. Bowley, *The Change in the Distribution of the National Income, 1880–1913*, 1920, p. 22; Stamp, p. 95; Colin Clark, *National Income and Outlay*, 1937, p. 110.

22. See pp. 164–6; and Cole, p. 95.

23. H. J. Laski, *The Personnel of the English Cabinet, 1801–1924* (reprinted from *Amer. Pol. Sci. Rev.*, vol. xxii, no. 1), 1928, pp. 18–19.

24. A Cecil, *British Foreign Secretaries, 1807–1916*, 1927, p. 134; R. T. Nightingale, 'The Personnel of the British Foreign Office and Diplomatic Service, 1951–1929,' in *The Realist*, December 1929, pp. 333–4, 341, 343; M. Ginsberg, 'Interchange between Social Classes,' in *Econ. Jl.*, December 1929, p. 563.

25. See Tawney, *The Religion of Inequality*, Appendix 1, ch 2.

26. See report in *Manchester Guardian*, 15 November 1929, of evidence submitted by Civil Service Commissioners to the Royal Commission on the Civil Service. For the years 1906–10 the percentage was 74.

27. R. F. Cholmeley, 'The Boys' Day School,' in *The Schools of England*, (ed.) J. Dover Wilson, 1928, pp. 113–14; Rev. F. A. Nairn, reported in *Times Education Supplement*, 5 May 1928.

28. De Tocqueville, *Democracy in America*, (trans.) H. Reeve, 1898 edn, vol. ii, bk. ii, chap. xx.

29. Clive Bell, *Civilisation*, 1928.

William Letwin

The Case Against Equality

Most people now believe in equality. To put it another way, most people believe that many aspects of social life should be reformed so as to get rid of inherited inequalities. That is why they support redistribution of income and wealth, within nations and among nations; why they sympathise with measures to extend powers of decision to workers as well as employers, students as well as teachers, voters as well as politicians and officials; and why they automatically assent to many similar exercises in 'democratisation', 'participation' and 'equalisation of rights'.

Most people also believe that equality as a goal is entirely self-evident, so that it neither need be nor could be justified by reasoning from any deeper principle. If that were so, one would be forced to wonder how anybody could ever oppose equality. Egalitarians accordingly tend to explain opposition as stemming from cynical efforts of favoured people to stay on top of the heap, or from the misguided and lethargic complaisance of people at the bottom of the heap. But in fact there is now little such opposition to be accounted for. Most of those who stand to lose by equalisation nevertheless feel themselves compelled – by decency or religious faith, as they suppose, and most frequently perhaps by a sense of guilt – to concede that equality should by right prevail. Nor, within free democracies, is there any great mass at the bottom of the scale who are so bewitched or oppressed that they regard inequality as justified or inescapable, or so enlightened as to understand that inequality may be beneficial to themselves. Most people heartily endorse equality as a goal, some acquiesce to it reluctantly, and very few deny it outright.

This essay is intended to disrupt the consensus. It calls into question the philosophical arguments which have been or might be advanced in favour of egalitarianism; points out ambiguities within the idea of equality; disputes the data which are supposed to reveal great and growing inequality; and identifies the destructive consequences which have already resulted from or may be expected from policies aimed at equalisation.

It may be alleged that this essay is unbalanced, because it gives no hearing to the defendants' advocates. Such a complaint would ignore the fact that libraries, newspapers and airwaves are full of pleadings for and avowals of faith in equality, whereas the case against egalitarianism is seldom stated or heard.[1] In any event, an effort, such as this one, to stir up serious debate about a vital principle which has so widely and so long been taken for granted, goes beyond partisanship. What is said here may indeed persuade some readers that to reject equality as a goal conforms with reason even if not with fashion. At the same time, proponents of equality should be grateful to anyone who locates weak points in their armour, thus giving them opportunity to reinforce their defences. Intellectual frankness should interest everyone in a dissection of a faith which has hitherto been largely unexamined.

Egalitarianism, as a systematic doctrine, goes beyond the inarticulate public faith in the obvious goodness of equality. As expounded in political tracts, official reports, philosophical essays and other considered utterances, egalitarianism seems to rest on three ideas: all persons should be equal; all existing inequalities can be reduced if not utterly eradicated by action of governments or by revolutionary change in government; all other political objectives must give way to equality, if any conflict arises between it and them. Full-fledged egalitarianism holds, in short, that equality is a desirable end, a feasible end, and the paramount political end.

Needless to say, the egalitarian position is seldom put quite so boldly. A simple belief that everyone should be equal in every way would seem ridiculous even in the eyes of avid egalitarians. Even they would not maintain that all human beings should be equal in height and weight, in the number of cigars they smoke, and in the frequency of their sojourns in jail. To make equality an ideal that is even remotely sensible, it must be narrowed. The most sensible limiting formula to have emerged is that people should be equal *only* in respect of certain goods which are both general and vital. The sorts of goods to which judicious egalitarians have accordingly confined their ideal are income, wealth, esteem, political power, legal rights and education. It is obviously easier for egalitarians to maintain that people should be equal in these essential respects (such as income) rather than in more particular and indifferent respects (such as consumption of strawberries). Nevertheless, as will be shown in what follows, no amount of such narrowing can give the ideal of equality a coherent and determinate content.

As to their second idea, that equalisation is practicable: here too egalitarians have tended to settle for a more confined and accordingly more defensible position. They hold that, although perfect equality is or may be unattainable, nevertheless it is always possible to move one step closer to equality. The premise which typically underlies this faith is that inequality – in all the dimensions that really matter – is made by human beings, is a product of human vice. Nature makes men equal. Man makes them unequal. This implies that social arrangements which have been fashioned badly can be refashioned so as to make them less bad. It is not, however, the moral reform of individuals (who might then bring about equalisation by private philanthropy) on which egalitarians pin their hopes, but rather enforced equalisation by government. The practical optimism of egalitarians will be shown to be intellectually unsound and politically dangerous.

As for their third idea, that equality is the paramount end of good government: liberal or democratic egalitarians frequently limit the force of this proposition by denying that equality is at all likely to conflict with the other principal ends of good government. Suppose, for instance, it were objected that equality and individual liberty necessarily clash in the context of any policy of enforced redistribution of income, inasmuch as anyone forced to pay a heavy tax is to some extent deprived of his previous liberty to spend his income as he chose. A large variety of answers is offered by egalitarians, most of which pretend to explain away this conflict of ends. One is that the deprivation of liberty on the part of the few, unwilling, rich 'benefactors' is more than offset by the enhancement of liberty on the part of the many beneficiaries – an argument which depends on the fallacy of confusing liberty to do something with ability or power to do it. Another is that property rights exist only within a framework of laws established by the state, from which egalitarians would have it follow that no person can properly be said to be deprived of his property (or denied freedom to use it as he chooses) when the laws governing property rights, which in the egalitarian view include the tax laws, are changed in a constitutional manner. Still another is that the fundamental liberty of a citizen in a democracy is his freedom to vote as he chooses, and the ancillary freedoms to discuss political questions, to belong to a party, and to criticise the government; whatever 'restrictions' the laws of a democracy may impose on a citizen are, according to this view, to be understood as voluntary obligations, entered into by each citizen through the vicarious action of his representatives, rather than as deprivations imposed on him by others. Such evasive answers are, however, quite eschewed by blunter breeds of egalitarians. They unblinkingly assert that when other ideals – liberty, stability, diversity or economic efficiency – clash with equality, those other principles must be sacrificed. I will indicate, in what follows, how the pursuit of equality jeopardises the preservation or furthering of other political goods.

How has it come about that equality now commands such widespread assent? Common among historians who lean toward egalitarianism is the thesis that equality, liberty and democracy are the first fruits of a struggle carried on for hundreds of years, a struggle by the common people against the rich, their masters. On this view, every member of the lower class who recognises his true interest demands equality; but it has taken centuries for enough of the lower class to learn this, to organise effectively for action, and to succeed partially; and the ultimate victory of equality awaits the abolition of capitalism, either by reform or revolution.

Every step of this sort of historical analysis could be shown to be an arbitrary theoretical assumption rather than an empirical finding. That every community consists fundamentally of 'classes'; that the class defines the 'interests' of its members; that the several classes are naturally at war with each other; and that perfect, stateless socialism, the reign of equality, will inevitably supersede capitalism, the reign of oppressive inequality – all these are postulates, belonging to a particular interpretation of human affairs, rather than self-evident truths or indisputable historical facts.

A proper historical attempt to explain how equality has achieved its present pre-eminence would have to investigate the diverse reasons why so many people – of the upper and middle sorts as well as the lower – have come to believe in, equality. One set of reasons, certainly not negligible, is a variety of ideas which have been put forward during the past three centuries. Among these have been interpretations of Christianity which stressed the equality of all men in the sight of God; philosophical writings which, besides many other effects, made equality one of the three watchwords of the French Revolution; the doctrinal pronouncements of socialists of many varieties; and, more recently, the writings of academic social scientists, especially of certain economists and sociologists. But these are only a few of the many activities which have contributed toward bringing about the present state of affairs.[2]

A historical account that took cognisance of all the actions and circumstances which might be invoked to explain the high esteem in which equality is now held would be a very elaborate work. Valuable as this would be, nothing of the sort is attempted in this essay. Occasional allusions are made to the history of equality as a goal and of equalisation as a policy, but the point of the book is to examine arguments and interpretations of fact which are in use today, rather than to trace the historical steps which brought them onto the stage.

In considering the arguments which have been advanced for equality, it is useful to disentangle various strands which are often interwoven in egalitarian thought. Although these strands are more or less similar inasmuch as they converge on a common conclusion, they are logically independent of one another and can therefore be scrutinised separately.

The presumption of equality

Most people who believe in equality regard it as an obvious presumption, a self-evident starting point for thought and policy, akin to an axiom, not needing to be supported by a foundation of reasoning.

Some believers in equality suppose that their case can be made satisfactorily, or in any event quite adequately illustrated, by a parable. The parable may be put in this form. Four children sit at the tea-table presided over by their mother. When the cake is served, she *naturally* gives each child an equal piece. To give one child a larger piece than the others would be wrong unless some compelling reason justified an exceptional departure from the rule of equality. And so, say the tellers of this story, equality is the obvious presumption, the rule which ought to be followed in principle in the allocation of all the world's goods.

Like any other parable, this one achieves its persuasive force by weaving into the simple plot a series of assumptions, unstated and unrecognised, yet vital to the effect. So here the cake stands for something which everyone wants. Moreover, in this case, the claimants are children, whose appetite for sweet things is known generally to be exorbitant. Further, being children, they are assumed to be incapable of making or buying more cake for themselves. In short, the parable introduces us, slyly, into a situation of scarcity, extreme and irremediable, where the allocation is authoritatively determined by a person assumed to be a benevolent despot.

It is easy enough to construct a parable that carries just the opposite message. A cocktail party is being given by a lavish host. Waiters circulate constantly, offering drinks and *hors d'oeuvres* of all sorts. The guests are distinguished middle-aged professionals, suave, sober and slim or slimming. When the guests leave, plenty of food and drink remains. The rule of allocation in these circumstances is that each guest consumes what he likes, and the outcome is that each guest consumes a different amount. So far from equality being the natural presumption, any effort by the host to make each guest consume the same amount would be taken as bad taste if not mad hunger for power. Instead of scarcity in the face of greed, this parable posits plenty in the presence of self-restraint.

If we wish to come closer to the circumstances in which people live most of their lives, we should think of yet another parable. It concerns a farmer who works a large plot of land and who, considering one year with another, grows an amount of grain proportional to the amount of effort he puts into seeding, weeding and harvesting. Neither a benevolent despot nor a lavish host provides for him, but he provides for himself; and within the limits set by the fruitfulness of land and climate, he can consume more or less as he chooses to work more or less.

If we now reconsider the story of the tea-table, it is clear that the mother might allocate the cake according to a large number of different criteria, each quite reasonable in itself. She might give every child as much as it likes, knowing that some like more than others. Even after all have had their fill, some cake may be left over and may spoil before the next meal; the possibility of waste is, all else being equal, a strong reason for letting people take as much as they like. If, on the other hand, there is not enough cake to go around, the mother might invoke the rule of first-come-first-served; eagerness is a traditionally accepted way of measuring desire. Of course, people who prize responsibility will be frightened by the thought that anybody should get as much as he likes; they would feel safer with a rule that people should get as much as is good for them and no more than that. To this we might retort that what feels good to a person, at least to a normal adult, is often the best evidence about what is good for him; certainly physicians often follow this rule. Again, the mother might distribute the cake according to merit, giving each child a piece proportional to the virtues which he has recently demonstrated, or proportional to her love for each. She might distribute it in accordance with her views of their different needs for nourishment, or her experience of how eating that cake affects the subsequent health of each child. In short, she can invoke numerous specific criteria within the general classes of desire, desert and need.

There is, thus, no fundamental, initial or general presumption in favour of equal shares for all. Equality would be adopted as a criterion only if the allocating authority were too ignorant, lazy or dogmatic to consider any more refined criterion. Equality would emerge, as a reasonable criterion, only if the children were equal in respect of desire, desert, need, or in some other relevant way. In short, equality is rationally defensible as a rule only when the persons in question are held to be equal, beforehand, in some predominant respect. Inasmuch as people are unequal, it is rational to presume that they ought to be treated unequally – which might mean larger shares for the needy or larger shares for the worthy. And so, the parable intended to sustain the presumption in favour of equality falls apart under critical scrutiny and seems if anything to suggest the opposite of what it intends.

Identity of essence

The first, probably the oldest and perhaps the most persuasive, foundation for the ideal of equality is the premise that all men are essentially identical. Adherents to this line posit an essence, core or 'nature' which is present in each human being, which identifies him as human, and which, because it is durable and universal, is to be regarded as more telling than all the contingent and changeable particularities that differentiate any human individual from all others. They assert, in effect, that the fundamental similarities among men are more important than the accidental or casual differences.

Secular variants of this position have identified the essence of man as one or another of the following: his ability to reason, to converse, to govern himself by deliberate peaceable assent, to create works of beauty, or to recognise right and wrong. Whichever of these they take as their starting point, egalitarian arguments of this sort pursue the same path thereafter. They maintain that, despite superficial and accidental differences among individuals – despite even the manifest inequalities among individuals in respect of their inessential attributes – all human beings are identical in possessing the essential attribute which makes them human, and therefore all human beings are essentially equal.

In this way, all the observed differences among individuals are over-ruled by the identity alleged to be essential. Essential why? Only because it marks off the species of man from all other kinds of things. Surely an attribute that differentaties one kind of thing from another is 'important', and well worth knowing about. But that is very far from saying that what differentiates this thing from another is therefore the central, fundamental, vital, crucial aspect of this thing. What distinguishes red flowers from other flowers is their redness, yet no connoisseur of flowers would regard redness as the pivotal, uniquely telling, in short, essential characteristic of a flower. In any event, the attributes which are essential as a tool in defining human beings, that is, in differentiating men from all other beings – attributes such as the powers to reason, converse, and the like – are not therefore the attributes which are central to every branch of public policy.

Yet even if we knew man's essential nature, it would not follow that because every human being necessarily possesses it – or for want of it would be described without hesitation as abnormal, defective, or even as inhuman – all men are thereby equal. To infer equality from such identity is to commit a fallacy.

In order to identify this fallacy, it is necessary to recognise that there are two broad ways in which things can be the same. One form of sameness is the one we call equality; the other form of sameness has no necessary relation to equality.

Simple examples can illustrate this distinction. For instance, two numbers such as 3 and 5 are the same in as much as both are numbers and moreover both are integers, odd, and prime; yet 3 and 5 are clearly unequal. Bears and dogs are the same in being hairy, but we would hesitate to declare that bears and dogs are equally hairy, which might imply that they have the same amount of hair. Brahms and Bruckner could comfortably be called the same in so far as both were composers, but to call them equal composers or even equally composers would go beyond what many critics care to affirm.

Clearly two distinct varieties of sameness are present here. Although the pairs of specimens share in each instance the same attribute, they do not exhibit that attribute in the same degree. We can recognise this disjunction by labelling the first sort of sameness as 'sameness in kind' and the second as 'sameness in degree'. 'Equality' is a synonym for the latter, but not a synonym for the former.

This distinction once made, a series of implications follow, which can illuminate and rectify the discussion of equality as a principle of ethics, law and politics. (1) Things which are the same in kind, that is, the same in respect of some attribute, may be equal or unequal in that respect; though it may happen also that despite the sameness of some attribute, no meaningful statement can be made about the subjects' equality or inequality. For instance, two trees may be the same in respect of being elms, but to say that they are equally or unequally elms is meaningless, as the quality of 'elmness' does not admit of quantification. It need hardly be said that in relation to height, age or any number of other attributes which all elms possess, the two may be equal or unequal. (2) Things which differ in kind cannot, in that respect, be either equal or unequal. For instance, a rock and a rabbit cannot be said, without further ado, to be equal or unequal. Of course, one might say that a rabbit can run faster than a rock, and thus conclude that they have unequal powers of locomotion, but this conclusion is possible only by imputing to both the same attribute, namely 'power of locomotion', as a precondition of comparing the degrees to which they possess it. Similarly with the common cliché that men and women are unequal. Taken at face value, it is meaningless, since being of different genders, men cannot in respect of gender be either equal or unequal to women. Taking it generously, loosely enough to recognise the intended meaning, it asserts that in respect of attributes which they share, men get preferential treatment: so that, for instance, men are paid more than women, pay less for bank loans, and so on. Things can only be equal or unequal in relation to qualities which they have in common and qualities which moreover can be quantified.

In short, to say that things are the same need not mean that they are equal, and to say that things are different need not mean that they are unequal. Much discussion of equality founders on these shoals.

It follows that the attempt to deduce the equality of men from the universal presence in men of an identical essence must be dismissed as resting on the fallacy which confuses 'sameness of kind' with 'sameness of degree'. Like the numbers 3 and 5, any two men may, while being identical in kind, be unequal in any or every possible matter of degree. Although all men have a power to reason, it does not follow in the least that all men have equal power to reason, or could have, or should have. Even if we accepted that all men are identical in essence, the conclusion that they are all 'essentially equal' could emerge only by logical trickery.

A theological variation on the same theme is exposed to similar criticism. We meet it most often in the statement that all men are equal in the sight of God. Perhaps this means that all men are identical in having immortal souls; yet it appears, according to the tenets of many sects, that this will not guarantee them equal treatment, for some souls will be raised to everlasting glory while others will be condemned to eternal damnation. Perhaps it is to be understood as meaning that in God's sight we are all minuscule – though not therefore equally small: perhaps that God's infinite mercy will redeem us all, though we be unequally unworthy of redemption. Perhaps again, God's infinite love for all men inclines him to treat as equal souls which are strictly speaking quite unequal. No such interpretation can enable mere human beings to leap the gap between sameness of attribute and sameness of degree.

Christianity may have been a powerful influence in propagating the beliefs that underlie contemporary egalitarianism. Not that the record is unequivocal, for while various strands of Christian dogma lay some stress on equality, there are others which strongly imply the opposite: such as the doctrine of election in Calvinism; or the phrase in the Anglican catechism which instructs the child to do his duty 'in that state of life' (that status or station, as we would say) 'unto which it shall please God to call me'. Even if it were true, as it may well be, that the present vogue of egalitarianism owes much to Christian teachings, that historical truth could not be mustered as a rationally compelling argument in favour of equality. Powerful as faith is, it cannot perform the office of reason.

Aboriginal equality

Some egalitarian positions base themselves on the premise that men are 'naturally' equal: that is, that men were equal while they lived in a 'state of nature', their original condition. That primitive paradisial equality was corrupted, according to this view, when men formed societies, for society brought in the unnatural domination and exploitation of some men by others, so engendering the malady of inequality. The cure is to reform society, so as to restore the natural, healthy condition of equality. Such, more or less, is the line promulgated by Rousseau, Marx and others, as well as by many who follow them unknowingly.

What is 'natural' in men, within this view, should be discernible by examining the condition of human beings before they have been exposed to and influenced by society. One way to do this is by examining the human individual in embryo. Such an examination, far from confirming the premised equality, reveals many differences and many inequalities among individuals. Attributes given from the moment of conception differ, and these lead to differences which accompany the individual throughout his life: among them are colouring (of skin, hair and eyes); gender; and abnormalities of structure or function, abnormalities which may be rated as defects (such as vestigial fingers) or as special blessings (such as hyper-acute hearing). Other of the differentiating attributes which accompany the individual from conception are potentialities rather than determined givens; and, although presumably nobody can fully realise all of his potentialities, nevertheless the ultimate performance of any individual is facilitated by and limited by the specific endowments with which he arrives on the scene. It is impossible therefore to maintain that all human beings are identical at the moment after conception and are made different only by their nurtures – unless one takes the radical, demonstrably false, position that all human beings are genetically identical.

One can insist on the falsity of 'natural' equality without in any way overlooking the extent to which the different concrete circumstances of each individual's life affect the way in which he shapes his life. As important, nevertheless, is the fact that individuals can exercise considerable choice about the concrete circumstances among which they prefer to live and which they accordingly arrange to live among. To attribute differences among individuals exclusively to the mystical operations of 'society' is to prefer faith to obvious fact: a faith frequently embraced because it yields certain desired political conclusions, particularly that men ought to be equal because they 'naturally' are equal – that is, that they would be equal if not for the distortions introduced by corrupt society.

Further to confute this faith we might point to many other differences among people which are not caused by human will, either of individuals or of communities. One such is difference of age, which carries with it many other differences, not least of which is that, all else being equal, the older one becomes (short of agedness and senility), the greater the advantages that accrue from accumulated experience. Hence the pre-eminence of older people at the tops of hierarchies, political and industrial as well as spiritual or social; and hence also the larger incomes of skilled older workers compared with incomes of relatively unskilled younger workers in the same occupation. Other natural differences in height, weight, musculature and other gross physical characteristics – 'natural' inasmuch as they persist despite identity of nurture- largely account for individual differences in such aptitudes as physical strength, speed and agility. Still another natural difference is in the physical details which make up a person's appearance, so that some individuals are held to be attractive, while others seem plain or ill-favoured. Although the criteria of good looks which prevail at any given place and time are laid down by social convention, and a person regarded as ugly here might be thought elsewhere to be distinctively handsome, nevertheless, in a deeper sense, differences in looks transcend social norms, because it is unimaginable that any human community should fail altogether to recognise beauty. The universal human capacity to perceive differences between individuals originates in the inherent, durable character of human beings and not in the variable standards – or, as some see it, the arbitrary and perverse standards – which prevail in one community or another.

Another way to test the proposition that men are naturally equal would be to examine the condition of adult human beings living in a 'state of nature', before they have formed society. Unfortunately this test cannot be performed empirically, because it is impossible to find human beings living in a 'state of nature'. Some peoples, it is true, are so 'primitive' that they live under forms of government which are rudimentary, sporadic and unstable; yet, though they may lack what we would call government, they do not lack community. In short, we cannot observe individuals (except for rare, dubious instances of wolf-children) who have lived outside society, isolated all their lives, regarding every other human being as an alien enemy. And therefore we can find no facts which would authorise us to assert or deny that men in a pre-social condition are naturally equal. In so far then as theorists have asserted that natural equality is the condition of men in a state of nature, they have had to rest their case on nothing more solid than pure hypothesis. It is an utterly shaky foundation, ready to be toppled by the counter-hypothesis that in a state of nature men are radically unequal.

It is true enough that society, as we know it, provides opportunity for individuals to differentiate themselves from one another and also to make themselves unequal. Or, to drop the filmy image of 'society' in favour of terms more tangible, individuals in civilised communities (and probably in all communities) make themselves different from one another – different enough at least so that they can be recognised as themselves – and they aim to be unequal, at least in so far as some at any rate aim to earn more, run faster, act more virtuously or achieve higher office. Yes these observations do nothing to sustain the view that it is society alone or only some sorts of society which create inequality among individuals who would remain naturally equal if they could stay outside society.

Finally, even if men were naturally equal, it would not follow in the least that they should be treated equally within a society. The natural condition of things is not necessarily the most desirable or morally the superior condition. Indeed, men sensibly exert themselves to overcome or modify many natural conditions. So natural equality, even if it could be known to exist and even if it is presumed to exist, could not constitute a rationally defensible imperative for treating people equally, in any or all respects, within 'post-natural' society.

Common enterprise

Some egalitarians maintain that men ought to be equal quite apart from whether they are or are not equal in essence or by nature. They rest their case on the view that society is a common enterprise, to which all persons contribute, and in whose benefits they are all therefore entitled to share fairly, that is equally. Each step in this argument is suspect, not to say demonstrably false.

Society is misrepresented when pictured as an enterprise. An enterprise entails entrepreneurs, who launch a project in order to accomplish a goal. But society was never launched, since human beings have never existed outside it; at no time did a number of asocial individuals, born and living in utter isolation from one another, all resolve to join together for the deliberate purpose of creating a society. Society is not a project, but simply the name we give to the fact that wherever we see human beings we see them living together in communities. Because society is not a project, it has no ends. Society may loosely be said to confer benefits on its members with just as little reason as the sun may be said to confer benefits upon the earth. Rather it is the members of a society who confer benefits on each other by co-operative efforts. Of course, co-operation would be impossible if people lived in total isolation from one another; though conflict would also be impossible, so that a pessimist might conclude that society does more harm than good. But any such calculation is beside the point. Society is incapable of acting; it is the inevitable condition of mankind; it is not an artificial enterprise endowed with ends and purposes by individuals who could have made it or not as they chose. And, strictly speaking, society contributes nothing; the only contributors are human beings, and the only beneficiaries are human beings.

Again, to say that all persons contribute to society says either nothing or too much. If the members are thought to 'contribute' in the sense that the collective entity would vanish on the departure of all its members, then the statement resolves into a mere tautology. Without parts there can be no whole, without a whole there can be no parts; each is a necessary element in defining the others, neither 'contributes' to the other. If, however, the members are thought to contribute in the more meaningful sense that they benefit not society but each other, then the question must arise in what ways their contributions are the same. And the answer is that various individuals make contributions of different kinds, catering to the various desires, tastes, motives and purposes of different beneficiaries; some of which contributions, being the same in kind, differ in degree. These evident differences and inequalities deny the implication that, because everyone makes a contribution, everyone deserves an *equal* reward.

Here we reach the step most unwarranted of all. That the labourer is worthy of his hire, that everyone who helps should enjoy a due share of the proceeds, is a widespread belief. But the notion that only an equal share is a due share does not command the whole field. Many believe that goods produced by a common enterprise should be allocated rather according to each person's need, desire, power or general merit. The only conclusion which can encompass all these competing views is that everyone must get a 'proper' share. Proper shares differ from fair shares as 'fair' is usually understood, namely as an approximation to 'equal'. To define equality as coextensive with fairness or justice – thus treating all that is equal as just, and all that is just as equal – does not settle the vast question of what constitutes justice but merely defines it away, and merely assumes that equality is the proper ultimate objective.

Generosity

Another view maintains that sympathy does, or certainly should, prompt each person to share his goods with less fortunate brethren. It holds that a human being armed with normal decency cannot stand by unmoved while others suffer want. The ideal of equality thus emerges as the tribute we pay to our consciences, as the inevitable consequence of a universal moral duty of every person to be generous to all others.

The premise is beyond cavil. A person lacking all impulse or power to sympathise with others would be a moral monster. But the purported inference will not hold. Compassion commands the able to help and to share when sharing helps; it does not instruct men to share and share alike in accordance with a mathematical equation. Heroes of chivalric legends who say 'your need is greater than mine' achieve inequality rather than equality; by giving all they had, they end up having less than the recipient. Lesser mortals who practise philanthropy typically end up retaining more than they have given away, yet that does not deny the authenticity of their action or its value to others.

Generosity and sympathy dictate that no man be allowed to starve in the midst of plenty. This suggests that a safety-net be provided in the form of a minimum income guaranteed to each member of the community, adequate to provide what are considered the basic necessities. Such a policy, commendable and practicable in a moderately wealthy community, may exceed the resources of a very poor community, where the effort to provide a safety-net would convert the rapid starvation of the particularly unfortunate into the slightly slower starvation of all: a dubious achievement.

In short, sincere generosity is compatible, according to the circumstances, with giving away all one has, or some of it, or none of it. To follow the rule that one should give just as much as will result in all men having equal amounts is to replace the virtue of compassion with an amoral mechanical formula, possibly as harmful in its consequences as the most vicious forms of selfishness.

Envy

Whereas some of the arguments considered here are cast in a moral mould, maintaining that equality alone can satisfy the commands of ethics or the requirements of justice, we turn now to an argument which founds the ideal of equality on convenience rather than right.

It maintains that inequality – or 'relative deprivation', a new name which combines melodrama with technicality – provokes envy among the less fortunate, and that envy corrodes the social fabric. Equality is therefore the price of social stability, because only if each person feels that the society benefits him about as much as it benefits everyone else will each desist from disruption, sabotage and sinister pursuit of his own private good regardless of harm to others.

Crucial to this position is the assertion, as a matter either of historical fact or of psychological probability, that inequality leads to envy. But historical evidence would seem to point in just the opposite direction. Five hundred years ago, when inequality was certainly more pronounced than now, envy was perhaps less deep than it is now. To go beyond 'perhaps' is impossible: it is difficult enough to assess the magnitude of envy felt by people who can be observed directly today; surmise, and inference from indirect and scanty evidence, give us evidence of only the flimsiest sort about the feelings of people long since dead. Yet popular turmoil was not a vastly more remarkable feature of late medieval Europe than it is in far less unequal societies today. Nor can cross-sectional comparisons of various societies today sustain the presumption. If one ranked all societies today according to, first, their degree of inequality and, second, their degree of social instability – tasks calling for an awesome amount of insight and subjective judgment – it might turn out that the two rankings correlated more or less closely. Yet if such a correlation emerged, which is doubtful, it would prove nothing to the purpose, since any number of other considerations might be the common causes of both inequality and social instability. The most obvious candidate would be a self-serving tyranny, which distributed goods very unequally, survived temporarily only by force of repression, and was destabilised not by envy but by outrage and hatred. Instability today results much more from such groups as dissidents in the Soviet bloc, black African nationalists, and Arab or Irish terrorists than from the 'relatively deprived' in the liberal democracies.

Psychology fails, as history does, to establish that inequality must inevitably result in envy. Some amateur tennis player may envy the world champion, but many admire him. The heights, seen from below, may inspire respect, reverence, awe, love, worship, trust, obedience or many other forms of deference, as readily as envy or disapproval.

If different individuals respond differently to a given set of circumstances, the circumstances do not *cause* any one of those reactions. If, for instance, this man loves strawberries whereas that man abhors them, it is not the strawberries which cause the one response or the other; in fact we say, if anything, that it is the 'preferences' or 'tastes' of the individual which account for his response. Similarly, since different individuals can and do respond to the superior position of others in many different ways, it cannot be maintained that inequality *causes* any one of those different responses. In short, envy is caused not by external circumstances but by something in the persons who respond enviously.

To argue that equality is an eligible cure for envy is to *assume* that inequality is evil and that envy is a natural reaction to it. If, on the contrary, inequality is natural whereas envy is corrupt, then the entire argument for equality as a cure for envy collapses. To try to eliminate envy by abolishing inequality is like trying to eliminate crime by abolishing law.

One might add further that, though envious people continue to exist and though many societies today exhibit some social disorder, there is no reason to suppose that the envious are among the main contrivers of disorder. Many of those who refuse allegiance, who work to destroy 'the existing order', whatever it may be, seem to be moved by abstract ideas untinged by private interest, by vices other than envy, or by virtue such as they understand it to be.

Democracy

Equality is sometimes said to be the inevitable outcome of democracy, the form of government which some regard as inevitable in any community whose members are truly free. According to this view, free men will sooner or later realise that their common business must be so organised that each citizen's voice counts just as weightily as every other's; and the majority, who in any normal community are less prosperous than some few, will always use their electoral preponderance so as to redistribute income and wealth downward; from which it follows that equality is implicit in the drift of history. To put it another way: anybody who regards democracy as the best form of government must accept as desirable the policies that naturally emerge from it, among them equality.

That modern democracies have engaged in redistributive practices, direct and indirect, is not open to doubt. But is this an inevitable tendency of democracy? Here there is much room for doubt. Modern non-democrative governments also engage in redistribution, sometimes fiercer than that practised by democracies. It would seem therefore that redistribution results from the widespread belief that equality, especially equality of income and wealth, is the paramount element of justice, rather than that it results inevitably from any particular form of government.

There is no conclusive reason to believe that the majority within a democracy will always aim to level income and wealth down to their level. For one thing, the disparity of incomes *within* the least prosperous half of any industralised community is quite considerable, with the result that those at the more prosperous fringe of the lower half may judge correctly that they have more to lose than to gain from redistribution and may therefore join in a majority of the higher income citizens who resist redistribution. Suppose, for instance, a community of three citizens whose incomes are £4,000, £5,000 and £5,400 respectively; on a vote to redistribute those incomes absolutely equally, the middle-income earner would do better for himself by voting against the measure (so keeping his £5,000) than by voting for it (which would reduce his income to the average of £4,800). The easy supposition that in democracies a majority would always have good economic reason to support redistribution is accordingly false. If people's votes were determined exclusively by a desire to get the highest possible income for themselves – the supposition made by those who believe that democracy entails redistribution – then whether a majority supported or opposed a given scheme of redistribution would depend entirely on whether the majority stood to gain or lose by it; and redistribution can go from the poor to the rich just as easily as from the rich to the poor, or it can easily go from both the rich and the poor to a majority in the middle.

But such a narrow, arithmetic view of the matter is mainly beside the point. In many modern democracies the majority party or coalition is formed less on the basis of income differentials than on the basis of ideals about how best to govern the community. Among the ideas that matter in modern democracies equality is certainly one, but another is economic efficiency. And as many instances show, the majority may believe that to give everyone the same income – or to come anywhere near giving him the same income – no matter how little or ineffectively he works is certain to destroy or severely diminish most people's incentives to work, so reducing the prosperity of each and all. Democratic majorities, in short, may and often do prefer policies that aim to raise everyone's income (as a result of general economic growth) to policies that aim to raise the incomes of some by reducing the incomes of others.

As equality is not in any way an inescapable by-product of democracy, the ardent democrat is free from obligation – suggested by the principle of love me, love my dog – to condone or endorse equality.

Response to risk

Some, following a line of reasoning put forward by John Rawls,[3] believe that equality is a necessary implication of a psychological law which dictates men's preferences when facing situations of risk.

Suppose, as Rawls invites us to do, that a person were asked to design the distribution of income for a community of which he would then become a member; yet the designer, though authorised to determine the distribution of income, is barred from specifying his own place in it, that being determined purely by chance. He is, in effect, empowered to lay down the rules of a lottery in which he will thereafter play, but prohibited from rigging the lottery so that he would be sure to win. Under these constraints, how would a rational man design the lottery? He would, says Rawls, in effect design it in such a way that each player would be sure to win about the same amount, thus ensuring that nobody – including himself – could lose catastrophically. By analogy, only a society which conferred equal or nearly equal outcomes on all its members would be safe for all its members, and therefore a rational man would prefer it to all others.

Among various defects in this analysis, we may notice first that it does not account for the attitudes manifested by the many people who engage in lotteries. Characteristic of every lottery is that the participant pays a fee to enter; he submits to a *certain* loss in exchange for a purely *contingent* gain. Now some people gamble compulsively; and some in ignorance that the odds are against them; and many others, who are moderate and knowledgeable, do it for the rare pleasure of deliberately courting controllable risk. But in principle a lottery, if it is 'fair', is so far from being irrational from the standpoint of the subscribers that probability theorists regularly take it as an arch-case of rational behaviour. To pay a pound for one chance in a hundred of winning a hundred pounds is totally in keeping with the dictates of reason and with the tastes of millions.

Consider, in this light, the design of societies, each of which is a lottery as far as Rawls's designer is concerned, since pure chance will dictate which of the possible incomes he himself gets. Let us restrict our examination to the following four societies, identical except for differing distributions of income:

- All get £7,500 each.
- Half get £5,000, the other half £10,000.
- One per cent get £3,000, 99 per cent get £7,545.
- One per cent get £100,000, 99 per cent get £6,566.

Now from the standpoint of disembodied reason, perfect rationality unembellished by any irrational preferences, all these four – and also an indefinitely large number of other – are perfectly equivalent. They are equivalent because their 'expected values' (the 'expected value' of a gamble is defined as the sum of the possible pay-offs, each weighted by the probability that it will occur) are equal, namely £7,500 in each instance; and the rational gambler, shorn of all other human attributes, pays attention to nothing but expected value. So it follows that the rational gambler, far from designing an egalitarian society, would regard it as no better or worse than an intensely unequal society. He might take the precaution, on his own behalf, of setting some lower limit below which nobody's absolute income should fall: a precaution akin to table-stakes which limit one's losses in a game of poker; but to interpret such precaution as implying a preference on the gambler's part for equality would be to overlook entirely his readiness to face the risk of loss for the chance of gain. No gambler aims at equality between himself and his co-gamblers.

But of course not everybody is a gambler. Once we leave behind the ideally rational calculator, we enter the realms of preference and are bound to notice that real human beings fall into three groups with respect to risk. Some avoid risk: they would prefer a certainty of £15 to equal chances of winning £10 or winning £20, and they tend to take out more insurance than is rational. Some are neutral: they subscribe indifferently to fair lotteries and to fair insurance. Some seek risk: they would prefer equal chances of winning £10 or winning £20 to a certainty of winning £15, and they under-insure themselves.

We may suppose, accordingly, that these will respond differently to Rawls's proposition. Those who are neutrally disposed toward risk would regard as equivalent every pattern of income distribution which yields the same expected volume of income. Those who like risk would prefer a society with wide disparities of income. And only those averse to risk would do as Rawls assumes, they alone would prefer a more equal distribution of income to a less equal and hence more risky distribution. From which it follows that Rawls's argument, if it held at all, would hold only for that fraction of men who are averse to risk.

How widespread is aversion to risk? Not sufficiently widespread to be a reliable clue to what is natural in men. Human nature may be reflected at least as well by the admiration which men willingly pay to heroes and others who thrive on riskiness. Apart from heroes and outright gamblers, every investor who knowingly buys risky shares instead of blue-chips, every entrepreneur who sinks his capital in a new enterprise, every writer who labours to produce a book which may or may not sell, every student who spends years of time training for a profession which will yield to him financial rewards that are quite unpredictable – all these and many more deliberately court risk. And as most people marry, eat food which may be contaminated, carry cash in their pockets, and cross roads, it may be said that nobody could get through a normal life without accepting many risks.

It may be said, however, that there are some risks which everybody would regard as senseless, even if those risks were 'fair' in the probabilistic sense. To pay a pound for one chance in ten thousand of winning £10,000 is reasonable; to pay a pound as the fee for admission to a social arrangement in which one has 9,999 chances of having no income at all during one's lifetime and one chance of having an annual income of £10,000 would be drastically unreasonable, even though the expected values of the two lotteries are equal. What makes for the difference is, of course, the differing degrees to which the risk-taker can 'afford' the loss. If a loss, however large or small absolutely, had the effect of preventing the gambler from ever playing again, then the game, though remaining a fair one in a hypothetical sense, becomes potentially unfair in the practical sense. On this account it is clear that no rational person would design a social dispensation in which some persons are left either entirely without income or with incomes far too low to sustain life even briefly. A rational designer would therefore, as we have already seen, set a lower absolute limit to incomes, so providing a safety-net; but only in a drastically impoverished society would the intention to provide everyone with an absolute minimum leave no surplus to be divided, equally or unequally, according to the designer's choice. With regard to any community living beyond the margin of subsistence, the rational designer could still implement, in greater or lesser degree, his own preference as between riskiness and risklessness. And accordingly, Rawls's conclusion must be rejected: rational calculation in accordance with human nature would *not* yield an egalitarian society, since the many human beings who prefer risky undertakings to 'safe bets' would rationally create a society which offered the possibility of great rewards as well as small rewards.

Quite a separate flaw in Rawls's argument is his assumption that the designer could feasibly prescribe the *distribution* of *goods in a society without thereby influencing at all the total volume of goods* available to be distributed. Suppose that the designer faced a choice between two dispensations: one that gave every member of a community £5,000, the other that gave half the members of of the same community £5,000 each and the other half £10,000 each. Which should he rationally prefer?

Many people would answer, as Rawls would, that the second dispensation is rationally superior, in as much as, compared with the first, nobody is worse off than before and half are better off. Sophisticated, or rather sophistical, objections may be raised to this 'natural' view.

It might be said, for one thing, that a larger income is not really better for the recipient than a smaller income. Such an assertion would rest, presumably, on some variant of the primitive idea that 'money isn't everything'. Yet giving full credit to this notion, issue could still be joined by positing a hypothetical measure of 'satisfaction' or 'happiness', and asking whether a community in which half of its members enjoyed 5,000 units of happiness per year and the other half 10,000 units of happiness ought to be rationally preferred to a community in which every member enjoyed only 5,000 units of happiness. Persons prepared to accept 'happiness' as a synonym for the *summum bonum*, or as a category comprehending all possible varieties of human good – spiritual as well as material, other-regarding as well as self-regarding, those accompanied by short-run pain as well as those giving short-run pleasure – must rationally affirm that the community each of whose members enjoyed either more or no less happiness is preferable. Indeed, to deny this would be to cut away the ground under Rawls's argument, for if more income (however 'income' may be defined) does not suit the recipient better than less income (all else being equal), then why should Rawls's rational designer pay the slightest attention to how much income he or anybody else gets? If more income were not better than less, it would not matter whether some people had lower incomes than others.

A second sophistical objection is that an equal distribution of income is in itself a positive good: in other words, that recipients of high incomes within an unequal society suffer sympathetic pain at the thought that others are less well placed than themselves, while the recipients of lower incomes suffer discontent at the thought that others are better placed. These disutilities, resulting from compassionate suffering on the one hand and envious suffering on the other hand, ought to be reckoned in as modifications on the distribution of 'private pecuniary' incomes – so say those who raise this objection. On this view, a community in which half receive £5,000 and half receive £10,000 in 'private pecuniary' incomes ought to be recognised as one in which everyone's 'psychic income' is really lower than their money incomes would suggest – standing, let us say, at adjusted values of £4,000 and £8,000. Nevertheless, even if we accept this qualification for the sake of argument, it will not do Rawlsians much good.

For one thing, the compassionate high-income recipient could diminish his suffering by voluntarily giving away as much as he liked of his income. This possibility means that the original distribution need not be made egalitarian by edict. Moreover, if we assume that each member of the community differs in the *extent* that he suffers psychically from any specific unequal distribution, then a regime of voluntary redistribution would be rationally preferable (from the standpoint of minimising each individual's suffering) to a regime of imposed equality.

But another line of reasoning more powerfully dissolves the second objection. Let us merely transpose the discussion into 'psychic incomes', which make due adjustments for sufferings arising from inequality. What now will the Rawlsian say to the choice between two arrangements, in one of which everyone gets an all-inclusive 'psychic income' of £5,000 and in the other of which half get 'psychic incomes' of £5,000 and the other half get 'psychic incomes' of £10,000? He must accept the latter as superior – unless he maintains that the latter alternative is unthinkable because it represents an impossibility, logical, psychological or moral. This would be tantamount to asserting that no person, or at least no moral person, could tolerate a situation in which he received a higher psychic income than anybody else. But to assert this would merely beg the whole question at issue, for if nobody can tolerate inequality, then it could only come about by malign accident; or, if it is said that no moral person can tolerate inequality, then this is merely to assert that inequality is immoral by definition.

Having disposed of those two frivolous counters, I return to the question of whether Rawls's designer can reasonably be credited with a facility for determining the distribution of income without affecting the total income available to the community. The answer must be that he cannot. Suppose for instance, a community all of whose members receive £5,000. Suppose now that one member were offered an increment of £10 worth of income in exchange for producing additional product valued at £10. Now, if he were permitted to keep the additional £10 for himself, he might undertake the additional work; but if a strict rule of equality were enforced, with the result that the incremental money income of £10 must be distributed equally among all members of the community, he might well decide that the gain accruing to himself was far too small to compensate him for the additional effort required. And if this could conceivably ever happen, it follows that the size of each person's income is not independent of the distribution of income. Accordingly, when Rawls's rational man designs a society with an equal distribution of income he is automatically, if unknowingly, designing a society such that some or all of its members are less well off than they need be in view of their tastes and productive potentials. Once alerted to this implication, rational men would respond by preferring the richer society to the equal society, provided that everyone in the richer society is at least as well to do as in the poorer equal society. A rational man would prefer, for instance, an arrangement in which everybody gets between (say) £7,500 and £15,000 to one in which everybody gets £5,000, assuming that the two were practical alternatives, so that one could move from one to another at will, merely according to whether private incentives were or were not permitted to operate.

This point can be underscored by noticing a vital distinction which tends to be overlooked simply because the thrust of Rawls's argument militates against recognising it. It is the distinction between the notions that people 'receive' certain incomes and that they 'earn' certain incomes. Rawls's rational designer might make plans about the relative incomes that each member of his projected society should 'receive', without saying anything about who would supply these receipts or how large the receipts would be in absolute measure. A government exercising perfect control over the conduct of citizens could dictate what fraction of the total output of the community should be allocated to each citizen; but, of course, as reason and experience alike tell us, the most perfectly dictatorial government cannot dictate the absolute size of the total output generated by the community – otherwise such governments could decree infinitely great accomplishments, instead of languishing, as dictatorships frequently do, at low levels of income. If, on the contrary, one thinks of a dispensation in which each person 'earns' his own income – in the precise sense that he enjoys an income equal to the marginal value product generated by his own efforts – then no Rawlsian designer, and no government, however dictatorial, can determine either the absolute size of its total output or the distribution of its members' incomes. This is so because the amount of income earned by each individual will be determined by the account of work he wishes to do and is able to do, as well, of course, as by the amount of output which the conditions of production (such as the level of technology and the supply of capital) enable his labour to generate. And it follows therefore that Rawls's doctrine applies, at most, to questions of distribution of output, as though the output to be distributed were somehow given magically or were totally insensitive to anything that the designer might do about distribution. The doctrine, in short, rests on ignoring the simple and basic fact that free rational human beings adjust the amount of work they do in accordance with incentives to work, at least one of which incentives is the possibility of increasing one's private consumption.

In short, Rawls's analysis of this point, which is far too elaborate to be dealt with comprehensively in these brief comments, is vitiated by his having assumed that all human beings do, or rationally should, avoid risk; and, secondly, that enforcing a more equal distribution of income need not depress the absolute level of everyone's income. Many human beings rationally enter risky situations and emerge from them unrepentant even if disappointed, and even those who stand most to benefit from equal distribution could rationally reject it in favour of an unequal distribution which might give them higher absolute incomes.

Marginal utility of income

One of the more common arguments for equality of income rests on the premise of diminishing marginal utility of income. This is the notion that if a man's income rises from £5,000 to £6,000 (while prices and all other relevant considerations remain constant), the additional utility provided by that additional £1,000 is less than the additional utility provided by the £1,000 that previously raised his income from £4,000 to £5,000.

Properly understood, this asserted principle must contain a kernel of truth. Income is generally desired for the sake of the consumption which it permits. And as to consumption, it seems clear that a law of diminishing utility operates. Passionately as the Englishman loves bacon and eggs for breakfast, the third helping of the morning or the sixth must be less thrilling than the first. It might be luxurious to have one's hair dressed every day rather than each week, but luxury would turn to boredom and finally exasperation as one's hair was dressed twice a day, four times a day, and at last continuously. And since the same waning of delight, followed by extinction of delight, must occur as anybody (other than an uncontrollable addict) consumes more and more of any given commodity in any given period of time, it may be concluded that the utility of money also must decline as one earns more and more of it within any given period – at least in so far as income is thought of as a means of access to consumption.

Now, taking it that the utility of income diminishes as income rises, it is easy, though fallacious, to suppose that if income were taken from the rich and given to the poor, the total utility experienced by the whole community would increase. Consider two men, one of whom earns £3,000 and the other £13,000. Then shifting £1,000 from the richer to the poorer increases the total utility available to the latter by more than it diminishes the utility available to the former, and so increases the total utility enjoyed by the two. Successive shifts of £1,000 each have similar effect, even though the increase in utility is less marked in each successive step; and the upshot is that the total utility of the two persons is maximised at the point where redistribution has made their incomes exactly equal. It would appear to follow that equality of income throughout a community is the essential condition for maximising the total utility which the total income available could confer on the members of that community.

But this conclusion is unsustainable, for the assumptions on which it is built are questionable at the least and most probably false.

First, the diminishing marginal utility of income is deduced from the diminishing marginal utility of goods and commodities being consumed. But income has other dimensions as well. Some people, at least, regard their incomes, in part, as accolades, the most tangible honours which their superiors can bestow, the tokens which best signal to themselves and everyone else the esteem which they deserve. People who understand honour as purely relative – who consider that one is honourable only in so far as one is honoured above others – and who regard the size of one's income as a proper measure of honour, would not experience any diminishing utility of income, not at least until their incomes were high enough to exceed by a safe margin those of people whom they regard as competitors.

Again, income is wanted not exclusively to sustain consumption but also, by most people, in order to accumulate savings. One motive, perhaps the dominant one, for saving is to meet emergencies, such as illness, unemployment or accident, and especially the most common of all emergencies, that of growing too old to work. The motive for saving may be said to be prudence; many experience it as fear. And to the extent that such fear is intense – a response to eventualities that are unknown because unexperienced, and unknowable because unpredictable – the marginal utility of income may diminish little if at all. No doubt some absolute level of savings should allay the fears of any rational person; but, until a fearful person had achieved that absolute level, each increment of income might easily be regarded as just as useful as each previously acquired increment of the same size. Nor is fear the crucial consideration: rather, any emotion or rational deliberation which persuades a person to set an accumulated target of some absolute size will have the same effect of rendering the marginal utility of income constant, so far as he is concerned, at least until he has achieved his target. To recognise this is to place oneself in a position to explain many of the instances where somebody who is apparently quite well-to-do continues to work at a killing pace.

Second, the utility of income is not a fixed characteristic of each individual which attends him unchanged throughout the whole of his life. Obvious facts attest the opposite. As people age, various appetites and aspirations may remain stable, but others will intensify, and still others fade. Besides, the specific contents of anyone's whole array of tastes visibly changes with time. An enthusiastic traveller may convert into a stay-at-home, a spartan may move toward lavishness, a libertine toward parsimony, a miser toward ostentation; anyone who has lived in one way may move toward another way. Apart from random changes in individuals, the tastes of whole civilisations may alter with time. It may well be that the desire of western men for material comfort – in terms of food, clothing and shelter, transportation, entertainment and leisure – has expanded more or less constantly over the past millennium. If so, then we must conclude that the total utility of any given real income has been shifting upward from one generation to another. So even though, all else remaining fixed, it seems intuitively certain that the addition of one pound to one's income carries with it an incremental utility which is smaller than the loss of utility which would come about if one's income were lowered by one pound – nevertheless, the total utilities which any given income would yield to the same person at different points in his life are just as certainly different. Or to put it in minimal terms, since the utility of income depends on tastes, and tastes are notoriously variable, we are not entitled to assume that the utility of income is stable for any given person over time. Or, as economists might like to express it, the utility of income is not stable intertemporally.

Third, as the tastes of each individual change from time to time according to the individual's peculiar life history, it must follow that the tastes of any two individuals will differ in their composition and intensity, from which it follows in turn that the utilities experienced by any two individuals with identical incomes would not necessarily and not typically be equal. An enthusiast may get more utility from £5,000 than his phlegmatic neighbour gets from £10,000; and were their incomes reversed, the enthusiast would get a total utility and marginal utility more than twice as large as the other's. The implications drawn from all this are often presented as a caution against blithely assuming identity when making interpersonal comparisons of utility. They may be put more frankly as the implication that, because people differ from one another in the intensity of their desires for income, the utility conferred on separate individuals by equal incomes must typically differ as well.

Once we reject the assumption that the utility of income is the same for all persons, then the view that redistribution of income from richer to poorer increases and ultimately maximises the community's total utility is shown to be untenable. No longer can it be said that, in a hypothetical community of two whose incomes are £3,000 and £13,000, the total utility of the two persons would be improved by moving to £4,000 and £12,000, and so on until each has £8,000. Instead we must now admit the possibility that a redistribution *away* from equality – say toward £2,000 and £14,000 – would bring about the highest total utility. And all warrant has disappeared for the view that the community's utility would be maximised at just the point where both persons had exactly equal incomes. Depending on the relative utilities of the persons in question, equality of income might be less rewarding than extreme degrees of inequality.

Fourth, even if we accepted for the sake of the argument that equality of income maximises the total utility which a given total income yields to the whole community, this would provide no moral justification for redistribution by coercion.

To be sure, if equality of income did maximise the community's total utility, that principle might be converted into a guide for voluntary conduct: a guide urging the rich man to diminish his private good for the sake of the 'public' good (defined purely as a sum of all private goods). But proponents of redistribution do not limit themselves to preaching voluntary generosity; indeed, they generally reject philanthropy as inadequate. They insist instead that the state must impose redistribution by law, because enforced redistribution is right.

But the assumed desirability of equality does not establish the rightness of enforced redistribution. One might as well maintain that the desired end of public health morally justifies the extermination of all persons who are ill. Neither does the fact that enforced distribution has been installed by democratic procedures make it morally right. One might as well maintain that the enslavement of a black minority by a white majority would be right if decided on by a democratic procedure, honouring to the hilt the rule of one man, one vote. Tyranny by a majority is not less tyrannical than tyranny by a minority; and even a democracy violates the wishes of some citizens whenever it adopts laws other than those which command universal assent. Neither the presumed desirability of an end such as equality of income, nor the presumed superiority of democratic government, can confer moral rightness on enforced redistribution.

This defect would persist even if one doubted whether the distribution of income which comes about in the absence of enforced redistribution could be justified morally. What possible principle of justice, asks the common-or-garden moralist, can make it right that an immoral pop singer should earn a hundred times more than a decent hard-working farm worker? One might, of course, answer (though far too briefly) that in as much as such pay scales emerge from voluntary bargains uncorrupted by force or fraud, they may be held to be morally innocent even if not morally commendable. But we need not maintain that the unregulated distribution of income is morally perfect in order to hold that redistributing income by coercive force is morally unfounded. Even if an existing situation is morally inexcusable, that cannot justify every and any effort to alter it. To hold otherwise would be to hold that the existence of any vice justifies any effort to extirpate it, no matter how violent or tyrannical.

Finally, it must be noted that equality is desired, within the framework of this argument, not as an end in itself, but rather as an intermediate or instrumental end: that is, as a means of achieving the ultimate end of maximising the total utility of a community. But this end (which economists call 'Pareto optimality' and the Utilitarians sometimes described as 'the greatest good of the greatest number') has repeatedly been shown to be unsustainable. For the present purpose it it enough to point out that the total utility to be maximised consists of the summed utilities of all members of the community, each of whom is treated as equal, in some fundamental respect, to all others. In short, the argument as a whole is circular, since it seeks to justify equality by reference to an end which has equality built into it as a premise.

Having shown above that the familiar theoretical arguments in favour of egalitarianism are unsound, I shall now demonstrate that every and any egalitarian policy is internally contradictory. That is, were a government to equalise any one material dimension of life, such as pay, consumption, burden of work, or wealth, it would necessarily and inevitably create inequality in one or more of the other dimensions.

Suppose that the government set out to equalise pay by assuring every worker the same wage. Yet this is too vague to serve as a practicable rule. Does it mean that every worker would be paid the same rate per hour of work done? But then, if workers were allowed any freedom to choose the number of hours they worked per week, some would earn more than others per week. Does it mean that every worker would be paid the same amount annually? But then, if different workers worked different numbers of hours per year – because of ill health, breakdown of machinery or involuntary unemployment – their hourly pay would be unequal. And if they worked different numbers of years during their lives (as differences of health and opportunity would ensure), their lifetime incomes would be unequal. In short, any rule imposing equality on pay per hour, day, year or life would necessarily impose inequality on pay realised during any other interval of time.

In order to avoid this paradox, an egalitarian government might arbitrarily fix on one interval of time, say one year, and equalise everyone's pay per year. To do so would achieve administrative convenience without, however, resolving the inherent contradiction. For any worker who suffered illness, absented himself from work for good reason or bad, or failed to find employment, would earn more per hour actually worked than those who laboured steadily through the year. Whether this outcome should be considered just or desirable is not at present the issue. The point is that even equality of pay, leaving aside all other dimensions of equality, is strictly unattainable because equal pay for an interval of any given dimension means, in practice, unequal pay for any longer or shorter interval.

Suppose that every worker were paid the same annual wage, then the potential annual expenditure per person would be unequal. At equalised annual pay of £5,000, each member of a family of four in which the husband and wife both worked could afford to consume £2,500 worth of goods and services, whereas the members of a family of four with only one member working could each afford to consume only £1,250. This inequality of consumption potential, generated within a régime of equal pay, would of course reach its extremes in families on the one hand, in which all of the members worked, and in those, on the other hand, in which none of the members worked.

Contradictions that would arise if, in order to cure this one the government undertook to equalise consumption allowances, are discussed on page 110.

If all workers were paid equally, they would almost certainly accumulate unequal amounts of wealth. If we assume that nobody inherits any wealth, but that different people have different propensities to save and are permitted to save as little or as much of their earnings as they individually like, then equal pay would even within one life-time produce remarkable inequality of wealth. (See pp. 129–30.)

If people were permitted, as they are in capitalist economies and even in some more or less socialist economies, to invest their wealth and draw interest or dividends, then equality of income (paid for current work) would be contradicted by inequality of total income – because the equal pay that some received for current work would be enlarged, unequally, by earnings from unequal wealth.

Furthermore, if inheritance were permitted, then inequality of wealth and of income might intensify over time, even while the rule of equal pay to each worker was strictly observed.

Therefore, any thorough-going effort to equalise income would need to forbid inheritance and private saving, unless it neutralised the disequalising effect of unequal wealth by prohibiting interest, dividends and any other form of return on investment. But such prohibitions would, at the limit, be unenforceable. Even though the bulk of private saving were displaced by forced public saving, implemented by high rates of taxation, even the most oppressive taxation conceivable would not extinguish every individual's desire to save privately. Even though private gifts and bequests were declared to be unlawful, they could not be extirpated absolutely without first dissolving all families, friendships and close human associations. And even though the possibility of 'unearned' income were stopped by putting an end to all private investment in producers' capital goods, it would still be possible for people to get 'unearned' incomes in non-pecuniary form by investing their savings in consumers' capital goods. Leaving aside the question of practicality, it stands out clearly that to prevent unequal accumulation of wealth – even while earnings from work were absolutely equalised – would require continuous and all-pervasive repression.

If all workers were paid equally, this would entail unequal 'sacrifice' by different workers. Different sorts of work are widely regarded as being unequally burdensome. Some jobs, such as those of miners and test-pilots, are more dangerous than others. Some, such as those of night-workers and drain-cleaners, are unusually disagreeable. Some, such as those of tool-makers and psychiatrists, require particularly long and difficult training. If persons doing such jobs were paid no more than those whose work is safer, pleasanter and easier to qualify for, then equality of pay would contradict equality of effort.

Since it might be expected that where all workers are paid equally, few would volunteer to do jobs which are especially burdensome, the need to have such work done would point to forcible direction of labour. And nothing can better illustrate inequality of burden or sacrifice than the practice of conscripting people into forms of service which, though highly valuable to the beneficiaries, are repugnant to the unlucky individuals forced to perform them.

Suppose a government tried to resolve the foregoing contradiction by establishing a rule which equalised pay per unit of effort, burden, discomfort or sacrifice – let us say, generally, per unit of disutility. Such a rule would immediately contradict the principle of equal income for each worker, for the income now earned by any given worker would be proportional to the disutility entailed in his work, and everyone agrees that some jobs are less agreeable than others.

But this is only the beginning of the troubles. If the difficulty of a job were measured in accordance with the difficulty experienced by any particular individual doing that job, then a person who found a job difficult because he lacked skill or energy or will would earn more per year than if he did a job for which he was better qualified or happier to do. Further, the more skill he acquired in any job, and the less difficult it thus became, the lower would be his annual income. In short, the rule of equal pay per unit of disutility would flatly contradict another possible and plausible rule: the rule of equal pay per unit of output. The former rule would encourage people to choose the work for which they were least suited.

If, on the contrary, the disutility of a job were measured without reference to how disagreeable any particular individual found it, then different workers would get the same pay for doing that job even though some found it far less demanding or disagreeable than others – a clear violation of the principle presumably embodied in the rule of equality.

Worse still, how could one realistically measure the disutility of a job, in itself or as felt by each particular person doing it? Wage rates established in free labour markets would offer no guidance on this point, because they are determined by the interplay of both demand and supply, whereas the disutility of any given kind of work affects only supply and does not exhaustively determine even that half of the picture. Nor could any sort of scientific or technical expertise answer the question objectively. Who can pretend to know exactly how much more disagreeable it is to operate a lathe at midnight than at noon? Of course, each individual can judge for himself how much extra pay it would take to induce him to exchange his present job for some other – though as such judgments involve comparison of known past conditions with predicted future conditions, they are liable to gross errors of estimation. Yet ignoring this imprecision, were an egalitarian to adopt the expressed individual tastes of each worker as the criterion for determining the pay of each individual, he would have abandoned all hope of equalising pay in any sense other than equal pay per unit of felt disutility, and he would authorise instead great inequality among the annual incomes earned by different individuals.

Any public authority charged with proportioning the pay for various jobs to the disutilities they entail could, in one sense, succeed all too easily. No matter how wrongly it decided, it would seem sooner or later to have decided correctly – because as long as workers are free to change jobs and as long as young people entering the labour force are free to choose their occupations, workers will shift out of underpriced occupations and into overpriced occupations, so that after a time workers in every occupation would or should feel that their pay fairly compensated for the disutilities of their work. Pay relativities imposed by fiat thus operate as self-confirming hypotheses, and the work of so-called expert bodies in assessing the relative disutilities of different jobs is a loose exercise in assessing loose public opinion or, worse, self-indulgence and self-righteousness passing themselves off as scientific knowledge.

Suppose now that an egalitarian government, having recognised that it could not achieve any sensible result by trying to equalise pay, turned instead to the strategy of equalising consumption. Suppose further that it aimed to achieve this goal by distributing an equal cash allowance to every person: man, woman or child.

This method would fail to achieve the goal. If any person saved more than another, his consumption during that period would be proportionately smaller. If any person needed to spend more on medical services than another, his consumption of all other goods and services would be accordingly smaller. A child whose education had to be paid for out of his cash allowance might be restricted to an inadequate diet. Equal consumption allowances, in cash, would fail to ensure that all persons achieved an equal level of satisfaction in consumption either at any given time or through the whole of their lives: different people are not equally skilled at turning money into real utility, and the real utilities that different people experience depend in no small measure on their different temperaments, especially on their different and to some extent self-determined capacities for enjoyment.

Contradictions and difficulties more serious would arise if a policy were adopted of equalising consumption by conferring on each person the identical bundle of real goods. Some such thinking presumably underlies present policies of medical care free of charge to the patient, free public education, subsidised public housing and transportation, subsidised meals and foodstuffs, and the like. No doubt subsidies in kind rather than in cash are favoured by many egalitarians because they are convinced that some people would spend cash consumption allowances unwisely, buying gin when they ought to be buying medicine, buying toys rather than schooling for their children, and buying luxurious cars rather than adequate housing. No doubt it is true that some people are improvident in such ways. But subsidies in kind do not of themselves overcome such failings, and therefore it might be considered necessary to force people to use the subsidy, as the laws now force reluctant children to attend free schools. In order to be sure that people who are thoughtless, ignorant or fearful actually went to the physician at times when according to expert opinion they 'ought to', it would be necessary to establish a medical equivalent of truancy laws and truant officers. Similarly with housing and all other public services offering subsidies in kind. Indeed, the proliferation of social workers in public employment may be interpreted partly as a step in the direction of pressing people into using subsidies in kind.

Forcing everyone to use subsidies in kind does not equalise real consumption. On the contrary, there is reason to believe that the real benefits which accrue, for instance, to different pupils from attending a school, even the same school, differ in amount, and would differ no matter how schooling were organised and no matter what misguided efforts might be made to homogenise all pupils and teachers. Again, it would be difficult to say that the real benefits conferred on one patient by having his appendix removed equal or do not equal those realised by another who had an aching tooth extracted. And how much benefit is realised by a person who never uses free medical care because he is never ill, but merely benefits by the curtailment of contagious diseases?

Above all, consider the inequality of consumers' real utilities that would result if subsidies in kind were carried to their logical conclusion, and an identical bundle of goods and services were distributed to each person. Because of ineradicable differences of taste, one person would take much pleasure from his weekly mutton chop while another would eat it with loathing, if at all. One would feel that his living quarters were cramped and his clothing ration needlessly lavish; another the opposite. Assuming that each person were perfectly cognizant of what was good for himself, and supposing that barter were permitted, almost everyone could improve his situation by trading goods which he liked less for goods which he liked more but his trading partner liked less. And this certainty that trading would take place – as it does in prisons and concentration camps, where equality of consumption is aimed at by giving each inmate the identical bundle of real goods and services – proves that giving each person the same amount of money leads to a higher lever of satisfaction for each person than does giving him a standard bundle of goods of equivalent monetary value. Leaving aside the small minority of people who do not properly know what they want or what is good for them, a cash allocation for consumption is best. But even then, as we have seen, an equal allocation of money would would not remotely result in equalised satisfaction.

A policy of equalising consumption by distributing identical bundles of goods and services to all would founder because, contrary to what egalitarians commonly say or imply, the 'needs' of different individuals are unequal. Infants need fewer calories and more milk than stevedores. Aged people need more medical attention than young ones. Large people need more clothing than small people. And habitual smokers, drinkers, drug-takers need more cigarettes, whisky or marijuana than other people do. These last examples cast doubt on whether 'need' is an objective category at all.

What is beyond dispute is that 'needs', so far as they can be recognised at all, are extremely abstract. Everyone needs food to stay alive, but no particular foodstuff is needed by anybody. Many people throughout the world live healthy lives without ever eating beef or milk or bread. Yet even if we overlook all such problems about the nature of needs (and the resultant impossibility of specifying objectively exactly what any person, much less every person, needs), it is clear that giving every person identical consumption allowances would contradict the common understanding that different people have different and unequal needs.

It would seem to follow that a more appropriate egalitarian policy would be to proportion each person's consumption allowance to his needs. What would be equalised is consumption allowance per unit of need. It becomes immediately apparent that to do this would contradict equality of total consumption and of total satisfaction.

As for practical implementation: a government following this policy would be obliged to assess the true extent of each person's needs. The technical difficulty, indeed impossibility, of doing so does not require close demonstration; suffice it to say that the armies of different nations evidently hold quite varied views about the 'needs' of the soldiers whom they provision. Nor is it any answer to say, as some do, that 'needs' are 'culturally determined'; for this is to concede that 'needs' cannot be discerned by scientific knowledge, which means that they can only be determined by arbitrary discretion, exercised either by persons in authority or by respondents to public-opinion polls.

Any government that undertakes to proportion consumption allowances to 'needs' would have to add, if compelled to frank disclosure, 'and we will decide how much you need'. Greater frankness would no doubt disclose that the government's view of how much people needed – like any government's view about how much old-age pensioners need – is really in large part a decision about 'how much the country can afford'. And this reduces the whole matter to nonsense, for if need means anything, it means something contrary to how much can be afforded.

Equal consumption allowances for all, whether in cash or kind, would grossly contradict the principle of equal sacrifice. Those four in ten inhabitants of any economically developed country who do not work, as 'work' is normally understood, would get just as much income as the six in ten who do work. So far as the 'privileged' minority consisted of mothers and children, aged persons and others normally exempt from earning their own livings, their position might be considered morally defensible albeit unequally favoured. But we can be certain that some persons, though qualified for work by age and ability, would not work because they received the equal consumption allowance without working. They – and there is no telling how numerous they might be – would be merely the extreme instances of a predictable general tendency: once the link between work and income was severed, many people would put less effort into their labour. The burden of work would be shared most unequally as between the most conscientious and the most self-indulgent workers.[4]

Laxness of effort, condoned by this dispensation, would tend thus to reduce the community's total output and so its real income. Granted that pay is not the only incentive to work (for effort may be stimulated also by self-esteem, public honours, emulation, esprit de corps, and fear of rebuke or punishment), granted further that each individual's equal consumption allowance would rise or fall (all else being equal) according to how hard he himself worked, nevertheless much of the incentive to work hard would have vanished. Any individual worker who increased his output by working harder – supposing him to live in a country of 50,000,000 inhabitants – would improve his own consumption allowance by only one part in fifty million of the additional output. He would be subject, in effect, to a marginal tax rate of 99.999998 per cent. Conversely, and more to the point, any worker who stopped working altogether would thereby reduce the real value of his own consumption allowance by roughly 0.000002 per cent. But if many workers responded to this individually negligible penalty, each shedding his own individual burden, the equal consumption allowance of all would fall disastrously.

Similarly, equal consumption allowances would render senseless any private saving with a view to private investment. In the absence of investment, as the community's capital stock wore out, its income would sink further and further.

Except in so far as government could replace private incentives to work and to invest by forcing or inducing individuals to act contrary to their separate, foreseeable private interests, equalised consumption allowances would result in equal economic misery. Worse still, from the egalitarian's point of view, the differential effects of coercion applied to some persons and of non-pecuniary rewards conferred on others would create new forms of inequality as the price of equalising consumption.

'From each according to his abilities, to each according to his needs' is often advanced as a socialist or Marxist formula for equality. Presumably Mr Callaghan was expressing something of the same sort when he said in 1979 that the Labour Party ought to go forward under the motto, 'Need, not greed.'

As for the second branch of the formula ('to each according to his needs'): comments made above about equal income per unit of need show that this criterion of equality contradicts many others. As for the first branch of the formula ('from each according to his abilities'): it can be interpreted as the basic outline for a system of taxation. In return for giving each person an amount of income proportioned to his needs, the state will exact from each person an amount of work proportioned to his abilities.

How anyone's abilities are to be determined is left conveniently vague. Most people have many different abilities, and it should be obvious, even without cataloguing all the kinds of ability which may pertain to work, that anybody could do many different jobs. Practically speaking, therefore, it would not be any person's abilities that determined what he would be required to contribute. Instead, some official would decide *which* of any person's many abilities would be drawn into service. Of two people whose abilities enabled them to be either a prime minister or a street-sweeper (among other things), one would be recruited to run the country and the other to sweep streets. From all of which it follows that burdens, purportedly allocated equally, 'by ability', would lead to considerable inequalities of burden.

Confronted with such contradictions and difficulties inherent in policies which aim at equality of reward, egalitarians often take refuge in a halfway house. Their end, they say, is not to establish outright equality; rather it is to reduce inequality, to compress it within tolerable limits.

Such refuge provides no safety. Any argument which discredits a full-blown egalitarian policy, such as those considered above, applies proportionally to partial and qualified policies of the same sort. If utterly eradicating income differentials between brain-surgeons and hospital orderlies would lead to great inequalities of burden, then coercively narrowing such income differentials would still intensify the inequality of burdens, even though it did not maximise them. And similarly for each variety of egalitarian policy.

To defend halfway policies as 'moderate' is to pretend that a mitigated vice is really a positive virtue. On such reasoning, an assailant who wounded but refrained from killing his victim ought to be lauded as a benefactor. Halfway to an undesirable goal is too far by half.

In short, the aim of equalising income, whether in terms of earnings or consumption, is typically advanced in statements so vague as to conceal the contradictions and intolerable implications which lie just below the surface. Equalisation, along any coherent line, would inevitably bring with it unintended consequences – oppression, inequity and poverty – which would repel many advocates of equality, if they recognised those consequences, and which would reveal the dream of equality as a nightmare.

It may seem that an opponent of egalitarianism could not consistently support the principles that go under the names of 'equality of opportunity' and 'equality before the law'. But this apparent difficulty is dissolved if we recognise that, in connection with these principles, 'equality' is a misnomer. What those precepts really mean is that certain rights should be enjoyed by everyone and not only by a few or many: a notion misrepresented by 'equality' but precisely conveyed by the term 'universality'.

That the demand for universality of rights came to be expressed in terms of equality is partly due to historical accident and partly to slovenly misuse of language. Though now embedded in our language, 'equality' is in the context an unfortunate term, because many people read into it the implication that everyone should possess and exercise these rights in equal degree.

Properly understood, 'equality of opportunity' means that everyone should enjoy the right to enter any occupation for which he is qualified by skill and that nobody should be denied access to an occupation arbitrarily or captiously: that is, on grounds of personal characteristics other than his ability to do the job. In so far as access to an occupation is controlled – whether by public officials, professional associations, monopolistic employers or monopolistic trade unions – that control should be exercised impartially and impersonally, which means without reference to extraneous considerations such as parentage, sex, age or religion. Insisting on this does not imply that anybody should be guaranteed whatever job he likes, when and where he likes it and independently of his skill, actual or potential. Opportunity does not mean that somebody must provide such jobs as people desire; it means rather that nobody may justly be excluded from work which he could do satisfactorily.

Similarly, 'equality before the law', properly understood, means that every citizen of a country should be subject to the same laws, none enjoying special privileges, none suffering special disabilities; and that every person should have the right to a fair trial – in other words that judge and jury should studiously overlook every personal attribute of the litigants, heeding only the merits of the case made out by each of them.

Emphasised in both settings is that the right in question ought to be enjoyed by everyone, and that those who supervise the exercise of the right (such as licensing authorities, judges or their private counterparts) should use their authority or power impersonally. So far is this from implying 'equality' that it means, in at least certain critical aspects, an insistence on inequality. For it means that, among all those who may aspire to a given appointment, the one who is best qualified should get it; and it means that the litigant who puts forward the better case should win the suit. Inequality results, obviously, when some people enjoy privileged access to occupations and privileged treatment at law. But inequality results also when such rights are held universally.

A given right, though held universally in its general form, may be held in different degrees within a particular setting. Consider, for instance, a community which upholds inheritance, so that everyone in it enjoys the rights to bequeath property and to acquire property by bequest. Yet within the context of a particular will, one man's rights may be superior to another's. The residuary legatee enjoys a right to inherit which is subordinate to the rights of those to whom specific bequests have been made: he gets what is left, if anything is left, after their rights have been satisfied. His right is conditioned by theirs whereas theirs are not conditioned by his; it might be said that their rights are hierarchically superior to his; but 'inequality' would be a deceptive way of describing this relationship, especially if anyone interpreted 'equality of right' as meaning that all heirs should share out the estate equally. Moreover, only a fanatic would carry a predilection for equality so far as to maintain that nobody's right to anything should ever be subordinated to anybody else's right – in that event, bus queues would dissolve into chaos, to mention only a trivial consequence.

Again, rights may differ in duration. One man may buy a licence to fish in a stream for one day, another for one month. We can comfortably say that those rights are unequal in respect of duration because time is quantifiable. It would, however, be entirely misleading to say that they had 'unequal rights' if in fact both enjoyed the same constitutional right to fish.

As this example suggests, the rate at which people exercise a right is often susceptible of measurement, and one can therefore speak precisely about equality or inequality in the rates at which various people exercise a right which all of them possess. But it would promote radical confusion to infer from unequal exercise of a right that the right itself is unequally enjoyed by the persons concerned. If two citizens both enjoy the right to walk in a public park, and if one walks there often but the other never, the fact that one exercises the right more often than the other in no way alters the fact that both enjoy the identical right. Similarly, if two men enjoy the right to marry (unlike slaves who could marry only with their master's permission), the fact that one man marries three times while the other remains single does not in any way impugn the bachelor's right to marry. Again, the fact that different freemen own unequal amounts of private property does not reduce any of them to the condition of a slave who was denied the right to own private property.

'Equality' in rights is thus liable to be misinterpreted as a demand that everyone should exercise each right to an equal extent. But this is absurd. The right of free speech does not mean that anybody need talk all the time, or that everyone should talk the same amount of time, or that nobody may remain silent. To force someone to use a right because others are using it would be tyranny, and this interpretation of equality would turn all rights into duties and burdens.

Even more absurd is the implication that it is good for everyone to be alike rather than different in respect of rights – so that, for instance, if everyone were subject to total censorship, this would be taken as 'equality' and therefore regarded as better than the 'unequal' condition where all but one enjoyed freedom of speech. What matters is that certain rights should be available to be enjoyed by everyone, and this idea can best be conveyed by using the term 'universality', or, in any event, by recognising that the word 'equal' in such phrases as 'equal rights for all' is used in a special sense, meaning no more and no less than that everyone rather than a privileged few should possess certain rights.

What policies and actions would be required to bring about 'equal opportunity'?

Universal opportunity requires nothing more than that arbitrary exclusion should be prohibited. Simple as this precept is, the effort to put it into practice would be attended by complex puzzles. Consider, for instance, entry into the trade of taxi-driving, which is commonly regulated by an official licensing authority. In so far as the authority granted a licence to any applicant who demonstrated reasonable skill and care in driving, universal opportunity would prevail. But would it not be still better from the standpoint of opportunity to abolish the licensing authority altogether, so that any person holding a driver's permit and meeting other minimal conditions (such as adequate insurance and a safety-tested car) could carry paying passengers without going to the trouble of asking someone's permission? Again, if a licensing authority is to exist, should it be permitted to deny a licence to anyone with a criminal record? To exclude persons who have committed offences such as drunken driving might be reasonable; to exclude persons convicted of shoplifting might be arbitrary; and to exclude any ex-convict on the ground that unreliability (betokened by any crime) unfits him for taxi-driving would be a doubtful rule. The practical exercise of any licensing power raises questions no less perplexing. And yet it is hard to feel certain that all licensing – even of medical practitioners, lawyers and pilots – should be repealed forthwith in the name of facilitating opportunity.

On the other hand, certain kinds of restrictions should be lifted. There is generally no legitimate occasion for a licensing authority to limit absolutely the number of persons who may practice a trade; the effect is to guarantee a higher income to those who have entered the gates, at the expense of their customers on the one hand and of their excluded competitors on the other. Neither is there any legitimate case for a closed shop: membership of a union is as arbitrary a condition of employment as membership of a political party, religious sect or fraternal order. Nor is it acceptable that apprenticeship to a craft, apprenticeship being enforced as a precondition of practice, should be restricted to descendants of master craftsmen. A massive number of exclusionary arrangements of similar sorts exist, and they could be excised with unambiguous gains to all except those now privileged by the exclusion of others.

Yet if there is much to be done in opening opportunity by abolishing arbitrary exclusion, it is also true that too much has already been done in certain directions. Not long ago a householder in Britain was prosecuted under an equal-opportunity law because he advertised for a cook of Scottish extraction. What he should have done if, as appeared, he wanted someone who knew how to cook in the Scottish manner, was to advertise the post just that way, so opening the post to any qualified person without irrelevant reference to his or her extraction. So far, so good. But suppose the employer really wanted to have a cook of Scottish extraction about the house, because she would remind him of Highland heaths and fill his ears with the tuneful rhythms of Gaelic. 'Scottish extraction' would then be, from the employer's standpoint, one of the qualifications for the job and not a prejudicial irrelevance. Other cooks might feel offended that they were denied an opportunity merely because they were not of Scottish birth. But is is far from obvious that every cook's right to practise her craft should be given priority over an employer's desire to hire a person who suits his taste. The contrary view would be in order where the employer is a public official, not entitled to satisfy his private taste when recruiting people into public service; or where the employer is a manager, recruiting employees on behalf ultimately of many thousands of shareholders; or where the employer, being a monopolist, controls the entire supply of a certain kind of job. But where the employer is a private person, one of very many who enters a given labour market and therefore unable substantially to influence overall conditions in that market, there are good reasons for permitting him to indulge his whims and eccentric preferences. Opportunity, the right to find suitable employment, while vital, is not the highest right of all.

The belief that nobody qualified by skill to perform a certain sort of work should be arbitrarily excluded from doing it carries an implication which offends the susceptibilities of egalitarians. This offensive implication is that a person may legitimately be excluded from any job for want of the skill to do it satisfactorily (or to learn how to do it satisfactorily). Since everyone is more or less defective in some skills – for want of natural endowments (such as acute hearing or physical strength) or acquired training – everyone will be legitimately excluded from some and, indeed, many occupations and specific positions. By what means they should be excluded is not the issue. Whether licence to practise is restricted by law, or the adequacy of an employee's skill is determined separately and variously by each employer, or the satisfactoriness of a producer's goods or services is judged exclusively by his customers – any such means of testing competence will effectively foreclose each person from certain kinds of work, even while each person enjoys a general right to choose and pursue the opportunities which attract him. Although everyone will be legitimately excluded from some forms of work, the unskilled will be excluded from more forms and especially from work and positions which are most highly esteemed and rewarded. What offends the egalitarian about all this is that 'equal opportunity' seems inevitably to produce inequality.

For the egalitarian, the only way out of this uncomfortable paradox is the hope that people's skills can be equalised. If this could be accomplished, then freedom of opportunity would result in equality of outcome. But can people's skills be equalised? Not if a person's skills depend in substantial degree on his genetic inheritance and if the genetic inheritance of different persons is not merely different but also unequal. It has therefore become an article of faith among radical egalitarians that inequality does not stem from genetic inheritance; if they believed otherwise they would be forced to concede that inequality is in some degree or other ineradicable.

It must be admitted that it is impossible to know for certain to what extent the excellences and deficiencies of normal adults have resulted from capacities which they inherited genetically and to what extent from subsequent development of their potentials. This admitted difficulty of analysis, however, lends no credence to the radical egalitarian's view that all, or practically all, differences in the skills of normal individuals stem from differences in upbringing. Inequality of skill, in their view, results nearly exclusively from inequality of what is called the individual's 'social environment'; and from this theory follows the conclusion that 'equal opportunity' cannot be achieved unless all persons acquire bundles of skills which, even if different in composition, are equal in amount. We may remark in passing that a conscientious observer would be baffled how to tell whether persons with different skills are equally or unequally skilful. Despite this not inconsiderable difficulty, egalitarians have fostered policies which aim at equalising people's skills – as distinct from raising everyone's skills, however unequal the end result.[5] Hence British egalitarians argue that all schools should be comprehensive state schools, so that all children get identical schooling whereby all would acquire more nearly equal skills, and thus a more nearly equal start in life. Presumably the same principle would apply to higher education as well, and this no doubt explains why British egalitarians have been among the staunchest supporters of polytechnics, technical colleges and the Open University.

Yet this recipe fails to produce the desired result. Only the wilfully blind would deny that different children emerge from the same school with very unequal skills, not to mention the striking difference in average skills of children at comprehensive schools in different neighbourhoods. Obviously, say radical egalitarians, this is because children come to school from unequal home environments. And this suggests policies which would 'enrich' the education of children from 'deprived backgrounds'.

Unfortunately, experiments in enriched education, especially for black children in the United States, have disappointed their promoters. Exposure to more and presumably better education has not substantially increased the educational attainments of deprived children, so far as those can be measured by the tests that statisticians have used. Such observations can always be countered by arguing that more of the same medicine is needed to effect a cure. But a quite different conclusion is at least equally plausible. Some people could become olympic runners if given enough good training; there are others whom no amount of training would raise anywhere near the pitch of excellence, or indeed to any acceptable level of competence because they are too small or too big, too young or too old, too weak or simply unwilling. Is there any good reason for supposing that such differences in physical capacity are not paralleled by differences in mental capacity, and indeed in combinations of capacities (intellectual, moral and physical), in all their intricate particularity, which enter into competence for any sort of work from the least to the most exacting?

The belief that children are born with unequal capacities to acquire skill does not foreclose the decision on how education should be allocated among them. Most would agree that every child should be taught how to read, write and do arithmetic: partly because it is difficult for any illiterate and innumerate person to look after himself; partly on the more elevated consideration that, as every normal person enjoys a capacity to reason, he should be provided with at least enough schooling to actualise that potential. It is beyond such universally stipulated minima that serious debate sets in. The broad issue is whether children are entitled to better and more education because their performance is deficient or because their performance is superior. Bluntly, is success or failure the better guide on who should get more education? If the student's success in 'absorbing' education is his ticket of admission to more, then education will be more efficient, in the normal sense that a given input will produce higher levels of output, and educational achievement will be unequal. If on the other hand, the student's relative failure in absorbing education entitled him to extra dosage, educational effort would be relatively inefficient, while educational achievement would be somewhat (though perhaps not much) more nearly equal. Nevertheless, if genetically transmitted capacities substantially affect educability, then no system of allocating educational effort will bring about equality of skill.

From the egalitarian's standpoint, however, unequal performance of different children at school transfers attention to the unequal education or training which children receive at home before and during their time at school. Nobody can deny that it is unequal. Some parents are more intent than others that their children should submit to education and better able to train their children to welcome and take an active part in their education. In other words, whether or not educability is inherited genetically, it is most certainly inherited culturally. This being so, strenuous egalitarians ought, if consistent, to hold that as the family transmits and perpetuates inequality, the family – as an institution for bringing up infants and children – should be demolished. Let all children, from birth, be brought up in common nurseries. Although this solution is seldom met outside utopian communities and science fiction, it is part of the unspoken, because as yet unspeakable, mental baggage of a coherent egalitarian position.

But would state infant-farms really establish equality of skill? Only, for one thing, if genetics makes no difference. And here it is worth noting that differences which are explained in terms of 'cycles of deprivation', in other words as manifestly accounted for by poor upbringing, may be genetic at root. It would not be astounding – though saying it may astound – that in old and reasonably open societies, where for generations individuals have risen or fallen in rough accordance with their merits, people owe their standing in large part to their genetic endowments. If so, deprived parents transmit relatively little because they are genetically unable to do better, and deprived children suffer from genetic deprivation as the root cause of the relative poverty of their home environment. Recognising this possibility does not argue for diminishing the respect due to each human being nor for praising such personal attributes as are largely the gifts of fortune. On the other hand, it does indicate that the goal of equalised skills, even were it worthy of being set up as an ideal, would be quite unachievable, and approachable only at the cost of adopting grossly repressive policies.

It is well within our power to achieve universality of opportunity by eradicating arbitrary barriers to entry. It would be a pity if the visionary quest for 'equal opportunity' distracted us from that desirable and feasible achievement.

Equality before the law, understood as meaning that every person should enjoy the full benefits of due process is now fairly well established as a constitutional principle in free democracies. Certainly, many antiquated privileges and disabilities have long since been abolished. Noblemen can no longer claim immunity from normal prosecution, wives are no longer barred from testifying against their husbands, heretics and dissenters are no longer treated as dubious witnesses. Nevertheless, trial and adjudication remain imperfect. Errors occur in particular cases, contrary to existing rules of procedure – as they always will; and some rules are overdue for remodelling – as some always will be. Nevertheless, the basic principles of fair trial are well settled, and there is widespread agreement that the rules of procedure and the rights which they confer should apply identically to every person before the bench.[6]

However, amidst this consensus on the principles that should prevail, some voices declare that those principles are violated in practice, systematically rather than accidentally and sporadically. According to such critics, judges import biases into the courtroom: biases which stem from their middle-class upbringing, professional training, affluence and elderliness. Those biases operate to the disadvantage of the poor, ignorant, young and heterodox, thus effectively if not formally denying them fair trial. Because such allegations assume that, when a judge decides against a revolutionary, a picket, an adolescent drug-addict or a black, it is his biases which are at work rather than a fair interpretation of evidence and law, the allegations are themselves expressions of prejudice.

A somewhat subtler and more insidious variation on this theme holds that, although different judges exhibit different biases, all judges – like all human beings – are biased. Therefore an unbiased trial – the gist of due process – is unattainable. If this were intended merely to remind us that human judges do imperfect justice, there could be no dispute. Of course judges are prone to illusion, superstition, preconception, ignorance and moods – some badly so, and others less than most people, especially after opposing lawyers have done their best to inform and guide them. But bias, the heart of this critique, goes far beyond ordinary fallibility.

Bias is supposed to be an unreflective, unbidden reaction of the individual to the formative circumstances of his life. It is supposed to result from 'conditioning' imposed on the individual by his social environment. Seen in this light, man is a victim to bias rather than the maker and chooser of views. If bias operated as such critics suppose, it should be impossible to find a middle-class egalitarian, a working-class conservative or an aristocratic socialist; and the extreme variability of views which characterises individuals nurtured in similar environments, as well as the changeability of views during the course of an individual's life, should be unthinkable. We may take it, accordingly, that rough justice – a more or less good approximation of justice – is not rendered impossible by the supposedly inevitable predominance of prejudice and bias.

Another ground on which it is alleged that fair trial is practically unattainable bears more directly on equality. It is that the poor fare less well in court than the rich, because the legal advisers whom they can afford to employ are less proficient. This supposition (it is no more than that) would be difficult to test factually. An investigation would need to begin by grading litigants according to their incomes and lawyers according to their proficiency. But the incomes of litigants are not generally public knowledge and the proficiency of lawyers is a matter of subjective assessment. Moreover, poor men rarely confront rich men in court, since they have few commercial dealings with each other. To be sure, cases do arise between poor people on the one hand and their more affluent employers, provisioners, insurers and lenders; but many such cases are heard by petty-claims courts or by informal tribunals, where the quality of attorneys matters little because the facts are largely stipulated and the questions of law trivial, not to mention that when a worker appears in a case involving industrial relations he is frequently represented by an able and specialised lawyer retained by a labour union.

Most serious civil cases involving poor men, it is safe to guess, are contests between one poor man and another – and the fact that half of these poor men lose their cases is unremarkable. If one of these two poor men had more money then he does have, he might get a better lawyer (supposing that he, unlike most people, knew how to find a good lawyer); but if both of the poor men had more money, and both had better lawyers, one of them would still win and one lose.

As to criminal cases involving poor men, it might seem that the defendant is always at a disadvantage, in as much as his resources are far slimmer than those available to the public prosecutors. But this is true also for rich defendants, many of whom are indeed convicted despite being able to afford expensive advocates. And if it is pointed out that most convicted criminals come from poor families, the explanation is that most crimes are committed by poor people. Even if it were possible to establish that a higher fraction of poor defendants are convicted than of rich defendants, this would still fail to prove that the difference is accounted for by the rich defendants having been able to buy superior legal services. In short, the allegation that the courts provide unequal protection to the poor and the rich is unproven, largely unprovable, and highly implausible.

Even were we to accept it for the sake of argument, what remedies would make sense? One would be to provide a minimally competent standard of legal service, free of charge, to anyone who requests it. This, a reasonable device for meeting the legal needs of persons who are virtually destitute, is already widely implemented (by private and public legal aid agencies, by public defenders appointed by courts, and by actions *in forma pauperis*) and might usefully be strengthened and broadened. The opposite pole would consist of establishing a nationalised legal service on the same model as the nationalised health service. To do so would be to solve a relatively narrow problem – the legal needs of the destitute – by reform on a massive scale, with massive unpredictable side-effects. It is like setting off a nuclear bomb in order to win a skirmish between small patrols, or executing a person to stop him for singing off-key. Besides, nationalising legal services would not produce substantive equality of legal services. There would still be better lawyers and worse lawyers, and so far as the quality of a litigant's lawyer affected his chances, victory would still go to the clients of the better lawyers; though now the quality of one's lawyer would be determined by the administrative methods for allocating lawyers to clients, sometimes by bribery and corruption, by all sorts of chance, and – as now, though less than now – by the client's skill in assessing the quality of various lawyers.

In short, no conceivable reorganisation of legal practice will ever assure substantive equality to all parties before the courts. Here, as in the field of equal opportunity, the path of wisdom is to make certain, so far as we know how, that judges and juries, prosecutors and police desist from action that is personal, prejudicial or arbitrary. Where we cannot devise positive remedies whose benefits would probably outweigh their costs, we do well to restrict ourselves to negative remedies, especially when the latter are more restricted in scope, and therefore easier both to understand and to control.

Enthusiasm for redistributive policies is constantly kindled and fed by the conviction that income and wealth are drastically malidistributed, even if not as much so as in the distant past, which is supposed to have been peopled exclusively by lordly plutocrats and starving peasants. And, indeed, extreme contrasts are still visible, as between destitute vagrants and millionaire pop-stars or property speculators. Yet these extremes are obviously exceptions, which could be and indeed are dealt with by special methods for relieving absolute poverty and for taxing away windfall gains. If the great bulk of incomes fell within some quite restricted range, say between £2,500 and £15,000; as indeed they do, and most of them moreover clustered around £5,000, then a reasonable observer might wonder what all the fuss was about.

The public is constantly bombarded, however, with allegations that the distribution of income is devilishly uneven. Underlying this conclusion is a set of facts of which the public at large are unaware and which even the best educated members of the public do not know how to interpret correctly. On the rare occasions when the underlying facts do emerge in black and white, they most commonly take the condensed form of comparing the incomes of the most highly paid and the most lowly paid. For instance, it might be said that the top fifth of income earners get over one-third of the national income and that the top 5 per cent get as much in total as the bottom 20 per cent. Comparing this with the presumed consequence of equality –

that any 5 per cent of the labour force would earn exactly 5 per cent of the national income, any 20 per cent exactly 20 per cent, and so on – the intelligent observer concludes that income is indeed distributed very unequally.

Moreover, the fact that some people, at any given moment, have higher incomes than others is taken as an infallible symptom of severe social disease. So deep-set is this presumption that most people, including many who more or less closely follow the debate, would reject as patent nonsense the proposition that a high measure of inequality would emerge from a society deliberately designed to be egalitarian. Yet it is easy to imagine just such a society and to trace its inexorable consequences.

Suppose a benevolent despot, dogmatically egalitarian, institutes an economic order dominated by the principle that every worker should earn the same life-time income as every other, provided only that he works from the morning of his twentieth birthday to the eve of his sixtieth birthday. A job would be available for each person; each would start at the same annual income, say £1,000; and each would get an automatic rise of 4 per cent every year. Of this, 1 per cent would compensate the worker for his increased productivity resulting from accumulated experience on the job – it being one of the despot's principles that workers should be paid in proportion to their productivity, though in deference to his paramount principle of equality he declines to reward each individual worker differentially in accordance with his own individual productivity. The remaining 3 per cent of the annual increase would compensate the worker for economic growth occasioned by accumulation of productive capital (all of which the workers own in common) and by improvements in technology.

Following from this thoughtful and beneficient arrangement, every worker would earn no more and no less than every other worker in his age group, and each worker would earn the same amount in the course of a full working life, though not all of them would survive to the age of sixty, the despot having been unable to reduce the death rate below one per cent for each additional year of age.

The outcome of all this, when scrutinised at any given moment, would give the misleading impression of great inequality. The workers most highly paid at any given moment, those then in their last year of work, would get nearly five times as much as the workers then just entering the labour force. The most highly paid 20 per cent of the workers would be getting among them 35 per cent of the national income, whereas the lowest paid 20 per cent would be getting barely 10 per cent. Furthermore, the best paid 5 per cent would be getting among them just as large a share of the national income as was going to the lowest paid 20 per cent. Presented without prologue, such a picture would convey a picture of desperate inequality; yet, as we have seen, it would in fact emerge from a perfectly egalitarian framework.

The lesson to be drawn from this paradox is that statistics which purport to show great inequality of income, which are almost universally interpreted as showing that, may be compatible with relatively little inequality in life-time incomes. In other words, much of the inequality which they apparently disclose may be nothing other than the momentarily uneven effects of economic growth on the one hand and of mortality on the other hand.

All else being equal, inequality of income increases as people die faster, simply because fewer people survive to enjoy high incomes. To be quite precise, the share of income received by the highest income earners increases. For instance, when the death rate is 1 per cent additional year of age (and with a 4 per cent annual rise in wages), the top 5 per cent of income earners get 10 per cent of the national income; should the death rate rise to 2 per cent, they would get 11.5 per cent. As this example shows, the effect of mortality rates is not very great – nor is it unambiguous, for while the share of the highest paid rises, so does the share of the lowest paid. Nevertheless, some of the reduction in inequality which has been observed within the past century may be accounted for by the sharp decline in rates of mortality.

Economic growth, on the other hand, has a remarkable effect in increasing the apparent degree of inequality within the hypothetical system established by the benevolent despot. If, for instance, while the mortality rate remained at 1 per cent, the 'growth rate' (to be precise, the rate at which every worker's income rises each year) doubled from 4 per cent to 8 per cent, the share of the national income going to the upper half would increase from 69 per cent to 83 per cent. And this hypothetical conclusion lends credence to the frequent observation that the level of inequality tends to be high in economies undergoing rapid economic growth.

In short, so far as we have gone, the principal cause of economic inequality – which in this example is purely fictitious because purely temporary – is economic growth, which many welcome, rather than any unfairness inherent in the 'system'.

Suppose now that our benevolent despot decides to improve the productive potential of his labour force by continuing some of them – let us call them professionals – in training until they reach the age of thirty. In order to give them the same life-time income as is enjoyed by ordinary labourers, he ordains for them a higher starting salary, augmented by an automatic annual increase of 4 per cent. The professionals, in their first year of work, would earn 14 per cent more than ordinary labourers of the same age, and this differential in their favour would persist every year up to retirement at sixty. As a result, the disparity between the lowest and highest paid worker will spread, from $4^1/_2$ times previously to $5^1/_4$ times now. The distribution of income at any given moment will appear to have become more unequal, despite the fact that everyone – labourers and professionals alike, those who being young now are paid little and those who being older are paid more – will have earned exactly the same life-time income by the time each one reaches the age of retirement.

This characteristic of our hypothetical state can be imputed to the real world, both empirically and normatively. Some of the apparent inequality of income observed in any country is no doubt due to the fact that certain kinds of careers curtail the span of one's working life. Apart from careers that require long training, there are careers (those of the professional athlete, aviator or stevedore) which for physical reasons end early; careers (those of the pop-star, dress designer or columnist) liable to sudden termination by a change in fashion and many others subject to curtailment by changes in technology. Some young people thinking of entering such careers must be supposed to recognise that, unless their annual incomes are higher than in other careers, their lifetime incomes will be lower; and inasmuch as this consideration affects their willingness to enter short-lived careers, it will tend to push up their annual incomes – so creating the deceptive appearance of extreme inequality in the distribution of income. Looking at the matter from the standpoint of equity, not even an extreme egalitarian could cavil at the proposition that workers who take on jobs which necessarily restrict them to short working lives should enjoy as large a life-time income as other people and must therefore necessarily get higher annual incomes than others.

So far, our despot's system has provided only jobs which guarantee pre-determined annual incomes. But suppose now that he encourages some of his subjects to go into private profit-making business. Recognising the inherent riskiness of such enterprises, he guarantees them too the same life-time income as everyone else, no more and no less. But in any given year the businessman may realise a profit larger than anybody else's earned income, or no profit at all, or a loss. In any given year, that is, the incomes of businessmen will be scattered over a far wider range than the incomes of labourers and professionals: a range stretching from large negative figures to large positive figures. As a result the inequality of income will appear, when measured at any given moment in time, to have increased, despite the fact that everyone still gets the same life-time income. Once again, we may use this indication from analysis of the hypothetical model to explain and to justify some part – albeit we cannot tell how large a part – of the unequal distribution of incomes observed in real economies.

And now let us add a final refinement to the despot's arrangements, supposing that he permits people to save privately and so to accumulate private hoards of wealth. But let us assume that, in order to preserve the equality of life-time income, he forbids inheritance and private investments which would return dividends to the investors.

Under these constraints, if everyone saved the same fraction of his income, then annual savings would be distributed unequally at each given moment – exactly as unequally as income. But as the amount of wealth owned by any person would consist of savings accumulated over the years, the distribution of wealth would be far more unequal than the distribution of income. And this would be so even though everyone who survived until retirement age would have accumulated exactly the amount of wealth, amounting in fact (had they all been saving at the rate, for example, of 10 per cent) to exactly 10 per cent of their total life-time incomes.

If, as is more realistic to suppose, each person saved a greater fraction of his income as his income rose, then the distribution of wealth would become still more unequal – even though the amount of wealth accumulated by each person at the retiring age would remain strictly equal. As the adjoining Table shows, the highest paid fifth of the despot's subjects would own over one-third of the community's total wealth (if everyone saved at the same rate, which remained stable throughout their lives), or almost two-fifths of the community's total wealth (if everyone saved according to exactly the same indicated programme of rates rising in accordance with incomes).

If, as it still more realistic to suppose, some people saved hardly at all while some saved a great deal, then the distribution of wealth would be still more unequal, and it would besides cease to be true that everyone retired with the same accumulation of wealth, even though all received the same lifetime incomes.

Studies of the actual distribution of income and of wealth reveal just this pattern: that the distribution of wealth is always much more pronouncedly unequal than the distribution of income. We can say that this would be caused, in the first place, by the cumulative nature of savings and wealth, even if inheritance and 'unearned' incomes were prohibited, and even if everyone who survived to retirement accumulated exactly equal fortunes, and, of course, the actual distribution of wealth is still more unequal because people with equal incomes save at different rates, because people tend to raise their rate of savings as their incomes rise, and because the outcome of investments is largely determined by chance.[8]

It remains to consider what would happen should the despot authorise inheritance and the earning of dividends by private investment. The answer is in one sense obvious. Inheritance and unearned incomes would tend to increase the inequality of income and wealth alike, not only in the momentary sense but also over people's life-times. In truth, the effects are more complex than that, since inherited capital can be dissipated as well as increased; and if we depart from the hypothetical despot's régime to look at our world, then we will encounter many instances of heirs living in genteel poverty, getting low unearned incomes from dwindling estates. We cannot confidently assume that any substantial part of the observed inequality of wealth and income is due to inheritance or to returns from investment.

In short, the evidence normally presented as proving that much inequality exists is illusory. It quite overlooks differences

Table 1 *Distribution of income and wealth*

Age	Number of persons[1]	Annual income per person[2]	Annual income of age group	Annual savings of age group at 10%	Wealth = Cumulative savings, at 10%	Annual savings of age group, accelerating	Wealth = Cumulative savings, accelerating[3]
		(£)	(£ millions)	(£ millions)	(£ millions)	(£ millions)	(£ millions)
20	1000	1000	1.00	.100	.100	.075	.075
21	990	1040	1.03	.103	.203	.088	.163
22	980	1082	1.06	.106	.309	.101	.263
23	970	1125	1.09	.109	.418	.114	.378
24	961	1170	1.12	.112	.530	.129	.507
25	951	1217	1.16	.116	.646	.145	.652
Total	5852		6.46	.646	2.206		2.038

1. Mortality rate is 1% per year.
2. Income increases at 4% per year.
3. Savings rate accelerates at 1% per year from 7.5% to 12.5%.

in age, length of working life, annual variability of incomes in risky undertakings, patterns of saving, success in investing, and the like. Some of what it measures are therefore differences which are purely temporary and accidental. Were adequate allowances made for these considerations, present estimates would be shown to exaggerate greatly the real degree of economic inequality in developed economies. Economic inequality, in the ethically significant sense, is far less pronounced than most people believe.

Table 1 considers a hypothetical community, which, for the sake of simplicity, I have assumed to consist exclusively of workers all of whom are aged exactly 20 or 25 or some year between. Every worker gets the same income as every other worker of his age; and every worker gets the same life-time income as every other, namely, £6,634. The inequality of income and wealth, as they appear at the moment that this distribution describes, is expressed in Table 2.

Opponents of egalitarianism are commonly mistaken for proponents of inequality. Egalitarians and neutral bystanders leap, naturally if unsubtly, to that conclusion. Nor is that conclusion confuted by the thinking of most anti-egalitarians. Those whose intuitive repugnance to equality is unfortified by reasoned argument are liable to believe that, in opposing equality, they must stand for inequality: an uncomfortable stance, as few today can subscribe to inequality without feeling tainted by deficient sympathy or excessive complacency. Some others expressly endorse inequality and urge those who benefit from it to defend the *status quo* or, better, to restore the *status quo ante* – so falling into a trap,

Table 2 *Shares of income or wealth*

	% Income	% Wealth		
		Savings at 10%	Accelerating savings[1]	Variable savings[2]
Lowest 20%	18.2	6.1	5.1	0
Lowest 40%	37.3	18.8	16.3	0
Lowest 60%	57.2	38.3	34.9	6.1
Highest 40%	42.8	61.7	65.1	93.9
Highest 20%	21.9	34.8	37.7	61.8

1. Half of each age group saves nothing, half saves 20% of income.
2. Savings rate accelerates at 1% per year from 7.5% to 12.5%.

for such politics without principle, pursuing self-interest, and the self-interest of a favoured minority at that, is bound in present circumstances to strengthen the hand of egalitarians.

The imputation that opposing equality necessarily means fostering inequality puts the anti-egalitarian in a false position, from which he can however extricate himself. The way out is by recognising himself for an anti-egalitarian, not an inegalitarian. Far from desiring inequality, he must refuse to regard either inequality or equality as ends. Policies intended to establish inequality, and policies intended to establish equality he should regard alike as misguided.

Vital in all this is the distinction between ends of policy and by-products of policy. For a policy to claim our support, its ends must be meritorious. But its by-products need not be; sufficient if they are tolerable. We do not breathe in order to generate carbon dioxide, neither should we stop breathing in order to avoid exhaling carbon dioxide. We do not produce goods and services in order to generate inequality, neither should we curtail production in an effort to achieve equality. For the consistent anti-egalitarian, both equality and inequality count as by-products only, lacking the character of ends in themselves, because, as we have seen, no persuasive argument exists to endow them with that character.

It may be said, of course, that when the by-products of a policy become noxious, the policy ought to be discarded despite the commendable ends it serves. So it should.

But neither equality nor inequality, to the extent we ordinarily experience, is intolerable. An anti-egalitarian may detest equality on grounds such as that it tends to be accompanied by uniformity and is therefore desired by many who hate and fear individuality, diversity and everything in human beings that makes them hard to understand and harder to control. Nevertheless, where equality or a closer approach to it came about purely as a by-product of policies aimed at ends which the anti-egalitarian judged desirable, the objection to uniformity would have no place, for no intention to produce uniformity (or equality) would have animated those policies. To insist that equalisation, occurring as a by-product, should automatically disqualify any and every policy, no matter how desirable in all other respects, would be exorbitant and self-defeating.

By contrast, a typical egalitarian detests inequality, even as a by-product, for a variety of reasons, many of which have been reviewed above. One more may be mentioned here. It is the fear that inequality feeds on itself, tending always to increase, until the day when one man will own everything and need will force all others into eternal slavery. That spectre makes egalitarians regard inequality, in any degree, even when it emerges as a by-product, as totally unacceptable. For that reason, as well as others, equality becomes for them the paramount end, the ultimate criterion of all policy. But the apprehension that any single germ of inequality will fatally contaminate a whole society is unfounded: no evidence, no argument demonstrates that inequality must always increase unless forcibly curbed. The degree of inequality that results incidentally from policies otherwise desirable can be presumed to be tolerable, in the absence of clear evidence to the contrary.

Here, as always, egalitarians will make much of persons who are absolutely destitute, ill-fed, ill-clothed, ill-housed, and unable to remedy their situation. Certainly there are such people, though the number of people officially labelled 'poor' is vastly exaggerated by the arbitrary level at which the so-called poverty line is drawn in highly-developed economies today. Certainly the plight of the really destitute should stir any decent onlooker to remedial action. Yet absolute poverty has nothing whatsoever to do with equality or inequality. If everyone were equal and equally poverty-stricken, their equality would not relieve their poverty. If only some were impoverished while others were rich, that inequality would not intensify the suffering of the poor. And the clumsiest, least sensitive and slowest way to relieve the poor would be by a policy of enforced equalisation. In short, to accept inequality as a tolerable by-product of otherwise desirable policies in no way incapacitates the anti-egalitarian from dealing with absolute poverty, a real problem deserving special attention, unlike the fictitious problem of 'relative deprivation', which is merely a sophisticated attempt to justify the intention deliberately to institute equality.

Another touchstone of outlooks on equality is attitudes toward the transmission of wealth by inheritance.

Testators acquire the substance of their estates by saving. People save at different rates and for different combinations of reasons. Among the common reasons, one is the wish to accumulate reserves so as to provide for one's widows, orphans and other dependents. Another is the wish to supplement income for work with income from profits and dividends. Still another is the wish to accumulate enough reserves to provide for oneself in case of illness and in the highly probable event of growing too old to work. Reasons prompting short-run savings, to pay for holidays, washing-machines, or Christmas gifts, are not significant in the present context. One very rare reason for saving, we may be sure, is in order to increase inequality.

By contrast with saving, which is deliberate even when habitual, the transmission of wealth by inheritance has a large accidental component. Though the testator usually chooses the legatees with some care, his control over how much they will get is limited by the accidents of how long he lives, how early or late he retires, how price levels move during his life, and so on. It is accordingly clear that in leaving his estate, even more than in gathering it, the testator has no intention to promote or undo inequality, and no great hope of realising such an intention were he eccentric enough to harbour it.

Quite apart from intention, it is by no means clear that inheritance must tend to increase inequality. Whether it does so or not will depend on the economic condition of heritors before they inherit, how much they inherit, and ultimately on whether they in turn spend it or pass it along. Precise and comprehensive detail about these questions is not available. Yet let us suppose, for the sake of the argument, we knew for certain that inheritance maintains and even extends inequality. What should be done about that?

For the consistent anti-egalitarian, the policy question is easy. Inheritance results from savings, and saving is desirable in as much as it swells the stock of capital, to the benefit not alone of the capital's owner but also of workers who use the capital and of consumers who use its products. Moreover, the intentions that animate savings are also commendable, in so far as people aim to look after themselves and their dependants. So, overlooking the unintended side-effects of heightened inequality, the anti-egalitarian would approve inheritance as an institution to be upheld by the laws.

The dogmatic egalitarian would readily conclude that inheritance should be abolished, because it contributes to inequality.

The moderate egalitarian would be in a quandary, supposing that the desirability of economic improvement and the desirability of individual responsibility occupied places in his hierarchy of values roughly as exalted as the desirability of equality. Most probably he would seek to resolve his quandary by following a 'middle way', which continued to recognise a legal right to devise and inherit but effectively crippled it by severe taxation. Egalitarians, dogmatic and moderate alike, would have used the side-effect – in real life a purported rather than certain side-effect – as a reason for thwarting inheritance and thus to some extent, even if not deliberately, discouraging saving. In the name of a ghost they would stifle a living thing.

Egalitarians of all shades are pursuing a will-of-the-wisp. They are deluded by loose thinking and utopian fantasies. Their conviction that equality is the highest good or at least one among the highest goods rests on incoherent intellectual foundations, suffers from internal contradictions, and takes its departure from an exaggerated estimate of how much inequality exists. They are grotesquely optimistic in supposing that equality will bring in its train all the other great goods such as liberty, fraternity, wealth, justice and general virtue. Even worse, they ignore the likelihood that, if they have their way, the ultimate outcome will be a decline into widespread poverty and tyranny.

Notes

1. Some authors who have challenged the egalitarian position are: Keith Joseph and Jonathan Sumption, *Equality*, London, 1979; G. Lowell Feild and John Higley, *Elitism*, London, 1980; and Anthony Flew, *Libertarians versus Egalitarians*, Berkeley, 1980.
2. Historic explanations recently offered for the rise of egalitarianism are Gerhard Emmanuel Lenski, *Power and Privilege*, New York, 1966; and Ernest Gellner, 'The Social Roots of Egalitarianism', *Dialectics and Humanism*, 4, 1979, pp. 27–43.
3. For a compendium of critical essays on John Rawls, see N. Daniels (ed.), *Reading Rawls*, New York, 1976.
4. For a systematic analysis of income redistribution programmes in the United States and of their tendency to reduce incentives, see Martin Anderson, *Welfare*, Stanford, California, 1978.
5. An excellent critique of egalitarian theories of education is in David F. Cooper, *Illusions of Equality*, London, 1980. A useful compendium of American views is given in Donald M. Levine and Mary Jo Bane, *The 'Inequality' Controversy*, New York, 1975, which takes as its point

of departure the study of Christopher Jencks *et al.*, *Inequality*, New York, 1972; London, 1973, 1975.

6. A most thorough study of equality before the law, in the constitutional practice of the United States especially, including an admirable bibliographical spread, is given in P. G. Polyviou, *The Final Protection of the Laws*, London, 1980.

7. An ingenious analysis of American statistics reaches a similar conclusion: see Morton Paglin, 'The Measurements and Trend of Inequality', *American Economic Review*, 65, September 1975, pp. 598–609. For a survey of statistical techniques, see F. A. Cowell, *Measuring Inequality*, London, 1977.

8. For the effect of chance on the outcome of investments and thus on the distribution of wealth, see E. Schwartz and J. A. Greenleaf. 'A Comment on Investment Decisions', *Journal of Finance*, 33, 1978, pp. 1222–7.

Hugh Dalton

The Measurement of the Inequality of Incomes

It is generally agreed that, other things being equal, a consider-able reduction in the inequality of incomes found in most modern communities would be desirable. But it is not generally agreed how this inequality should be measured. The problem of the measurement of the inequality of incomes has not been much considered by English economists. It has attracted rather more attention in America, but it is in Italy that it has hitherto been most fully discussed. The importance of the problem has been obscured by the inadequacy of the available statistics of the distribution of income in all modern communities. To such stat-istics as we have, no very fine measures can be applied. The improvement of these statistics is the business of statisticians, but the problem of measuring and comparing the inequalities, which improved statistics would more precisely reveal, should be capable of theoretical solution now. No complete solution is presented in this essay, but only a discussion of certain points of principle and method.

First, as to the nature of the problem. An American writer has expressed the view that 'the statistical problem before the economist in determining upon a measure of the inequality in the distribution of wealth is identical with that of the biologist in determining upon a measure of the inequality in the distri-bution of any physical characteristic'.[1] But this is clearly wrong. For the economist is primarily interested, not in the distribution of income as such, but in the effects of the distribution of income upon the distribution and total amount of economic welfare, which may be derived from income. We have to deal, therefore, not merely with one variable, but with two, or possibly more, between which certain functional relations may be presumed to exist.

A partial analogy would be found in the problem of measuring the inequality of rainfall in the various districts of a large agricultural area. From the point of view of the cultivator, what is important is not rainfall as such, but the effects of rainfall upon the crop which may be raised from the land. Between rainfall and crop there will be a certain relation, the discovery of which will be a matter of practical importance. The objection to great inequality of rainfall is the resulting loss of potential crop. The objection to great inequality of incomes is the resulting loss of potential economic welfare.

Let us assume that the economic welfare of different persons is additive, that the relation of income to economic welfare is the same for all members of the community, and that, for each individual, marginal economic welfare diminishes as income increases. Then, if a given income is to be distributed among a given number of persons, it is evident that economic welfare will be a maximum, when all incomes are equal. It follows that the inequality of any given distribution may conveniently be defined as the ratio of the total economic welfare attainable under an equal distribution to the total economic welfare attained under the given distribution. This ratio is equal to unity for an equal distribution, and is greater than unity for all unequal distributions. It may, therefore, be preferred to define inequality as this ratio minus unity, but for comparative purposes this modification of the definition is unnecessary. Inequality, however, though it may be *defined* in terms of economic welfare, must be *measured* in terms of income.

Starting from this definition, it is clear that, if we assume any precise functional relation between income and economic welfare, we can deduce a corresponding measure of inequality. It is also clear that, under this procedure, no *one* measure of inequality will emerge, whose appropriateness will be independent of the particular functional relation assumed.

The procedure suggested may be illustrated by two examples. Take, first, the hypothesis that proportionate additions to income, in excess of that required for 'bare subsistence', make equal additions to economic welfare. This is Bernoulli's hypothesis, except that economic welfare is substituted for satisfaction.[2]

Then, if w = economic welfare and x = income, we have:

$$dw = \frac{dx,}{x}$$

or
$$w = \log x + c$$

If $x_1, x_2, \ldots x_n$ are individual incomes, whose arithmetic mean is x_a and geometric mean x_g, the corresponding measure of inequality is, by our definition:

$$\frac{n \log x_a + nc}{n \log x_g + nc} = \frac{\log x_a + c}{\log x_g + c}$$

If we assume that, when $x = 1$, $w = 0$, then $c = 0$, then our measure of inequality becomes $\dfrac{\log x_a}{\log x_g}$. It may, at first sight, be thought that a still simpler, and practically equivalent, measure will be $\dfrac{x_a}{x_g}$, but this simplification raises a question to which further reference will be made.

The hypothesis, however, is not satisfactory. Apart from the difficulty that only income in excess of that required for 'bare subsistence' is taken into account, it is clear that too rapid a rate of increase of economic welfare is assumed, when income becomes large. After a certain point it is pretty obvious that more than proportionate additions to income will generally be required, in order to make equal additions to economic welfare. To be even tolerably realistic, a formula connecting income with economic welfare should satisfy the following three conditions: equal increases in economic welfare, at any rate after income is greater than a certain amount, should correspond to more than proportionate increases in income; economic welfare should tend to a finite limit, as income increases indefinitely; and economic welfare should be zero for a certain amount of income, and negative for smaller amounts. These conditions are satisfied if we assume that the relation of economic welfare to income is of the form $dw = \dfrac{dx}{x^2}$, so that $w = c - \dfrac{1}{x}$, where c is a constant. For then however large x becomes, w can never become larger than

c, and, when x is less than $\dfrac{1}{c}$, w is negative.[3] If we adopt this formula, which appears to be a good compromise of its kind between plausibility and simplicity, the corresponding measure of inequality is:

$$\frac{nc - \dfrac{n}{x_a}}{nc - \dfrac{n}{x_h}} = \frac{c - \dfrac{1}{x_a}}{c - \dfrac{1}{x_h}}$$

where x_h is the harmonic mean of the individual incomes, and c, as already stated, the reciprocal of the minimum income, which yields positive economic welfare.

Both the measures of inequality obtained here are simple in form and have a certain theoretical elegance. But neither is readily applicable to statistics. The arithmetic mean is, indeed, easily calculated from perfect statistics, and fairly easily approximated to from imperfect statistics, but the corresponding calculations for the geometric and harmonic means are very laborious, when the number of individual incomes is large, and the corresponding approximations, especially for the harmonic mean, are practically impossible, where the statistics show more than a small degree of imperfection. The first of the two measures, moreover, involves an estimate of the income necessary for 'bare subsistence', and the second an estimate of the minimum income which yields positive economic welfare. And neither of these estimates are easily made. Nor, of course, have we really any precise knowledge of the functional relation between income and economic welfare.

Failing such precise knowledge, we may still lay down certain general principles, which shall serve as tests, to which various plausible measures of inequality may be submitted. We have, first, what may be called the principle of transfers. Maintaining the assumptions laid down in the second paragraph of the essay, we may safely say that, if there are only two income-receivers, and a transfer of income takes place from the richer to the poorer, inequality is diminished.[4] There is, indeed, an obvious limiting condition. For the transfer must not be so large, as more than to reverse the relative positions of the two income-receivers, and it will produce its maximum result, that is to say, create equality, when it is equal to half the difference between the two incomes. And we may safely go further and say that, however great the number of income-receivers and whatever the amount of their incomes, any transfer between any two of them, or, in general, any series of such transfers, subject to the above condition, will diminish inequality.[5] It is possible that, in comparing two distributions, in which both the total income and the number of income-receivers are the same, we may see that one might be able to be evolved from the other by means of a series of transfers of this kind. In such a case we could say with certainty that the inequality of the one was less than that of the other.

Let us now apply the principle of transfers to various measures of dispersion used by statisticians for measuring inequality in general. A distinction may be drawn between measures of relative dispersion and measures of absolute dispersion. Measures of relative dispersion will be simply numbers, while measures of absolute dispersion will be, in the present case, numbers of units of income. Most of the general measures of dispersion proposed by statisticians are measures of absolute dispersion, but are easily transformed into measures of relative dispersion, when divided by an appropriate divisor.

Consider first the mean deviation from the arithmetic mean. This measure is the sum of two parts, one of which comprises the deviations above, the other the deviations below, the mean.[6] It is a bad measure, judged by the principle of transfers, for it is unaffected by transfers within either part, provided that no income previously above the mean is reduced below it, and conversely. The transfer of a given sum from incomes above the mean to incomes below it, as, for example, by the provision of old age pensions for persons of small incomes from the proceeds of a tax on large incomes, would obviously reduce the mean deviation. But it would be unaffected, if such pensions were provided by a tax levied on those whose incomes were just below the mean, or if additional comforts for millionaires were provided from a tax on those whose incomes were just above the mean, provided that none of the latter were reduced below the mean by the tax.

The mean deviation is a measure of absolute dispersion. If we divide it by the arithmetic mean, we obtain what we may call the relative mean deviation, which is equally insensitive to transfers wholly above or wholly below the mean.

Consider next the standard, or mean square, deviation from the arithmetic mean, that is, the square root of the arithmetic average of the squares of deviations from the arithmetic mean. The standard deviation is perfectly sensitive to transfers,[7] and thus passes our first test with distinction. Dividing the standard deviation by the arithmetic mean, we obtain what may be called the relative standard deviation. This, too, is perfectly sensitive to transfers.

Consider next Professor Bowley's quartile measure of dispersion

$$\frac{Q_3 - Q_1}{Q_3 + Q_1}$$

where Q_1 and Q_3 are quartiles.[8] This is a measure of relative dispersion. It is sensitive to transfers, in so far as these involve movements of the quartiles, but not otherwise. In this respect it is somewhat more sensitive than the mean deviation, but much less sensitive than the standard deviation.

An interesting measure of dispersion, which has not, I think, hitherto attracted the attention of English writers, is Professor Gini's mean difference, which, as applied to incomes, is the arithmetic average of the differences, taken positively, between all possible pairs of incomes.[9] It may be shown that this mean difference is equal to the weighted arithmetic mean of deviations from the median, the weights being proportionate to the number of incomes, increased by one, which are intermediate in size between the median and the income whose deviation is being considered.[10] The mean difference, thus defined, is a measure of absolute dispersion. Dividing it by the arithmetic mean, we obtain a measure of relative dispersion, which may be called the relative mean difference. The mean difference, whether absolute or relative, is perfectly sensitive to transfers.

Another interesting measure of inequality is based upon what some writers have called a Lorenz curve.[10a] This is a simple and convenient graphical method of exhibiting any distribution of income, provided that our interest is confined to proportions, rather than absolute amounts, both of total income and of the number of income-receivers.

Along the axis Ox are measured percentages of the total income, and along the axis Oy the minimum percentages of the total number of income-receivers, who receive various percentages of the total income. For example, if the richest 20 per cent of the population received 75 per cent of the total income, this fact would determine one point ($x = 75$, $y = 20$), upon the Lorenz curve. A perfectly equal distribution would be represented by the straight line *OP* inclined at an angle of 45° to either axis. An unequal distribution would be represented by a curve, such as *OQP*, lying below the line *OP*. If *MP* is perpendicular to *OM*, *OM* = *MP* = 100, and an obvious measure of inequality is the area enclosed between the Lorenz curve and the line of equal distribution *OP*. The larger this area, the larger the inequality.

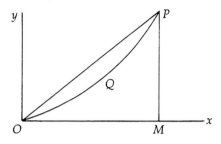

A remarkable relation has been established between this measure of inequality and the relative mean difference, the former measure being always equal to half the latter.[11]

Something will be said below concerning Professor Pareto's well-known measure of the inequality of incomes. But this measure cannot be tested, with reference to the principle of transfers, since it is based upon a supposed law, according to which, if the total income and the number of income-receivers are known, the distribution is uniquely determined.

So far, then, as tested by the principle of transfers, the standard deviation, whether absolute or relative, and the mean difference, whether absolute or relative, are good measures; Professor Bowley's quartile measure is a very indifferent measure; the mean deviation, whether absolute or relative, is a bad measure; and Professor Pareto's measure evades judgment. But the scope of the principle of transfers, as a test of measures of inequality, is narrowly limited. It can only be applied to some cases – and by no means to all – in which both the total income and the number of income-receivers are constant, and distribution varies.[12] It cannot be applied when either the total income or the number of income-receivers varies, or when both vary simultaneously. For these more general cases further tests are required, and three general principles suggest themselves as serviceable for this purpose.

We have, first, what may be called the principle of proportionate additions to incomes. It is sometimes suggested that proportionate additions to, or subtractions from, all incomes will leave inequality unaffected.[13] But, if the definition of inequality given above be accepted, this is not so. It appears, rather, that proportionate additions to all incomes diminish inequality, and that proportionate subtractions increase it. This is the principle of proportionate additions to incomes just referred to. A general proof of this principle presents difficulties, and is not attempted here, but the proof in two important special cases is easy. For, first, assume, using the same notation as in the fifth paragraph, that the relation of income to economic welfare is $w = \log x$. Then, if δ be the inequality of any given distribution, we have

$$\delta = \frac{\log x_a}{\log x_g}$$

Let all incomes be multiplied by θ and let δ' be the inequality of the new distribution.

Then $\delta' = \dfrac{\log \theta + \log x_a}{\log \theta + \log x_g}$ and since $x_a > x_g$, we have $\delta > \delta'$, if $\log \theta > 0$, that is to say, if $\theta > 1$.

Similarly, $\delta < \delta'$, if $\theta < 1$.

That is to say, proportionate additions to all incomes diminish inequality and proportionate subtractions increase it.[14] This is true, if x is the total income of any individual. *A fortiori*, it is true, if x is surplus income in excess of 'bare subsistence'. For equal proportionate additions to surplus income involve larger proportionate additions to total income, when the latter is large, than when it is small. A series of transfers from richer to poorer will, therefore, transform proportionate additions to surplus incomes into proportionate additions to total incomes.

Next assume that the relation of income to economic welfare is

$$w = c - \frac{1}{x}$$

Then, if δ be the inequality of any given distribution, we have

$$\delta = \frac{c - \dfrac{1}{x_a}}{c - \dfrac{1}{x_h}}$$

Let all incomes be multiplied by θ and let δ' be the inequality of the new distribution.

Then

$$\delta' \quad = \quad \frac{c - \dfrac{1}{\theta x_a}}{c - \dfrac{1}{\theta x_h}}$$

and we have $\delta > \delta'$, if $(x_a - x_h)\,(\theta - 1) > 0$.
But $x_a > x_h$. $\therefore \delta > \delta'$, if $\theta > 1$.
Similarly, $\delta < \delta'$, if $\theta < 1$.

That is to say, proportionate additions to all incomes diminish inequality, and proportionate subtractions increase it.

If the principle of proportionate additions to incomes thus enunciated be provisionally accepted as true generally,[15] and not merely for the particular hypotheses just examined, a second principle follows as a corollary. This may be called the principle of equal additions to incomes, and is to the effect that equal additions to all incomes diminish inequality and equal subtractions increase it. Here, again, a direct general proof presents difficulties, though several writers have regarded the principle as so obvious that no proof is required.[16] But as a corollary of the preceding principle the proof is easy. For, let the total additional income involved in proportionate additions to all incomes be redistributed among income-receivers in such a way as to make equal, instead of proportionate, additions to all incomes. Then the addition to maximum economic welfare attainable is the same in both cases. But the addition to economic welfare actually attained is obviously greater, when additions to incomes are equal, than when they are proportionate. Therefore, inequality is smaller after equal additions have been made than after proportionate additions have been made, the total additional income being the same in both cases. But proportionate additions reduce inequality. Therefore, *a fortiori*, equal additions reduce inequality.[17]

The third principle may be called the principle of proportionate additions to persons, and is to the effect that inequality is unaffected if proportionate additions are made to the number of persons receiving incomes of any given amount. This, again, is easily proved. For the maximum economic welfare attainable and the economic welfare actually attained will both have been increased in the same proportion, and hence their ratio will be unaltered.

We may now test, by means of these three principles, the measures of inequality which have already been tested by means of the principle of transfers. Simple mathematical operations yield the results shown in Table 1.

Here the three absolute measures of dispersion give one set of identical results, and the four relative measures another. None of the seven measures passes the test of proportionate additions to incomes, but the relative measures come nearer to doing so than the absolute measures.[18] The relative measures pass the test of equal additions to incomes, but the absolute measures do not. All seven measures pass the test of proportionate additions to persons. We may therefore eliminate the three absolute measures from further consideration. As between the four relative measures, the order of merit established by reference to the principle of transfers may stand, so far, unchanged, viz:

1 and 2. Relative standard deviation and relative mean difference (bracketed equal).
3. Bowley's quartile measure.
4. Relative mean deviation.

Can Professor Pareto's measure be brought into this order of merit? This is a relative measure, which is only applicable when distribution is approximately of the form

$$y = \frac{A}{x^a},$$

where x is any income, y the number of incomes greater than x, and A and a constants for any given distribution, but variables for

Table 1

Upon	Effect of		
	Proportionate Additions to Incomes	Equal Additions to Incomes	Proportionate Additions to Persons
Absolute Mean Deviation	Increased	Unchanged	Unchanged
Relative Mean Deviation	Unchanged	Diminished	Unchanged
Absolute Standard Deviation	Increased	Unchanged	Unchanged
Relative Standard Deviation	Unchanged	Diminished	Unchanged
Bowley's Quartile Measure	Unchanged	Diminished	Unchanged
Absolute Mean Difference	Increased	Unchanged	Unchanged
Relative Mean Difference	Unchanged	Diminished	Unchanged

different distributions.[19] Assuming this formula for distribution, which, as Professor Bowley has shown,[20] is the same thing as assuming that the average of all incomes greater than x is proportional to x, Professor Pareto treats a as the measure of inequality, in the sense that, the greater a, the greater inequality. It follows mathematically that 'neither an increase in the minimum income nor a diminution in the inequality of incomes can come about, except when the total income increases more rapidly than the population'.[21] In other words, increased production per head is both a necessary condition and a sufficient guarantee of a diminution of inequality.

Professor Pareto's law, about which much has been written both by way of criticism and of qualified appreciation, implies a uniformity in distribution, which makes it impossible to apply either the principle of transfers or the principle of equal additions to incomes. Like the four other measures just considered, it is unchanged both by proportionate additions to incomes and by proportionate additions to persons. It has been suggested that this measure, where it is applicable, will be in general accord with other plausible measures of dispersion.[22] But, in view of the investigations of Italian economists, this is very doubtful.[23] It seems on the whole more likely, though the question requires further study, that, in order to bring it into general accord with other measures, the Pareto measure should be inverted, so that, the greater a, the smaller inequality. But such an inversion will explode Professor Pareto's alleged economic harmonies, and it will follow, according to his law, that increased production per head will always mean increased inequality!

According to Professor Gini,[24] many actual distributions of income approximate to the formula

$$n = \frac{1}{c}s_1{}^\delta, \text{ or } \log n = \delta \log s - \log c$$

where s is the total income of the n richest income-receivers and δ and c are constants for any given distribution. He proposes δ as a measure of inequality, or 'index of concentration', as he prefers to call it, such that, the greater δ, the greater inequality. This formula is a more convenient variant of Professor Pareto's, such that

$$\delta = \frac{a}{a-1},$$

and, as a diminishes from any quantity greater than one down to one, δ increases up to infinity.

The equation $\log n = \delta \log s - \log c$ is easily transformed into that of a Lorenz curve. For, if N is the total number of income-receivers and S the total income, we have

$$\log N = \delta \log S - \log c$$

$$\therefore \log \frac{n}{N} = \delta \log \frac{s}{S}$$

Putting $\frac{n}{N} = \frac{y}{100}$ and $\frac{s}{S} = \frac{x}{100}$ we have the equation of a Lorenz curve

$$\log \frac{y}{100} = \delta \log \frac{x}{100}$$

or

$$\frac{y}{100} = \left(\frac{x}{100}\right)^{\delta}$$

The area enclosed between this Lorenz curve and the line of equal distribution is:

$$\frac{1}{2}(100)^2 - \int_{x=0}^{x=100} y\,dx$$

$$= \frac{1}{2}(100)^2 - \int_{0}^{100} 100 \frac{x^{\delta}}{(100)^{\delta}}\,dx$$

$$= (100)^2 \left(\frac{1}{2} - \frac{1}{\delta+1}\right)$$

Thus, the greater δ, the larger is the above area, and the larger the relative mean difference.[25] There is thus some ground for believing, though I do not here definitely commit myself to the belief, that *reciprocal* of Professor Pareto's measure is a mere variant of the relative mean difference, in the particular case, when distribution is approximately according to Pareto's law. In this particular case, then, Professor Pareto's measure would have no independent significance, and, in the more general case, when distribution may depart widely from Pareto's law, the measure has, of course, no general significance at all. It will, therefore, be provisionally set aside in this discussion.

Returning to the four measures set out in order of merit on page 147, this order is based on theoretical advantages. But account must also be taken of practical applicability to statistics. Both the relative mean deviation and the quartile measure are more easily applicable than either of their two rivals to perfect statistics, and applicable, with less risk of serious error, to imperfect statistics. As for perfect, or nearly perfect, statistics, the advantage of the former pair over the latter relates only to laboriousness and not to accuracy, and is not, therefore, a matter of great importance. But, as for markedly imperfect statistics, such as are actually available, the advantage relates to accuracy as well as to laboriousness and is, therefore, vital.

The provisional conclusion which suggests itself, is as follows. When statistics are so imperfect that neither the relative standard deviation nor the relative mean difference can be applied with any expectation of reasonable accuracy, we must make shift with the relative mean deviation and the quartile measure. It is some palliation of the comparative insensitiveness to transfers, which is a defect of both the latter measures, that each is sensitive to many possible transfers, to which the other is insensitive. If, therefore, both give the same result in any particular comparison, their evidence is to some extent corroborative.

If statistics are so far improved that the relative standard deviation and the relative mean difference are applicable, these are to be preferred to the two measures just mentioned. If a single measure is to be used, the relative mean difference is, perhaps, slightly preferable, owing to the graphical convenience of the Lorenz curve. Probably, however, it will be desirable, at any rate for some time to come, not to rely upon the evidence of a single measure, but upon the corroboration of several. Given perfect, or nearly perfect, statistics, it is worth while considering whether corroboration may not also be sought from the measure

$$\frac{\log x_a}{\log x_g},$$

applied, for the sake of simplicity, to total incomes, and not to surplus incomes in excess of the requirements of 'bare subsistence'. For this measure passes our test of proportionate additions to incomes, which none of the other four survivors do. In most practical cases, no doubt, these five measures will give results pointing in the same direction, but in some cases they may not do so.

Meanwhile, the chief practical necessity is the improvement of existing statistical information, especially as regards the smaller incomes. This paper may be compared to an essay in a few of the principles of brickmaking. But, until a greater abundance of straw is forthcoming, these principles cannot be put to the test of practice.

Notes

1. Persons, *Quarterly Journal of Economics*, 1908–9, p. 431.
2. A discussion of the distinction, if any, between economic welfare and satisfaction lies outside the scope of this essay.
3. If it were practicable to fix a unit of economic welfare, it would have to be fixed, in relation to the unit of income, so that both these attributes of c would hold good. There is no theoretical objection to this.
4. Compare Pigou, *Wealth and Welfare*, p. 24.
5. Inequality is certain to be diminished by a series of transfers such that all transfers from A, the richer, to B, the poorer, still leave A richer than, or just as rich as, B. But if some of the transfers make B richer than A, it is possible that the effects of the series of transfers might cancel out and leave the inequality the same as before.
6. Thus if S_1 is the sum of the deviations of incomes greater than the mean and S_2 the sum of the deviations of incomes less than the mean, the mean deviation $= \dfrac{1}{n}(S_1 + S_2)$, where n is the total number of incomes.
7. For, if δ be the initial standard deviation of any distribution of n incomes, and δ' the standard deviation after an amount h has been transferred from an income x_1 to an income x_2, all other incomes remaining the same, we have $n^2(\delta^2 - \delta'^2) = 2h(x_1 - \delta'^2) = 2h (x_1 - x_2) - 2h^2$. Therefore $\delta = \delta'$, only if $h = o$ or if $h = x_1 - x_2$.
8. Compare Bowley, *Elements of Statistics*, p. 136.
9. See, for a discussion of this measure, Gini, *Variabilità e Mutabilità*.
10. Gini, *Variabilità e Mutabilità*, pp. 32–33.
10a. Originally proposed by Mr M. O. Lorenz (1907), *Publications of the American Statistical Association*, Vol. ix, pp. 209 ff. M. Séailles also recommended it, apparently independently, in 1910 in his *Répartition des Fortunes en France*, pp. 56–7. Sir Leo Chiozza Money had

already given hints of this measure in his *Riches and Poverty*, first published in 1905.

11. For a mathematical proof of this see Ricci, *L'Indice di Variabilità*, pp. 22–24. The proof was first given, apparently, by Professor Gini. Another most elegant proposition, due to Professor Ricci (*ibid.*, pp. 32–33), is that, if any straight line be drawn parallel to the line of equal distribution, then all the Lorenz curves, to which this straight line is a tangent, represent distributions having the same relative mean deviation.

12. Professor Pigou (*Wealth and Welfare*, p. 25 n.) uses the following argument to prove that, in these circumstances, a reduction in the standard deviation will probably increase aggregate satisfaction. 'If A be the mean income and a_1, $a_,$ . . . deviations from the mean, aggregate satisfaction, on our assumption

$$= nf(A) + (a_1 + a_2 + \ldots) f' + \tfrac{1}{2}! (a_1{}^2 + a_2{}^3 + \ldots) f'' + \tfrac{1}{3}! (a_1{}^3 + a_2{}^3 + \ldots) f''' + \ldots$$

But we know that $a_1 + a_2 + \ldots = 0$. We know nothing to suggest whether the sum of the terms beyond the third is positive or negative. If, therefore, the third and following terms are small relatively to the second term, it is certain, and, in general, it is probable that aggregate satisfaction is larger, the smaller is $(a^2 + a^2{}_2 + \ldots)$. This latter sum, of course, varies in the same sense as the standard deviation.' This argument would be strong if all deviations were small, that is, if inequality were already very small. But when, as is the case in all important modern communities, a number of the deviations are very large, it is quite likely that successive terms in the expansion will go on increasing (numerically) for some time, and this is specially likely as regards the series of alternate terms, which involve deviations raised to *even* powers. This likelihood will vary according to the form of the function f, but it seems clear that the third and following terms cannot, in general, be neglected. It follows that, in general, there is no certainty and only a somewhat low and problematical degree of probability that a reduction in the standard deviation will increase satisfaction. There is no reason to suppose that it is not at least equally probable that a reduction in certain other measures of dispersion will have the same effect. One good test of the relative appropriateness of various measures of the inequality of incomes would be the relative probability that a reduction in such measures would increase economic welfare (or satisfaction), on the assumption that both the total income and the number of income receivers were constants. But the evaluation of such relative probabilities presents difficulties.

13. See, for example, Taussig, *Principles of Economics*, II, p. 485.

14. If we write $\delta = x_a / x_g$, instead of $\delta = \log, x_a / \log x_g$, proportionate additions or subtractions will leave inequality unaffected. It follows

that x_a/x_g is not a mere simplification of the measure $\log x_a/\log x_g$ arrived at above, but is a distinct, and inferior, measure.

15. The additions must, of course, be genuine. Inequality in this country would not be diminished by reckoning everyone's income in shillings, instead of in pounds. Units of money income in any two cases to be compared must have approximately equal purchasing power.

16. 'An equal addition to everyone's income ... obviously makes incomes more equal than they would otherwise be.' Cannan, *Elementary Political Economy*, p. 137. See also Loria, *La Sintesi Economica*, p. 369.

17. Alternatively, the total additional income being given, a distribution involving equal additions to all incomes may be evolved from a distribution involving proportionate additions to all incomes by means of a series of transfers from richer to poorer.

18. It should be noticed that, if we are comparing the inequality of two distributions by means of a measure which is unchanged by proportionate additions to incomes, it is not necessary that the unit of money income in the two distributions should have approximately the same purchasing power.

19. Compare Pareto, *Cours d'Economie Politique*, II, pp. 305 ff, and *Manuel d'Economie Politique*, pp. 391 ff.

20. *Measurement of Social Phenomena*, p. 106.

21. *Cours*, II, pp. 320–1.

22. See, for example, Pigou, *Wealth and Welfare*, pp. 25 and 72.

23. See Bresciani, *Giornale degli Economisti*, August 1905, pp. 117–8, and January 1907, pp. 27–8. Ricci, *L'Indice di Variabilità*, pp. 43–6, Gini, *Variabilità*, p. 65 and pp. 70–1. Compare also Persons, *Quarterly Journal of Economics*, 1908–9, pp. 420–1, and Benini, *Principii di Statistica Metodologica*, p. 187. Professor Benini inverts Professor Pareto's measure, but apparently without realising that he has done so.

24. Benini, pp. 72 ff.

25. This index δ has been used by several Italian writers in enquiries into distributions of income. See, for example, Savorgnan, *La Distribuzione dei Redditi nelle Provincie e nelle Grandi Citta dell' Austria*, and Porru, *La Concentrazione della Ricchezza nelle Diverse Regioni d'Italia*.

John Charvet

The Idea of Equality as a Substantive Principle of Society

I am concerned here with the idea that a principle of equality must constitute the basis of any good, just, or fully human society. A principle of equality as the basis of such a society could, however, be largely formal. It could be the principle which states that equals should be treated equally, from which it follows that unequals should be treated unequally, and this is formal because it doesn't of itself tell us how any of the particular members of a society should be treated; we first have to identify in what respects anybody is to be counted as equal to anybody else before we can say anything about how they should be treated. Such a formal basic principle of society would thus be a relatively trivial and uninteresting affair. What I am interested in is the possibility that there could be a substantive principle of equality – a principle which of itself could tell us how the particular members of a society should be treated: namely all should be treated equally.

A principle which tells us that all members of a society ought to be treated equally could only arrive at its conclusion that this is what ought to be done, if in the premises of the argument there is some statement about the actual equality of these men. In the arguments that I shall consider, however, it is not supposed that men are equal in such matters as their physical and mental qualities. The respect in which men are said to be equal is sometimes put in the form of an assumed actual natural equality, by which is meant that no man can naturally claim any kind of authority over any other men. In respect of authority all men are naturally equal.

The classical argument for this position, as it is found in the books of the modern political philosophers from Hobbes, proceeds by initially removing men hypothetically from all social relations, and putting them into the so-called state of nature.

They then assert that men in such a state must be supposed to be free and equal. And this I take to mean the following: if, having put men hypothetically in such a state, one asks: 'In virtue of what could one man claim to exercise authority over any other man?' the answer must be: in virtue of nothing whatever. In such a state nothing could count as a valid ground for one man to claim such authority. Now this is true because the hypothesis has removed the conditions in which the exercise of authority by one man over others makes sense. That is, authority only makes sense, in the context of social relations and human practices and activities, where some men, on the basis of the possession of attributes or qualities considered relevant to the carrying on of such practices and activities, can legitimately claim a superior position over others; so if one removes this context one necessarily removes the conditions in which one can talk meaningfully about authority. And so they conclude that all men are naturally in a state of equal authority towards each other, which is to say that no authoritative relations exist naturally between men.

In the beginning this argument was directed towards politically authoritative positions and concluded from its premises that political superiority, since it could not exist naturally, could only exist with the consent of all the members of society, but also that, since each man is naturally his own master – lord of himself and subject to no other – such men could only enter society on equal terms. The condition for membership of the society must be the same for all. Thus at the basis of society is an initial principle of equality that appears to be of a substantive nature. While this argument was at first directed towards political authority, it naturally leads to a more general attitude towards superior positions and the construction of a derivative principle: namely, the principle of equality of opportunity. For if one begins with the premise that no man can naturally claim a superior position over others, and yet recognises both that human abilities vary and that for human activities and practices to be carried on, superior positions will be necessary or beneficial, then one will conclude that the opportunity to attain such positions must be open equally to all. That is, that the legitimate title to the occupation of such positions must be merit alone: the possession of the natural abilities considered relevant to the carrying on of the required activities. And since the fact of possessing a pedigree of a certain kind or money of a certain amount cannot of itself give one these abilities, to admit this as a legitimate basis for a claim to exercise authority over others would be to admit that, independently of any specific activities or relations, some people had a legitimate claim to exercise authority over others, and this would be to admit something inconsistent with the premises.

Now, the principle of equality of opportunity as derived above from an initial principle of equality, together with assumptions about the desirability of differentiated positions, is also a substantive principle of society, for it specifies in what ways opportunities to attain superior positions are to be allocated between the members of society: namely, equally to all. But there is something wrong with this argument which arises out of the initial hypothesis of a state of nature. For it is difficult to see what sense can be attached to talk about individuals in a state of nature as human beings at all, that is, as beings possessing the attributes of humanity. We are inclined to think of humanity as essentially social, as only developing in a social context, and not possessable by individuals independently of their having entered into social relations. If this were the case, to talk about beings in a non-social state could have no relevance at all to a different type of being existing in a social condition.

However, in his article 'Justice as Fairness',[1] Rawls has attempted to reformulate the classical argument while removing the difficulty of the initial hypothesis of a state of nature. Rawls's argument is the following: instead of a state of nature we begin by assuming a number of mutually self-interested men already engaged in a well-established system of practices. From time to time individuals engaged in the practice may be expected to make complaints that they are being treated unjustly. We may then suppose that the participants in the practice discuss among themselves on what principles such complaints are to be adjudicated. Rawls asks us to imagine that they adopt the following procedure: each man is asked to propose the principles on which he would like his complaints to be judged, and that no complaints will be tried until everyone agrees on the principles by which the complaints are to be judged. It is further understood that the principles once accepted will be binding on all future occasions so that a man will not be inclined to propose principles to his immediate advantage when on future unknown occasions they may work to his disadvantage. One would expect such men, Rawls says, to agree on certain general principles which each man sees as a guarantee that his present and future interests will be protected. Now Rawls also assumes that all participants are roughly equal in power and ability, so that no one can of himself dominate the others, and no one knows what his future position in the practice will be. Given all this, Rawls says, his men will naturally agree on equality as an initial principle, that is, that the advantages of the practice should be distributed equally. This will be so because each man, wishing to protect his interests and not knowing what his future condition will be, can only acknowledge equality as such a guarantee. But equality is only an initial principle, and assuming them to be reasonable men, they will accept that departures from such an initial position may be justified, in the sense of being beneficial to all. Departures in the direction of unequal positions will then be accepted, provided that all gain from them, and that such positions are open to all to attain. On this argument, then, we have as an initial substantive principle of a just practice – or of a just society seen as a system of practices – equality; and equality of opportunity as a secondary derivative principle. Both these principles, however, may be over-ridden by a superior consideration, which is that departure from them makes *everybody* in the practice better off.

Before examining the validity of this reformation of the classical position, I shall consider the notion of equality of opportunity as a substantive principle, for I think it can easily be seen that this notion ends in absurdity. But since it is logically derived from the initial principle of equality together with an assumption that unequal positions in human practices will be necessary and beneficial, then it would allow that either this assumption is wrong, which seems implausible, or the principle of equality, as we have it in the above arguments, must be false.

If one starts by considering the opportunity to attain superior positions in adult practices, one is rapidly led backwards into arguing that the opportunity to obtain the education that will enable one to claim superior positions should be equal for all. But one can't stop at schools, for the development of one's abilities doesn't begin there, but in the family, where being brought up by certain parents will give one an initial start over one's contemporaries less favoured in their parents. But entrance into more favoured families is not carried out on basis of merit, but on the arbitrary practice of mere birth. This, however, can be remedied by removing children from families altogether and bringing them up in state nurseries. But at this point I can couch the argument in more general terms. The principle of equality of opportunity requires that, in the development of one's natural abilities, one should not be put in an advantageous or disadvantageous position with regard to one's competitors as the result of an association with other human beings who help and encourage one to develop. Parents, teachers, friends, etc., all help or hinder one's development, and having access to those who help rather than hinder, or help more or hinder less, gives one an unfair advantage, unless the access itself is awarded on merit. But since it is absurd to suppose that one could control access adequately in this way, the only two other possibilities are: that all those through associating with whom individuals develop themselves should be equal in their capacities to help such development: or that there should be no such association at all. And both these are absurd fantasies. What I am saying is this: the principle of equality of opportunity requires that in the successful development of oneself no one should be dependent on any other human being or human practice unless this dependence is equal for all; but since it is accepted that men's abilities and capacities vary, the condition for the satisfaction of this requirement is that no one should be dependent on anyone else, and the condition of no dependence between men is that of having no society at all, and so no men.

However, it might be said that Rawls's argument doesn't require that equality of opportunity should be realised in all cases for it may be over-ruled by a higher consideration: namely, that all gain from not having equality of opportunity in particular cases. But this argument supposes that equality of opportunity in itself is a good, although it may be over-ruled by a higher good – everybody being better off. And this must be the case if equality of opportunity is to be a principle at all. But what I'm saying is that as a principle it cannot be satisfactorily formulated, that is, formulated without incoherence or contradiction. For a complete formulation of it renders it incompatible with any form of human society, while it is being put forward as a principle of a good human society. To say: 'But we can use it without contradiction in specific areas such as entry into the civil service or education', begs the question: 'Use what?' For if you are using the principle of equality of opportunity then you are using an incoherent notion, but that you can talk sensibly and be understood in specific areas is because you need not be said to be using this principle at all, but applying the formal principle of equality – that equals should be treated equally – and providing reasons for thinking that certain distinctions hitherto made, class or money, etc., should not now be taken as constituting inequalities relevant to treating equals equally in such and such an area of human activity.

Now if the idea of equality of opportunity as a substantive principle of the just society is false, and it is logically derived, together with the reasonable assumption that human practices require superior positions, from the principle of equality as we so far have it, then there must be something wrong with this principle of equality. What was wrong with the classical argument for equality was that it purported to be talking significantly about the human condition, while removing the context in which any such talk could be meaningful. And in fact these writers only achieve what appears to be relevant because, while removing man's social context, they leave him with attributes which he could only have developed in such a context.

However, the reformulation of this position by Rawls is in no better state. For, although he assumes his men to be engaged in a well-established system of human practices, and thus can legitimately allow them human attributes, he makes two further assumptions necessary for his argument which are incompatible with his initial assumption – namely, that his men are roughly equal in power and ability, and that no one knows what his future position in the practice will be. To make these two further assumptions is merely to reintroduce the state of nature by the back door. For in so far as his men are engaged in a well-established practice they will necessarily be occupying certain present positions within the practice, and have legitimate expectations as to what their future positions will be. If this were not so they could hardly be said to be engaging in a practice at all. But if they occupy such positions then some will have more power and authority within the system than others, and indeed have more or less definite future expectations of its continuity or acquisition. Such men cannot then be said to be equal in respect of power, ability and future expectations. If they are then asked to debate on what general principles claims of injustice within the system are to be adjudicated, there is no reason to suppose that they would all agree on an initial principle of equality. For at least some have established positions of authority which get their legitimacy from the accepted purposes and standards of the practice together with their possession of the required attributes for the occupation of such roles. For them to agree to accept equality as an initial principle would be for them to agree to a principle that has no conceivable relevance to their position. Rawls wants to say that all will accept equality as a guarantee against being done down by the others, since no one knows what his future position will be. But since this cannot be true, equality cannot serve as a guarantee to those with established positions and expectations. Rawls's argument would only be true if his men engaged in the practice do not have established positions in the practice and so consequently are not engaged in the practice at all. It follows, therefore that equality could only make sense as a principle to those in inferior positions who want to destroy the superior positions of others; and if this is all that is going on, it deserves not the slightest attention.

So Rawls's argument is merely a restatement of the classical position and rests on the validity of its starting point – a state of nature in which something significant claims to be being said about men, who have no social relations of any kind. And if the derivative principle of equality of opportunity is self-contradictory, it is because the initial principle of equality from which it is derived is self-contradictory also. For it asserts, as a basic principle to govern men's social relations, a principle which only makes sense in a condition in which men have no social relations. The contradiction within the notion of equality and its related principle, equality of opportunity, can be further brought out by considering the egalitarian argument in the more complex form than it has in the writings of J.-J. Rousseau.

Rousseau starts off with the traditional rigmarole about the state of nature, in which individuals possessing human attributes pursue their lives independently of each other, and so independently of all social relations. These men, Rousseau argues, cannot be supposed to be corrupt or vicious, for corruption and viciousness between men can only exist in a social context. He then provides an argument to show how with the emergence of social relations corruption accompanies it. The argument is this: in a state of nature men are conscious only of themselves and not of other human beings; they consequently cannot compare themselves with others to see whether they are more beautiful, stronger, more able, and so on, than others. Once social relations develop, however, men become conscious of others as well as of themselves; but at the same time social relations only develop once men start carrying on common activities together. But carrying on common activities such as hunting, dancing or whatever involves standards of performance in terms of which some people can be judged superior to others. Now, since men have become conscious of others, they become conscious of themselves as occupying certain positions in relation to others through the activities they carry on together. Some men are respected more than others, and men begin to desire to achieve positions of superiority for the respect that is carried with them in the eyes of others. They then come to be concerned with the opinions that others have of them, and wish to wrest from others those opinions that most flatter them. Thus they learn to appear what they are not; deceit and lying emerge, together with pride, vanity contempt, vengeance, and so on. Men have become corrupt, and are henceforth involved in a struggle for power or superiority.

Now, the essence of what has gone wrong is that men have become dependent on each other by becoming dependent for their own self-respect on the opinions that others have of them. They cannot do without others, for only others can make the judgments which will provide them with the self-respect they need; and yet at the same time others constitute threats to them, because others can withhold the judgments they look for or give judgments that cannot possibly satisfy. In these circumstances individuals are left in a perpetual state of unease and restlessness, out of harmony with themselves and others, alienated; they haven't a chance of achieving happiness. If, however, this condition of humanity is to be altered, the remedy must strike at the roots of the evil: namely, at the very dependence of men on each other. One must create a form of society in which no one is dependent on any other man.

The concern for the respect of others Rousseau calls *amour propre*, which we see emerges only in a social condition. However, the *amour propre* of a man, Rousseau says, leads him to desire first place for himself – to be superior to others. But since all men desire this, and since not all can by definition be satisfied, it results in a perpetual struggle and conflict between men. In these circumstances, Rousseau says, the condition of a good society is that the *amour propre* in men be destroyed or at least suppressed, and this can be done if they substitute a demand for equality in the place of the demand for superiority. Now this is fair as equality acts as a guarantee that no one will suffer from its realisation, that is, no one will be made inferior to any other. This equality resolves at the same time the problem of the dependence of men on each other, or the living in the opinion of others, which is the root of the problem. For equality necessarily destroys the conditions – that is, inequality – in which the *amour propre* of a man can get a grip in his relations to others. *Amour propre* can begin to emerge and wreak its havoc only if the conditions exist in which some people can achieve superiority over others. And if *amour propre* cannot get a grip on a man's activities, then there is no scope for him to be concerned with the opinions or judgment of others, and so no possibility of his achieving or not achieving the respect of others. Thus equality, in constituting the condition which suppresses *amour propre*, constitutes also the condition which destroys the dependence of men on each other, and thus all the evils of the human situation. Man ceases to be corrupt, alienated, unhappy.

However, all this is of course an absurdity, for it involves, as the condition of the good, just or fully human society, the suppression of that element in man – namely, his *amour propre* or desire for the respect of others and of himself – which constitutes his specifically human characteristic, and requires, as the condition for the overcoming of man's alienation, the total alienation of his humanity. For, as Rousseau has shown, human society emerges only with the emergence of activities that men carry on together, which involve standards of performance and so inequalities of performance. Thus, given that men are conscious both of themselves and others, and thus of themselves in relation to others, the condition of a human society is also the condition for the existence of *amour propre* or the concern for the respect of others and of oneself in relation to others. So men in so far as they are human are necessarily dependent on each other in the manner described, and Rousseau's argument involves the establishment as a principle of a human society, a principle which makes human society impossible.

But having argued for equality as the solution to all human problems, Rousseau then admits that distinctions within society are both necessary and permissible, provided that individuals in attaining differentiated positions do not owe their positions, either superior or inferior, to the will of any other men. That is, if inequalities are to be permitted, they must not contradict the basic principle of society, namely the non-dependence of men on each other, and this can only be so if a man is not dependent for the position he occupies on the will of any other man. And this, as we have seen, is the essential implication of the principle of equality of opportunity – that in occupying a position of a certain sort, I must not owe it to the relations I may have had with any other man: i.e., the relations must be either equal for all or non-existent. But this, as we have also seen, is a fantasy. Thus, if distinctions are admitted in society, then it will necessarily be the case that dependence of men on each other will have been recreated. Consequently the admission of distinctions and of equality of opportunity as a derivative principle must necessarily contradict the basic principle from which it is derived – equality as a condition of non-dependence. And that this is possible is because the basic principle itself is self-contradictory.

The Rousseauan argument introduces the notion of respect, and since then people have argued from a notion of equality of respect, which is owed to all men, to an egalitarian society. So I shall now consider this argument, and in the first place in relation to the form it has in an article by Bernard Williams, called 'The Idea of Equality'.[2] Williams's argument is as follows: men are beings with purposes and intentions, who are also conscious of these. Now, in judging a man, one may do so solely in terms of his public achievements: whether he is a good administrator or academic or whatever. But clearly one can also enter into a man's own attitude or consciousness of his life: that is, see him not only from the external point of view, but from the internal point of view, of how he himself sees his efforts and understands his activities and performances. To treat a man in a fully human way and with respect for him, Williams says, is to adopt this internal point of view, and all men are equally owed this effort of identification. But while at first sight nothing much seems to follow from this – that is, it would appear compatible with an hierarchical society based on birth – Williams wants to say that, in following out its implications, one is led in the direction of an egalitarian society. The consciousness a man has of his role in society, Williams argues, is the product of that society itself, and can be increased or diminished by social action. Now, what keeps stable hierarchies together is a belief in the necessity of the social orders of the society. But this will involve false consciousness, for people will not be fully conscious of the roles they actually occupy in society, but see them in a false light. Now suppose that, while the lower orders retain their false consciousness, some members of upper orders come to a clearer and truer view of their roles: that is, they no longer see them as necessary. Then, in order to preserve the society, it will be necessary to prevent the lower orders developing the awareness of their roles that would undermine the stability of the system. Consequently an element of conscious deceit enters the system, but also an element of contempt, as the upper orders will necessarily see the lower orders as self-deceived. These elements destroy the equality of respect that is required for a just society, and so the argument leads to a demand for a socially egalitarian society.

This argument, however, rests on two notions – the notion of seeing one's role as necessary, and the consciousness one may have of one's role – which are insufficiently explored by Williams. With regard to the former notion of seeing the structure of one's society as necessary, which involves false consciousness: what has to be the case is that the members of that society take what is their social structure to be what must be. But suppose they are not aware of any other possible social structure than their own. Now, the idea of their accepting the social structure as what must be, or as necessary, becomes problematical. For it is not clear what could be meant by this, other than merely repeating that they accept their social structure with no questions asked. But merely accepting something with no questions asked or doubts raised is different from believing it to be necessary, for the latter supposes that one raises the question as to alternatives and finds no answer. But then those who merely accept something cannot be said to possess false consciousness with regard to what they accept, because there cannot be anything false in merely accepting something. One is accepting it for what it is, not for what it is not. Furthermore, the notion of necessary is relative. Nothing is necessary in itself but always in relation to something else. So that to be aware of alternative forms of society, and still assert that one's own form is necessary, would only involve falseness, if what one was asserting was that of all the possible forms of society, this one is the only possible one:

that is, necessary for human beings – which would be like pointing to a tree and saying this is the only possible tree. Whereas what one could be asserting or believing is that one's form of society was the only possible good, just or fully human one, or necessary for *them*. This may, of course, involve false consciousness, but all I want to say is that the notion of necessary won't do the work for you, and that there could be hierarchical societies based on birth and accepted by all, either as necessary or not, without false consciousness, and so without inequality of respect.

What is needed to get from false consciousness to egalitarianism is a much stronger notion of false consciousness. Now, false consciousness is concerned with the way in which one identifies oneself in relation to other people; and self-identification here means identifying the capacity in which one wishes to be recognised and respected by others. What I now propose to do is to consider three general ways in which a man might identify himself, and see how these might be related to the notion of false consciousness.

The first case is of a man who doesn't identify himself as an individual at all, but as a mere cog in a machine, as it were, a member of an organic body that has no existence apart from the body. Now, this as it stands is incoherent, because such a man could not be said to identify himself in any way whatsoever. For identifying oneself involves identifying oneself as an individual. So if this is going to be a possible case, one has to say that, while he is capable of seeing himself as an individual, he persists in talking and acting as though he were not. Now this would be a clear case of false consciousness because one is saying both that he has the consciousness of himself as an individual and yet refuses to recognise it.

The second case is of a man who identifies himself satisfactorily as an individual, but as an individual whose identity consists in occupying a certain role in society. He is an individual peasant who never thinks of himself outside his role of being a peasant.

The third case is of a man who stands back from his role and thinks of himself as someone: an individual who could be or could have been any number of things, and who merely happens to be a peasant. He doesn't identify himself with any particular role, but as a man apart from any role.

Now, if the third case is to be taken as the standard of true consciousness then the second case will have to be considered a case of false consciousness. For the peasant in the second case clearly could see himself in the manner of the third case, but refuses to do so. And it would follow from this that a social structure which prevented or discouraged individuals from identifying themselves properly as men would thereby be deficient, and if we take hierarchical societies as typically producing men of the second type of consciousness, this will constitute an argument against hierarchical societies and for egalitarian ones. So what we have to consider is whether the third case can meaningfully be taken as the standard of true consciousness.

To decide this, consider the fourth case of a man who, while occupying a certain role, realises that he has abilities which cannot be satisfied in his existing role, and consequently feels frustrated. Such a man would, of course, no longer be a clear case of the second type, for he would no longer identify himself with his role of being a peasant, but as someone with abilities and ambitions to occupy another role. He stands back to a certain extent from his role and considers himself apart from it. Nevertheless he is not a case of the third type, for it would not follow, if this man's consciousness of himself is taken as the standard, that the second is suffering from false consciousness. The fourth case differs from the second in that he has good grounds for thinking he has abilities that could be better realised in another role, which the second case entertains no such thought. So that, unless one were to say *a priori* that everyone has good grounds for thinking in this way, the second case cannot be represented as suffering from false consciousness in relation to the fourth. And no such assertion could be made.

So what one needs to arrive at the third case is the notion of a man who identifies himself as a man apart from any role or any particular abilities he may have to occupy a role. In so far as self-identification is identifying the capacity in which one wishes to be recognised and respected by others, this man then desires to be identified and respected as a man and not as a role-occupier. But what would it involve to be identified and respected as a man? Clearly in the first place this would involve being recognised as a member of the species man possessing the attributes of humanity, a language speaker, who is conscious of himself and a free agent.

Now, being a free agent is what one is potentially in being a member of the species man, but not what one is necessarily, for one may refuse to recognise it or identify oneself in this respect, and this would be a variant of the first case – a case of false consciousness. Being a free agent, then, or being a man or human being in the sense of realising or actualising in oneself the attributes of humanity, can be seen as achieving a certain performance, which indeed all men are capable of and most men achieve to some degree. To be identified and respected as a man is to be identified and respected in one's capacity as individual free agent. But what is it to respect a man in this capacity? The answer to this lies in the notion of self-respect. For self-respect is that without which a man hasn't a chance of performing anything adequately except evil, for its loss or absence involves the loss or absence of the belief that one has the potentiality for a certain performance; and thus in the extreme case, where it is lost in relation to everything, it is the abandonment of one's humanity – one's capacity for action. To respect a man, then, in this fundamental way of respecting him in his capacity as free agent, is so to behave towards him as to help him maintain his self-respect; while not to respect him can be either to behave towards him in such a way as to try and destroy his self-respect (to beat him down, make him feel nothing, a mere worm) or (what is the more dominant mode of not respecting a man) blandly to ignore the demands of his self-respect, as though there were none – which is to ignore his humanity. But not all men can equally be given this respect, only all men in so far as they possess self-respect to some degree. For to him who possesses none, none can be given – it would be a mere meaningless gesture, for there would be nothing in him for your respect to maintain; it would be respecting him for something that he isn't. One cannot respect a child of a certain age.

If being identified and respected as a man is being identified and respected as a free agent, nevertheless free agency is not an activity on its own separable from other activities such as being an engineer, or civil servant, citizen or husband, for it clearly enters into one's performance of these roles and could only be exercised in some such specific context. Nor could one be said to be performing such roles or carrying out such activities without the activity of being a free agent. And even if one were to say free agency is primarily connected with morality or being a good man, or achieving the virtues of humanity, it is not the case either that being a good man is an activity separate from and of the same nature as the performance of specific roles mentioned earlier. For just as free agency enters into one's specific activities, so the activity of being a good man consists in the manner in which one carries on one's specific roles. It is to do with the relations one achieves – relations of justice, generosity, magnanimity, and so on – with those with whom one is connected through the specific roles one occupies. Thus roles and the performance of roles are a fundamental part of the human and moral world, for it is only through specific activities and relations that the activity of being a good man can be realised at all, and thus that the respect of others and of oneself can be acquired.

But then the activity of being a man or free agent and the activity of being a role-occupier of a certain sort, while different activities are nevertheless necessarily related, so that being identified and respected as a man is not something that can be categorically opposed to being identified and respected as a role-occupier of a certain sort. One does not have to stand back from one's role and identify oneself as a man apart from one's role, for all one need do is identify oneself as a man *in* one's role or roles. But then the second case – the man who identifies himself as a peasant and doesn't think of himself outside his role – cannot be represented as a case of false consciousness, for identifying himself as a man *in* his role is what he is perfectly capable of doing. To be a free agent is not to choose in conditions where no restrictions or dependencies exist; it is merely to act and have the courage of acting, that is, accepting responsibility for what one is doing. But action always takes place in a specific context, and a specific context is always one full of limitations and dependencies. To see roles as restrictions on our humanity is to see what is a necessary condition of our humanity as an impediment to it. To assert the third case above as the standard of true consciousness that a man may have of himself is to be involved in such an incoherence. For the condition of its being realised is that one does not identify with any role. Now one may still have a role, but not identifying with the role means not accepting the standards and purposes of the role as relevant criteria for judging one's life-activity, one's performances, one's being anything at all. And this means that, in so far as one carries on the role, one carries it on without reference to those aspects of it which alone can make the activity meaningful – its standards, purposes, and so on. That is to say, while carrying on the role in some minimal sense, one is thoroughly alienated from it. But to lose the meaningfulness of roles is to lose the foundations of human and moral world.

Now, if this is the standard of true consciousness, those poor unfortunate persons who will identify with their roles will appear as retarded in their degree of self-conscious humanity. To raise them then to the highest standards of humanity, equality might be seen as a necessary condition. For equality as a basic and substantive principle of society destroys all traditional roles and equally alienates everybody. But now we have as the condition in which everyone can equally be respected – as a man without arrest or restriction – a condition in which all are equally alienated from the circumstances in which anyone an be respected. Once again, we have as a principle to govern a truly human society a principle which makes human society impossible.

As with other attempts to make of equality a substantive principle of society, equality of respect as a condition of the good, just or fully human society is incoherent and self-contradictory, for it is only through the existence of common activities and practices, and so of roles, that a human society comes into being at all, and the species man acquires the attributes of humanity.

That throughout this argument the various forms of egalitarianism that I have considered have turned out to be self-contradictory should not be surprising. For the whole direction of egalitarianism's effort, as is clear from its origins in those totally alienated men – the free and equal men of the state of nature – has been an attempt to conceive of a man's existence as a man apart from his existing under the necessary restrictions, limitations and dependencies involved in being a member of a human society, and consequently in being a member of the human race.

Notes

1. John Rawls, 'Justice as Fairness', in Peter Laslett and W. G. Runciman (eds), *Philosophy, Politics and Society, Series II, Oxford 1962*, pp. 132–57.
2. B. A. O. Williams, 'The Ideal of Equality', in *Philosphy, Politics and Society*, pp. 114–20.

Sidney and Beatrice Webb

Inequality of Income and Inequality of Personal Freedom

We believe that, apart from the poverty of the poor, so gross a disparity between the income of one citizen and another as is inherent in the present advanced stage of the capitalist organisation of industry, is in itself injurious to the commonwealth. The extremes of inequality are known to all men. In every newspaper, capitalist or labour, we find now and again sensational paragraphs drawing attention to the gross disparity in the incomes of selected individuals – between the few shillings or dollars a week of the labouring man or woman, and the hundreds of thousands of pounds or millions of dollars a year credited to the super-capitalists of Great Britain and the United States. But a more significant fact is the inequality of the way in which the national income is shared between one class of society and another.[1] To take, as a leading instance, the United Kingdom at its wealthiest period – the years immediately preceding the Great War. The inhabitants of this country were then producing, in the aggregate, each year, commodities and services priced at a total, in round numbers, of two thousand million pounds, besides drawing a couple of hundred millions of pounds a year from investments in other countries. One half of this aggregate of commodities and services, out of which the whole people had to live, was taken by the one-ninth of the community which was at that date liable to income tax, comprising, therefore, all the families that had as much as £160 a year income. Nearly one-third of the remaining half (say, three hundred millions sterling) fell to the share of that *nouvelle couche sociale*, the black-coated proletariat of humble clerks and teachers and minor officials, along with the smallest shopkeepers and traders – comprising, with their families, the two-ninths of the population who were not manual working wage-earners, but who nevertheless did not get for their work as much as £160 a year per family. There remained, out of the aggregate product, for the two-thirds of the population who were manual working wage-earners and their families, somewhere about eight hundred millions, which, after making the necessary deductions for sickness and other spells of unemployment, worked out, for the male adult male worker, at an average weekly income throughout the year of something like twenty-five shillings on which to maintain his family. And this glaring inequality in the distribution of the national income was not peculiar to the United Kingdom, or to those particular years. It is characteristic of every capitalist society. The statistics for France, so far as they can be ascertained, were no less extreme in their inequality. Those for the German Empire were apparently much the same. Even in the United States, with all the boundless resources of North America, there stood revealed, so far as the statistics extend, a parallel inequality in the way the national income was shared. To put it another way: in 1890 the total income of that country was so divided that 40 per cent was received as the reward of owning, and 60 per cent as the reward of doing.[2]

The nation 'chooses inequality'

It is therefore clear that a nation, in deciding to establish or to continue the private ownership of land and capital as the basis of the industrial organisation of its people, deliberately chooses inequality. We must face this now with our eyes open. The outrageous disparity in capitalist countries between one man and another, and between one class and another, independently of their merits, and often in the inverse ratio of their industry and social utility, is not produced by any defect in the working of capitalism, but is inherent in its very nature. It is not a transient phenomenon, but a permanent feature. By leaving in almost unrestrained private ownership practically all the differential factors in wealth production – such portions of its land and capital as are for the time being more advantageous than the worst in economic use – we cause the resultant 'rent' or surplus value, to the extent, as the statistics indicate, of at least a third of the aggregate product, to fall into the lap of the more fortunately situated members of the property-owning class, irrespective of their rendering any service whatsoever to the community. 'The widow,' says Carlyle, 'is gathering nettles for her children's dinner: a perfumed seigneur, delicately lounging in the *Œil de bœuf*, has an alchemy whereby he will extract from her the third nettle, and name it Rent and Law.' A similar 'surplus value' over and above the maintenance conceded to the workers concerned is being produced, year in, year out, throughout all capitalist industry down to the marginal cultivation in each case. This statement does not imply that 'all wealth is created by labour', meaning manual labour. The mining engineer, the captain of the merchant ship, the passenger superintendent of the railway, the bank manager, the literary or scientific writer or teacher, the inventor, the designer, the organiser, and those who under various names actually spend their lives in initiating and directing enterprises of social utility, together with the innumerable other 'brain-working' participants, may all be assumed to be co-operating in the making of the product, and to be legitimately earning a maintenance for their families and themselves. How far their several incomes bear any relation to the social values of their respective services is a disputable question, to which no convincing answer has been found. But, apart from all these incomes, there is normally a surplus accruing to the class of legal owners of the instruments of production, merely as a consequence of this ownership, irrespective of whether or not they are the organisers or directors, or are otherwise co-operating in production in any way whatsoever. This surplus goes, in fact, in all capitalist societies, very largely, and as it seems, even increasingly, to persons who are not, in respect of this income, producing anything. It will be obvious that this incident of the individual ownership of the differential factors in wealth production – of the soils, sites, mines, factories, and shops superior in productivity to the worst in economic use, or, where agreements or amalgamations among most of the separate proprietors have led to monopoly, of the tribute on the consumers that this monopoly permits – is not dependent on the lowness of wages: it remains unaffected by the remedial expedient of raising every member of the community to a prescribed national minimum. In so far as any such mitigation of the poverty of the poor increases their efficiency in wealth production, and thereby the aggregate output, the total of 'rent' may even be increased. If the widow is enabled to gather seven nettles instead of three, the seigneur lounging in the *Œil de bœuf* may find himself extracting from her more nettles than before.

The law of inheritance

And the effect of this diversion of a large part of the national product to the mere payment for ownership is cumulative. The small rentier may consume all his dividends in supporting himself and his family, but the larger the rent-roll or dividends the greater is normally the balance over personal expenditure, a balance automatically invested, through the highly organised banking and financial system, in additional instruments of production, yielding still further dividends. The possessor of what may be deemed a moderate fortune may lose it or dissipate it; but nearly all the super-capitalists know how to secure themselves and their heirs against any such calamity. Hence it is now axiomatic that, under the reign of capitalism, those who own the most, not those who work the most, get, in fact, the largest incomes; and those who own the least get, in fact, the smallest incomes, however hard they work. And the gulf is always widening. It is this automatic heaping up of individual fortunes – by the older economists termed, apparently with unconscious irony, 'the reward of abstinence' – that accounts for that ever-multiplying monstrosity of capitalist civilisation – the millionaire. Moreover, under the laws of inheritance that all capitalist nations have devised or developed, the payment for ownership not only intensifies the inequality of income between contemporaries, but also creates an hereditary class of property owners, the members of which find themselves legally entitled to levy, generation after generation, to the end of time, a tribute upon the toil of their contemporary fellow-citizens. It is necessary to emphasise this point. *The ownership of land and capital by private individuals, coupled with the legal institution of inheritance, is bound to result, however much it may be humanised by philanthropy and restrained from the worst excesses by a systematic application of the Policy of the National Minimum, in a division of the community into two permanent and largely hereditary castes – a nation of the rich and a nation of the poor.*
The evil effects of this gross inequality between the incomes of individuals and of classes are manifold. They may be summarised under four main headings: an altogether inefficient con-

sumption of the commodities and services annually available for the nation's maintenance; the encouragement of parasitic idleness; and, consequent on these, a widespread lack of good manners and a constantly operating dysgenic influence on the race.

The inefficient consumption of wealth

'For anything I know,' wrote the second President of the United States to Jefferson, 'this globe may be the Bedlam, *le Bicêtre*, of the universe.'[3] The events of the last hundred years almost seem to strengthen the suggestion that, in a universe of transmigrating souls, our particular planet may have been assigned to be the lunatic asylum for the solar system. At least, the way in which the most civilised communities upon our globe consume or use the commodities and services produced by the arduous daily toil of their millions of men and women, appears to be consistent with this hypothesis. We are not referring to the delirium of social lunacy of the four years of the Great War of 1914–18, during which nearly all capitalist governments of the world used up the entire product of the labour of their respective nations, devastated fertile land, burnt innumerable buildings, and deliberately destroyed plant and machinery, in order to kill and maim some thirty millions of the youngest and strongest of their male adults. Let us think, rather, of the normal consumption of the annual product in peace time – a consumption which is taken for granted, and accepted by the well-to-do citizen with the same sort of self-complacency as is the illusion of being God Almighty by the peaceful lunatic.

The report of the cosmic inspector

Imagine the report of the Spirit Expert in Scientific Consumption deputed by the government of the ALL GOOD to investigate the progress towards sanity of the inmates of the planetary lunatic asylum. 'I cannot agree,' he writes, 'with my colleague, the Inspector of Scientific Production, that the inhabitants of the Earth are showing any approach to sanity. I need not discuss what is sanity. It will be remembered that we are forbidden, by our instructions, to inquire into the ultimate aims or ideals of the Earthians, seeing that the rightness of ends as distinguished from means has always been a matter of controversy even in the Court Circle of the ALL GOOD. I take as the test of the sanity of individuals or races, sanctioned by the law of the universe, the capacity of selecting the appropriate means to a given end, as verified by the subsequent event. The end or ideal of the Earthians is not in dispute. They are never tired of asserting to each other, with fatuous smiles, that the end they have in view is the health and happiness of the whole community. They admit that, in the earthly state, this depends, in the first place, on the effective application of the necessary commodities and services. My colleague tells me that, in the production of most commodities and of some services, they are showing signs of increasing intelligence in the use of materials and the organisation of manual labour and brainwork. In the consumption of wealth they seem to me to be going from bad to worse. Former generations produced less, but what they did produce they seem to me to have consumed more intelligently. Take the three primary necessaries of earthly life – food, shelter and clothing. I first made it my business to review the consumption of clothing. In the Idle Quarter, there were a number of women, each of whom prided herself on consuming in the manufacture of her garments the whole year's toil of from one hundred to two hundred garment workers. I overheard one of them say, in a debate on possible economies, that the whole annual product of one worker would barely suffice to supply her 'with a hat and a nightgown'. A younger woman, about to be married, had provided herself, for her exclusive use, of no fewer than seventy-nine nightgowns, besides other garments on which many hundreds of persons had worked for more than a year. In order to consume the toil of one or two hundred persons on the garments of one woman, labour had to be wasted in barbaric decoration, in using materials which would not last long in wear, and in providing separate suits for each occasion (I observed one woman, closely attended by a worker, changing her clothes five times in the day); and, most idiotic of all, in discarding whole wardrobes of garments once or twice a year in order to introduce a new fashion. As Earthians are apparently valued according to their capacity to consume without producing, this inefficient consumption of the garment workers' toil was imitated by women of more limited means, so that the clothing of the whole population reflected the fantastic and unhygienic habits of the wealthy members. Passing from the

Idle Quarter to the homes of the garment workers themselves, I found these persons living day and night in the same clothes – ugly, badly fitting, scanty and foul. Their children were attending school in leaky boots; and, in hot weather and cold alike, were wearing rags of the same thickness and texture. The explanation was simple. These makers of garments were each of them restricted, for the whole year, to what could be produced by a single person working for one, two, or three weeks, as against the hundred or two hundred persons working for fifty-two weeks to equip each woman of the Idle Quarter. This example is typical. Hence, as a means to attain the end of the health and happiness of the whole community, the consumption of clothing on Earth cannot but be considered as a symptom of insanity.

'Then as to the shelter which the climate of these parts of the Earth makes essential. The homes in the Idle Quarters are often so large, and contain so many empty rooms, that the constant labour of from five to twenty-five persons is required merely to keep them clean, and to serve the daily needs of the so-called occupiers, who might or might not have wives and children to share them. Meantime, even in the wealthiest cities, 20 per cent of the total population of herded together in one- or two-roomed tenements. I actually discovered a number of cases of two or more families working and living in a single room, the resulting indecency and disease being unfit for publication.

'Even in the matter of food – the one absolute necessary for continued existence on Earth, the consumption is madly inefficient. It is noteworthy that the Earthians have now discovered the facts with regard to the consumption of food. They know, within a narrow margin, exactly the quantity and quality of food required for healthy, human existence; they know that less than this means starvation and more than this means disease. And yet, if we compare the normal consumption of food-values of the bulk of the inhabitants with the normal consumption of food-values in the Idle Quarters, measured in the labour required for their production, we find it ranging in the proportion of something like one to twenty, with the result that the mass of the people, and those who are working hardest, are habitually undernourished, whilst a select few, who are very often absolutely unproductive, are not only wasting food, but are actually making themselves inert and deformed in consuming it.'

So far the imaginary report of the Spirit Inspector on Earthian

Consumption. The mundane economist not merely confirms this criticism but even pushes it further. The present inequality of income conspicuously leads, not only to inefficient consumption, but also to the production of wrong commodities. The power of commanding from the world just what commodities and services the several owners of the unequal incomes elect to enjoy, vitiates, at a blow, all the assumptions of the earlier economists that production would, on the whole, be automatically directed to the satisfaction of human needs, *in the order of their urgency*. It gives us the state of things in which a vast amount of labour is lavished on the most futile luxuries, whilst tens of thousands of infants are perishing from lack of milk, innumerable children are growing up without adequate nurture, millions of men and women find themselves condemned to starved and joyless lives, and the most urgent requirements of the community as a whole – to say nothing of the essentials to the well-being of future generations – remain unprovided for. Under a system of private property in the means of production, the 'effective demand' of individuals affords no sort of assurance of the fulfilment of the most indisputable national needs.

The vitiation of effective demand

Unfortunately this is as true of the one-third or the two-fifths of the total income which makes up the expenditure of the toiling masses, as of the vastly larger incomes dispensed by the middle and upper classes. To quote the words of an American writer: 'Under present conditions the bad example of the rich is a greater evil than their indulgence, because it spreads inefficiency so widely. The effort to imitate or keep pace with the idle rich is infectious and demoralises even the poor. It breeds luxurious habits, not only among those who can afford them, but among those who cannot. Obviously this has a very depressing effect on consumptive efficiency throughout the community.'[4]

The wastefulness of consumption

It is, indeed, amazing that there should have been so much study of the means of increasing the aggregate production of commodities and services, and so little attention to the manner in which they are consumed or used. Yet the very utility of any commodity depends on the way in which it passes into consumption. It is obvious that a given aggregate of commodities and services may result in much more if it is consumed and used in one way than in another. This is plain, so far as the organisation of an industry is concerned, to every administrator. The 'captain of industry', applying to his enterprise what he calls 'scientific management', is keenly aware that his task is so to direct motive and stimulus in the whole staff, and so to apply to his processes all the resources of science, as to secure that the raw material, the various components, the sources of power, and the available labour-force shall be employed in such a way that the greatest possible total result is produced from a given supply. But he will return after his day's work to his 'well-appointed' home – the 'appointment' of which probably consists essentially in avoiding all labour-saving appliances and making necessary a whole group of domestic servants – to eat an unwholesome dinner on which ten times as much labour has been expended as on the meal by which his labourers maintain their health; and to encourage his wife to crowd his house with indiscriminate articles of furniture and ornamentation which have no merit beyond the amount of labour that has been wasted on them. In 'good times', he will respond to every caprice of his wife and children, 'Get it, it only costs money.' The contrast between the economical 'routing' towards maximum production of every item in his factory, and the thoughtless application of the products themselves, when they come before him as, within the limits of his own income, a cheque-writing director of consumption, can only be characterised as extraordinary. To any observer of the operations of a factory, it will be obvious that five tons of coal wastefully consumed do not constitute so large an item in the national wealth as three tons used in such a way as to produce a larger product. What is true of the consumption of fuel in a factory is equally true of the consumption of individual consumers of the factory's products. Thus, even with regard to national wealth, it is quite incorrect to say that its amount depends wholly on national production. The aggregate wealth of the nation can be as much augmented by an improvement in consumption as by a mere increase in production. The introduction of 'summer time' – to give only one instance – is roughly estimated to have represented to the United Kingdom the equivalent of twenty million pounds annually; or as much as the whole product of one of its coalfields.

The effect of 'rationing'

That the great inequality of incomes, which is an inevitable result of private ownership in the means of production, leads, in itself, to a flagrantly wasteful consumption of the aggregate product, has now been recognised by the modern economist. Quite apart from the fact that it destroys all possibility of 'marshalling the assets', in such a way that all the most urgent needs of the community may be supplied before the less urgent, the very glorification of expenditure as expenditure leads to the purchase and consumption of commodities merely because they are costly. What is even of greater permanent importance is that there is practically no inducement to discover in what way the available production can be employed to greatest advantage. Hence, until the stress of the Great War drove our statesmen temporarily to think, there was, in Britain as in the United States, neither research nor education in the question of efficient consumption. In Britain, the temporary system of rationing the rich and poor alike, so far as regards some essential foodstuffs, had as one of its great advantages, that persons with leisure, training and opportunity devoted themselves to discovering, not only the obviously useful facts as to food values and food preparation, but also labour-saving appliances in homes, and a more economical and hygienic fashion in clothes. It is suggested that an equally stringent 'rationing', not of meat and sugar, but of family incomes, would have had even more useful results. All the ingenuity and devotion of the wealthy women housekeepers might then have been diverted from a rivalry in conspicuous expenditure to an emulation in discovery of how to maintain the most charming home on the prescribed equal incomes! We suggest, indeed, to those to whom art is foremost, that an entirely new aspect would be given to design and workmanship, and to the construction and furnishing of homes, if every consumer, the most gifted and fastidious as well as the most reckless in expenditure, could escape the temptations of lavish cost and transient fashion, and found himself confronted with the problem of how to get the necessary utility and the greatest beauty out of the expenditure of the socially prescribed income available for every family.

The encouragement of parasitic idleness

In times of unemployment and increasing vagrancy the wage-earners are perpetually reminded that 'it is a law of nature and morality that if a man does not work neither shall he eat'. To enforce this law of nature and morality we see the country studded with such brutalising institutions as the Able-bodied Test Workhouse, the Casual Ward, and, in the last resort, the gaol. With characteristic modesty the spokesmen of the insurgent unemployed have hitherto replied that the obligation to work on the part of an individual citizen must necessarily depend on his being granted the opportunity; and, greatly daring, the Labour Party has introduced into the British Parliament a 'Right to Work Bill'. The socialist declares that a more correct answer to the middle-class criticism would be the enactment of an 'Obligation to Work Law', providing that any adult able-bodied person who was discovered not actively engaged in work of national importance should be – not cruelly punished by imprisonment in an Able-bodied Test Workhouse, a Casual Ward, or a gaol – but, with all courtesy, deprived of the income which enables him to live in idleness. The socialist believes that the establishment by law of a class legally enabled to live idly on rent and dividends amounts to the establishment in the community of a set of persons who are privileged, and thereby almost irresistibly tempted, to place themselves habitually above 'the law of nature and morality that if a man does not work neither shall he eat'. The loss to the community which such social parasitism entails is serious enough, but the effect on the parasites themselves is even more disastrous. Those who are 'above the law' do not, as we have already seen, escape an extraordinary callousness and insolence, none the less injurious because they are usually themselves unaware of it, which makes the sufferings of those who do not belong to their own class seem as unreal and as unsubstantial as if they were the sufferings of another species. The crippled conscience of the propertied class is blind to the truism that the man or woman who consumes without personally contributing to the world in the production of services or commodities is a social parasite for whose very presence the world is the poorer. Consciously or unconsciously such a person, not being infirm or superannuated, is, as Ruskin vainly taught, a thief; and a thief whose depredations are none the less real, and nowadays none the less resented, in that they are made with the sanction of the law. Even the intellect of the parasitic class is affected. This may be seen, not merely in the fact that it is not the families which have inherited millions that usually produce either scientific discoverers or geniuses in art or literature. Only by a subtle deadening of intellect can it be explained why it is almost impossible to make the average wealthy person even understand, still less believe, the obvious economic truth that the world is actually the poorer, not merely by the amount of the food and clothes that he consumes without equivalent personal production, but also by all that he spends on his personal desires and caprices; that, in his case, 'spending money' is not only not 'good for trade', but actually represents the abstraction from the world's stock of the services and commodities maintaining all those whom, by his purchases, he 'commandeers' to his behests, which might otherwise have been devoted to the improvement of the narrow circumstances of the average citizen or to the advancement of science and the cultivation of the arts. It needed all the shock of the Great War to open the intellects of a small proportion of the wealthy to this truth; and they, it is to be feared, have now let it pass out of their minds.

The life of unconscious theft

This life of unconscious theft, of which the idle members of the propertied class have an uneasy suspicion, together with the callousness and insolence that it breeds, as regards the sufferings of any but those who belong to their own class – subtly degrading as it is to the rich, has its obverse in its effect on the minds and characters of those who have not been able, in the same way, to place themselves above the world's law. The resulting servility, on the one hand, and on the other, the envy, or even the simple-minded admiration for a life which is essentially contrary to all principles of morality, is as demoralising to the poor as it is to the rich. The bounties of the rich to the poor actually make matters worse for both of them. All charity – apart from personal friendship – is demoralising to giver and receiver alike; and gifts among those who feel themselves socially unequal carry with them, however well intentioned and well devised, the poisons of patronage and parasitism. The habitual respect and deference given to men and women who are wealthy, merely because of their wealth – irrespective of goodwill, personal charm, or artistic or intellectual achievements – is as damaging to those who are thus respected and deferred to, as it is to those who pay this homage to riches. Not the least of its evils is that it falsifies social values, and actually obstructs the recognition, and therefore the imitation, of the qualities of character and intellect that are in themselves admirable. It is not too much to say that, in the Britain or the United States of today, the very existence, in any neighbourhood, of a non-producing rich family, even if it is what it calls well conducted, is by its evil example a blight on the whole district, lowering the standards, corrupting the morality, and to that extent counteracting the work alike of the churches and the schools.

'Above the law'

If the man himself works for a living, in business or finance, law or administration, but receives for his services an income which places him among the wealthy, he may, by the daily service that he renders, be saved from some of the personal demoralisation; though the exaggerated respect which he is paid by reason of his large income brings its own perils. But his wife and children can hardly escape the various results of their own habitual over-consumption and under-employment. The occupation of the wife will almost certainly be socially unproductive, whilst the climate of servility which she meets in household and shop is dangerously enervating. The children grow up in a corrupting atmosphere of material luxury. They cannot escape the feeling, though it may never actually come into their intellectual consciousness, that they are, in the sense already explained, 'above the law'. The formal schooling that they receive is itself perverted by the class atmosphere. Such of them as are not quite exceptionally gifted with ambition, with a passion for self-sacrifice, or with that intellectual curiosity which is the wellspring of science, almost inevitably content themselves, if they take up any occupation at all, with 'walking through the part' which the family position has obtained for them; achieving with a demoralising mediocrity of effort only mediocre results; and practising, in fact, throughout life, a policy of 'ca' canny' of which a craftsman would be ashamed. Nor are matters improved by the makeshift occupations – philanthropic, artistic or merely social – which untrained and undisciplined men and women of leisure miscall their work. What is required for intellectual and moral hygiene, as well as for equity, is that, in return for all the 'orders' on the world that any person gives by the expenditure of his income in a particular way, he should set himself, by his own personal service, to fulfil the 'orders' that other members of the community give, or would give if they had at their own disposal their reasonably fair shares of the national income. If he prefers to 'live his own life', not obeying other people's orders, let him at least refrain from giving orders; that is, from consuming more than he himself produces. Other economic relations between one man and another mean a self-deception and a self-complacency which is nauseous.[5] It is extraordinary that the individualist philosophers who are always dilating on the bracing effects of competition for a livelihood, as tested by market values, should accept with equanimity the demoralisation and degradation which, on their own showing, a life of parasitism imposes upon the offspring of those whom these same philosophers regard as having proved themselves to belong to the finest stocks. It is not easy to see how such reasoners escape the inference that the progress of the community and of the race imperatively demands the abolition, as regards dividend-producing wealth, of the right of inheritance, and with it the opportunity of living without work; if only in order that the young people of each generation – even their own children – may not be deprived of the beneficent results of the competitive struggle.

The lack of good manners

But there is another and quite opposite justification for inequalities in income and personal freedom, which is nowadays more often pertinaciously held than openly expressed. It is very widely felt that good manners, a high standard of refinement, personal charm and even human dignity, are dependent on the existence of a set of families, all the better if hereditary, who are 'above the law' of nature and morality that he who does not work shall not eat. The very hall-mark of the 'gentleman' and the 'lady' of today is the absence in their daily lives of any need for personal drudgery, for obedience to the commands of others, and for incessant regard to pecuniary considerations; the whole resulting in a freedom to develop new faculties of social advantage, though not productive of exchangeable commodities or services. Combined with this is the attraction, as an individual quality, of an easy habit of command, a form of personal dignity often accompanying the habitual utilisation, virtually coercive, of other people's services.

The corollary of bad manners

We note in passing that those who advertise the social benefit of an aristocracy of good manners, to be based, as an indispensable foundation, on wealth and freedom from any enforceable obligation of service, seem to regard as of no consequence the deterioration of manners brought about by the combination, in the daily lives of the vast majority of the race, of poverty and servility. In the modern industrial state, whether of the Old World or of the New, we see the obverse of the 'gentleman' and the 'lady' in the typical denizens of the urban slum. The brutality, the coarseness, the inconsiderate noises, the mean backbiting and quarrelsomeness that characterise no small proportion of all the residential quarters open to the wage-earning population compel the more 'respectable' of their inhabitants, as they say, to 'keep themselves to themselves', because they find social intercourse impossible. It is a pathetic incident of the 'bad manners' that – far more than selfishness, cruelty or failure of mutual help – characterise the slums that every one insists on being termed a 'gentleman' or 'lady'; whilst the honourable appellation of man or woman is used only, with an adjectival swear-word, as a term of abuse!

But the fact we want to emphasise is not the brutalisation of the poor but the vulgarisation of the rich. We deny that the leisure class of the modern industrial state supplies any standard of good manners. On the contrary, as the elder aristocrats themselves deplore, one of the specific evils of the modern capitalist community, with its apotheosis of profit-making, on the one hand, and of luxurious idleness on the other, is a degradation of manners, more pernicious because more exemplary, than the coarse brutalities of the slum.

The effect of loss of function

It is interesting to notice that, in the history of the world, the class of persons who were, by the coercive utilisation of other people's labour, themselves relieved from industrial toil, had originally their own distinctive social function, other than that of 'existing beautifully'. They hunted for the food of the tribe; they fought in its defence; they performed the priestly offices on which its well-being seemed to depend; in Greece they were the philosophers and artists, in Republican Rome the statesmen and the jurists, and often the conquerors or administrators of subject-peoples. It has been reserved for the century of capitalism to produce an extensive class of persons, absolved from productive work, of whom a large proportion of the men, and nearly all the women, have no specific function, and disclaim the obligation of any social service whatever. We have already commented on the degradation of manners and morals, and the subtle corruption of other people's manners and morals, which is involved in the existence of a functionless rich class. But there is another cause for the deterioration, among the wealthy families in our modern societies of advanced capitalism, of what used to be counted as the social graces of a leisure class. These social graces went best, it will be admitted, with such aristocracies as those of the Court of Louis the Fourteenth, the old landed families of Carolina or Virginia, or the Samurai of Japan, the very essence of whose lives was a personal abstention from the conscious pursuit of pecuniary gain, and the maintenance of a rigidly defined caste system. It is evident, however, that such a division of activities cannot endure, because it has no root in nature. If the capitalist class would breed true to feudalism by producing only statesmen or soldiers, sportsmen or dilettanti, a stable mediaeval inequality might be maintained. But Nature takes no notice of capitalism. Statesmen and dilettanti are as rare among its scions as they are in the class which produced Wolsey and Richelieu. Its energetic spirits have for the most part vulgar ambitions, vulgar capacities, and vulgar tastes in excitement. They are competitive rather than co-operative: they like success, which means money-making and the personal power and prestige that money-making leads to; and the gambling element in big business flavours it attractively for them. The specially active men arising in the old families nowadays vie with the crowd of the newly

enriched in the making of profit by the organisation and administration of the instruments of production. This influence becomes,
even in the richest circles, all-pervasive. The 'leisure class' of
today, in Britain and France, no less than in America and Australia – far from being above and beyond the pursuit of pecuniary
gain – is dominated by the desire for amassing more wealth,
without any very nice discrimination between the different forms
of production and the various kinds of profit-making that the
law permits. There is no longer an aristocracy, a bourgeoisie, and
a working class. There is a plutocracy and a proletariat; and it is
in the proletariat that the old distinctions survive as ideals, and
are miserably aped in practice; whilst in the plutocracy the big
shopkeeper dines with the viscount, and all are rich tradesmen
together.

The outcome of the attempt to combine the aristocratic ideal
of a leisured class with the bourgeois pursuit of pecuniary gain
is a state of manners which – at least to our taste – is unlovely
to the last degree.[6] The ostentation of leisure, the choice of conspicuous and futile expenditure, the estimation of everything by
its price, the measured appreciation of every person according,
not to his quality or his achievements, but to his wealth, the
consequent uncertainty as to everybody's 'social position', the
sycophancy towards millionaires, the almost irresistible arrogance given by the consciousness of possessions, and the subtle
insolence that is involved in the conception that other persons
with whom you habitually consort are social inferiors – all these
characteristics of the society of all capitalist countries appear to
us to reduce to an absurdity the claim that, in the present capitalist civilisation, it is upon the existence of a leisured class that
good manners depend.

The emergence of really good manners

The socialist does not restrict himself to this negative criticism.
He believes that a new conception of what is 'good manners' is
emerging in the modern democratic state, as an outcome of its
democracy. When a definite system of social castes ceases to be
maintainable, and social intercourse necessarily becomes general
and promiscuous – as in the common membership of democratic-
ally elected bodies, or in the common use by all classes of the
omnibus, the tramway, the American railway car, and now

the British 'third class' compartment – there is only one alternative to bad manners, and that is the common standard of mutual
courtesy. This, in fact, constitutes the good manners of the
remoter parts of contemporary Japan, where the nobleman or
the millionaire uses the same ceremonious politeness to the port-
ers as these do to him, and the great landlord to every one of
his hundreds of peasant cultivators of rice and radishes, as his
tenants themselves employ to the superior that they recognise.
A similar extension of the conception of mutuality in a humane
courtesy lies at the root of the typical 'civilisation' or urbanity in
which modern France, owing to the traditions of the Revolution,
is seen to excel, let us say, the Prussia of 1871–1918. It will be
remembered that, already in 1879, Matthew Arnold took, for
the text of his criticism of both the aristocracy of birth and the
aristocracy of wealth of the Britain of his time, 'a striking maxim,
not alien certainly to the language of the Christian religion, but
which has not passed into our copybooks: "Choose equality
and flee greed".'[7] With Matthew Arnold, socialists believe in
'choosing equality' as the essential element in good manners.

This fundamental condition of good manners was accepted by
those who have, from time to time, been recognised as exemplars
in the matter; but only as regards such as were admitted to
membership of their own particular social caste. At all times, in
well-mannered sets, all who were in the set have been expected,
in social intercourse, to treat each other as equals. Already we
extend this conception of social equality to the dinner table. We
do not, when there is only just enough of anything to go round,
seek to take for ourselves more than an equal share. We do not,
nowadays, think it compatible with the manners of a gentleman
to give the governess a cheaper wine that is served to the other
persons at table, nor even to put off the servants' hall with
inferior meat. But towards the great unknown mass of our fellow-
citizens, *who are really sitting down with us to eat at the world's
table*, this principle of good manners is observed only by a tiny
minority, even among those who think themselves well bred.
And this again is inevitable, because Nature still obstinately
refuses to co-operate by making the rich people innately superior
to the poor people. It is quite easy for the natural aristocrat to
be exquisitely courteous to poorer mortals. His privilege is not
challenged: the common man is touched by his condescension
and eager to show that he knows how to respect genuine worth

– that, as he phrases it, he knows a gentleman when he sees one. But the rich are not born with this natural superiority: they are in the lump as other men are; and their upbringing in comparative luxury tends to make them petulant, and expect a precedence to which their characters do not entitle them. Having no natural superiority, they are forced to assert their artificial privilege by insolence, and to demonstrate their power by expenditure. Without such insolence and such expenditure, they might as well be their own parlour-maids and butlers, who are often better looking and better mannered, and indeed could hardly obtain good situations if they were not.

Under such conditions it is useless to preach good manners and reasonable economy to people who combine average character with exceptional riches, not to mention those who are below the average, and are born mean, loutish, selfish, stupid, as happens just as often to those who count their incomes in thousands as in shillings. Bad manners become, if not literally compulsory, at least practically inevitable; and as in each class the accepted standard of manners is simply what everybody habitually does in that class the great majority of people come to think it no more a breach of good manners to be insolent and extravagant than to spend and consume, by themselves and their families, and thus to abstract from the world, just whatever income the accident of fortune gives them, irrespective of whether or not the consumption is necessary for the fullest performance of their duty to the community.

What stands in the way of the universal adoption of the democratic conception of good manners in the United States as well as in the Britain of today is, in fact, the inequality of material circumstances and personal freedom among the families which are, in our modern promiscuity of intercourse, driven into personal contact. It is for this reason that the best manners are to be observed – we venture to record what is our own opinion – not in the 'Upper Ten Thousand' of Britain or the 'Four Hundred' of New York, but in certain strata of society where a practical equality of material circumstances happens to prevail, and where social position depends on quite other circumstances than relative possessions. We may instance the academic families resident in university centres, the still surviving skilled handicraftsmen of old-fashioned vocations, and the ministers of religion in denominations which have remained poor and lowly. The socialist contention is that, if we are to be gentlemen, not only must we intuitively refrain from taking more than our equal share of the good things of life, but we must also embody, in our social institutions, and especially in the way in which we collectively allocate among the whole of our fellow-countrymen the means of civilised life, that fundamental maxim, 'choose equality and flee greed'.

The dysgenic influence

There remains yet another indictment of the social stratification resulting from the inequality of personal riches, and the dominance given to it in capitalist society. Mr Bernard Shaw, who more than any other socialist has brought into prominence both the evils resulting from disparity of personal riches and the ideal of equality of income as a fundamental part of the socialist creed, has given expression to this indictment in a characteristically challenging form. 'I do not believe,' he says, that 'you will ever have any improvement in the human race until you greatly widen the area of possible sexual selection; until you make it as wide as the numbers of the community make it. Just consider what occurs at the present time. I walk down Oxford Street, let me say, as a young man. I see a woman who takes my fancy. I fall in love with her. It would seem very sensible, in an intelligent community, that I should take off my hat and say to this lady: "Will you excuse me; but you attract me very strongly, and if you are not already engaged, would you mind taking my name and address and considering whether you would care to marry me?" Now I have no such chance at present. Probably when I meet that woman, she is either a charwoman, and I cannot marry her, or else she is a duchess, and she will not marry me. I have purposely taken the charwoman and the duchess; but we cut matters much finer than that. We cut our little class distinctions, all founded upon inequality of income, so narrow and so small that I have time and again said in English audiences of all classes throughout the kingdom, "You know perfectly well that when it came to your turn to be married, you had not, as a young man or a young woman, the choice practically of all the unmarried young people of your own age in our forty million population to choose from. You had at the outside a choice of two or three; and you did not like any of them very particularly as compared to the one you might have chosen, if you had had a larger choice." That is a fact which you gentlemen with your knowledge of life cannot deny. The result is that you have, instead of a natural evolutionary sexual selection, a class selection which is really a money selection. Is it to be wondered at that you have an inferior and miserable breed under such circumstances? I believe that this goes home more to the people than any other argument I can bring forward. I have impressed audiences with that argument who were entirely unable to grasp the economic argument in the way you are able to grasp it, and who were indifferent to the political arguments. I say, therefore, that if all the other arguments did not exist, the fact that equality of income would have the effect of making the entire community intermarriageable from one end to the other, and would practically give a young man and a young woman his or her own choice right through the population – I say that argument only, with the results which would be likely to accrue in the improvement of the race, would carry the day."[8]

We may perhaps differ in the present state of our knowledge of eugenics about the weight to be given to this plea for perfect freedom of sexual selection according to momentary impulse. But we must remember that, a generation before Mr Bernard Shaw, it had been pretty conclusively demonstrated by Francis Galton that the introduction of the motive of pecuniary gain – what Mr Bernard Shaw calls 'money selection' – resulted in the progressive sterilisation of the most promising stocks.

'Money selection'

To Francis Galton's statistical demonstration of the socially disadvantageous consequences of the preference for heiresses of the most successful men of each generation, we may now add the adverse influence upon the birth-rate of the selection by the French peasantry, and generally by the petite bourgeoisie, of an only daughter as the wife for an only son, in order to accumulate the petty inheritances. In Britain and the United States we see this as the tendency to 'marrying in', among wealthy families, in order to 'keep the money in the family'. Akin to this is the very common preference by parents who are keenly alive to their daughters' pecuniary advantage for sons-in-law of superior means, even with the drawbacks of age, weak health, lack of will-power, or deficiency in mental attainments. We see this deflection of sexual selection in its gravest form when the search for a husband or a wife endowed with the desired fortune leads, in circles high and low, to the acceptance of some one who is physically disqualified for healthy marriage, and even the morally degenerate, or the feeble-minded. The obverse of this 'money selection', in all its forms, which no one can believe to be other than eugenically disadvantageous, is the intensification, among the least provident and most casual of all classes, notably in the poorest stratum of irregularly employed labourers of our great cities (who are to a large extent condemned to a perpetual interbreeding), of a reckless propagation that may well be eugenically as adverse in its consequences to the community as the exceptional restriction of the birth-rate among the provident and the prudent.

The reaction of money selection on politics must be treated separately; but we may quote here the epigram made by Stuart Glennie at the expense of a gentleman who obtained the means of entering parliament by marrying the daughter of a rich manufacturer. He described him as MP by sexual selection'. The gentleman, as it happened, justified his success at the poll; but that entirely accidental fact does not diminish the intensity of the flashlight thrown by the sarcasm on the power of inequality of income to corrupt the House of Commons, which contains not a few 'members by sexual selection', and in like manner the whole system of representative government.

Inequality in personal freedom

There is another inequality in the capitalist state, which is perhaps more intensely resented by the modern artisan, and is more difficult to bring to the comprehension of the governing class than the inequality of income; namely, the disparity in personal freedom. Freedom is, of course, an elusive term, with various and conflicting meanings. To some simple minds freedom appears only a negation of slavery. To them any one is free who is not the chattel of some other person. The shipwrecked mariner on a barren island and the destitute vagrant wandering among property-owners protected by an all-powerful police, are 'free men', seeing that they 'call no man master'. But this sort of freedom is little more than freedom to die. In the modern industrial community, in which no man is able to produce for himself all that he needs for life, personal freedom is necessarily bound up with the ability to obtain commodities and services produced by other persons. Translated into the terms of daily life, personal freedom means, in fact, the power of the individual to buy sufficient food, shelter and clothing to keep his body in good health, and to gain access to sufficient teaching and books to develop his mind from its infantile state. Moreover, as we cannot regard as a free man any one with none but vegetative experiences, freedom involves the command at some time, of at least some money to spend on holidays and travel, on social intercourse and recreation, on placing one's self in a position to enjoy nature and art. We can, in fact, best define personal freedom as the possession of opportunity to develop our faculties and satisfy our desires. Professor Graham Wallas suggests the definition of 'the possibility of continuous initiative'. In this sense freedom is a relative term. It is only the very rich man who has freedom to consume all that he desires of the services and commodities produced by other persons, and also the freedom to abstain from all personal toil that would stand in the way of his 'continuous initiative', and stop it by absorbing his energy and his time. Any poor man has a very limited freedom. To the propertyless wage-earner freedom may mean nothing more than the freedom, by dint of perpetual toil, to continue to exist on the very brink of starvation. Hence inequality in income in itself entails inequality in personal freedom.

'Equal before the law'

We have grown so accustomed, under the reign of capitalism, to the grossest disparity in personal freedom among nominally free citizens, that we fail to recognise how gross and how cruel is the inequality even where we profess to have adopted equality as a principle. Both Britain and America are proud of having made all men equal before the law. Yet no one can even ask for justice in the law courts without paying fees which (though the statesmen and the wealthy refuse to credit the fact) do, in actual practice, prevent the great mass of the population from obtaining legal redress for the wrongs that are constantly being done to them. The very object with which the legal tribunals are established is to give men security for their personal freedom – to prevent this being impaired by assaults, thefts, extortions, defalcations and failure to fulfil contracts and pay debts. In every city of Britain and America the vast majority of the population never appear as plaintiffs in the civil courts, not because they are not assaulted and robbed, cheated and denied payment of what is due to them – every one must know that these evils happen much more frequently and, at one time or another, much nearer universally, to the poor and friendless than to the rich – but because they cannot afford, out of their scanty earnings, even the court fee, let alone that of the lawyer. But the disparity in personal freedom between the rich and the poor is seen most glaringly when the one and the other are charged in the criminal court with an offence against the law. The rich man, except in extreme cases such as murder, practically always receives a summons; the poor man is still often, for the same offence, peremptorily arrested, as was formerly always the case, and taken to prison to await trial. On a remand, the rich man easily procures bail, while quite a large proportion of propertyless defendants find themselves returned to the prison cells, a procedure which, coupled with their lack of means, does not, to say the least, facilitate their hunting up of witnesses who might prove their innocence, or their obtaining help in their defence. It is needless to recount the further advantages of the rich man in engaging the ablest lawyers and expert witnesses; in obtaining a change of venue, and successive remands, or in dragging the case from court to court. When sentence is imposed, it is, in the vast majority of cases, a pecuniary fine, which means practically nothing to the rich man, whilst to the poor man it may spell ruin for himself, his little business and his household. To the average police magistrate or clerk to the justices, it is quite a matter of course that a positive majority of those whom they sentence to small fines go to prison for one, two or six weeks, in default of payment. Ruinous as prison is known to be to the family of the prisoner as well as the prisoner himself, the poor are sent to prison, in the United States as in Britain, by thousands every year, merely because they cannot immediately produce the few shillings or dollars that they are fined for minor offences, which rich men commit daily with practical impunity. No inequality in personal freedom could be more scandalous than this practical inequality of rich and poor before the law courts, which characterises every capitalist community, and which, though known to every judge and every practising lawyer for a century, has remained unredressed.[9]

The psychological reaction

But all this springs directly from the disparity in incomes, a material interpretation of personal freedom which does not exhaust the question. There is a psychological aspect of personal freedom which arises merely from the relation between one man and another. Even when the wage-earner is getting what he calls 'good money' and steady work, he resents the fact that he, like the machine with which he works, is bought as an instrument of production; *that his daily life is dealt with as a means to another's end.* Why should he and his class always obey orders, and another, and a much smaller class, always give them? It is this concentration of the function of command in one individual, or in one class, with the correlative concentration of the obligation to obey in other individuals of another class, which constitutes the deepest chasm between the nation of the rich and the nation of the poor. In one of his novels Mr Galsworthy vividly describes the contrast between the daily life of the English country house and the daily life of the labourer's cottage. The rich man, and his wife and children, get up in the morning at any time they please; they eat what they like; they 'work' and they play when they like and how they like; their whole day is controlled by the promptings of their own instinct or impulse, or is determined by their own reason or will. From morning till night they are perpetually doing what is pleasant to them. They fulfil their personality, and they exercise what Professor Graham Wallas rightly calls their 'continuous initiative', by giving, day in day out, year in year out, orders to other people. The labourer and his family are always obeying orders; getting up by order, working by order, in the way they are ordered, leaving off work by order, occupying one cottage rather than another by order of the farmer, being ejected from home by order of the landowner, attending school by order, sometimes even going to church by order, relying for medical attendance on the 'order' of the Poor Law Relieving Officer, and in some cases ordered in to the work-house to end a life which, under the British constitution, has always been legally and politically that of a freeman. From morning till night – save in rare hours of 'expansion' usually expiated painfully – he 'working class' find themselves doing what is irksome or unpleasant to them. What is called in Britain the governing class (which includes a great many more persons than are engaged in political government) is, typically, the class that passes its life in giving orders. What are called the 'lower classes' are those that live by obeying orders.

When authority is acceptable

Now let no one imagine that these lower classes, or the socialists who champion them, or indeed any persons with common sense, object to one man exercising authority over another. What is resented in the capitalist organisation of industry is both the number and the kind of the orders given by the rich to the poor, by the owners of land and capital to the persons who gain their livelihood by using these instruments of production. The authority of the capitalist and the landlord has invidious characteristics. It is continuous over the lives of the individuals who are ordered; it is irresponsible and cannot be called to account; it is not in any way reciprocal; it does not involve the selection of the person in command for his capacity to exercise authority either wisely or in the public interest: above all, it is designed to promote, not the good of the whole community, but the personal pleasure or private gain of the person who gives the order. No one but an anarchist objects to the authority of the policeman regulating the traffic in the crowded street; to the authority of the sanitary inspector compelling the occupier of a house to connect his domestic pipe with the main drain; to the authority of the Medical Officer of Health enforcing the isolation of an infectious person; or even to the demand note of the tax-collector. No one resents the commands of the railway guard – 'take your seats' or 'all change here'. All these orders are given in respect of particular occasions in the citizen's life, and by persons assumed to be selected for their fitness for the duty of giving these particular orders. The persons exercising command are themselves under orders; they are responsible to superior authority; and they may be called to account for bad manners or for 'exceeding their powers'. Moreover, their orders are, in the best sense, disinterested, and have no connection with their personal gain or convenience. We may complain that the official is going beyond his function or is unmannerly in his methods. We may object to the policy of the national executive, or deplore the legislation enacted by parliament. But in obeying these orders all men are equal before the law; and all men have the same right of appeal to the superior authority. Finally, in political democracy, the persons who are subject to the authority are exactly the persons who have created it; and they can, if and when they choose, sweep it away. In their capacity of citizen-electors they may exercise collectively, through the parliament and the government of the day, an ultimate control over the stream of orders they are called upon as individuals to obey.

In this connection it is interesting to notice the socialist inter-pretation of a phrase much in vogue in the twentieth century. We often hear at labour meetings of the desirability of a man 'controlling his own working life'. But this does not mean that each man or woman is to be free to work at starvation wages, or for excessive hours, or under the most unpleasant conditions. This is the freedom demanded for the worker by the capitalist. Against it the socialist and the organised workers have carried on a war of attrition for a century, the victories in that war being factory laws, mines and railways regulation laws, minimum wage laws, and the like. What the insurgent worker means by 'the worker's control over his own life' is, on the contrary, the sort of control exercised by means of his trade union, through an executive council and officials, whom he and his fellows have elected, and can depose. These agents of the workers stand or fall, paradoxical as it may sound to those who still ignorantly regard trade unions as tyrannies, according to their ability to maintain and increase the personal freedom of the persons who elect them. The revolt of the worker is not against authority as such, but against the continuous and irresponsible authority of the profit-making employer. Where is the warrant, he asks, for the power of the owners of factories and mines, land and machinery, to dictate the daily life and the weekly expenditure of hundreds of their fellowmen, and even, at their pleasure, to withdraw from them the means of life itself? This power is not derived from popular election. It has no relation to the ascertained merit or capacity of those who wield it. It is, in many cases, not even accompanied by any consciousness of responsibility for the moral or material well-being of those over whom it is exercised. Not only is there no necessary connection between the particular orders which the workers find themselves compelled to obey, and the security or prosperity of the commonwealth: there is often a great and patent contradiction, orders to adulterate and cheat being quite common. From the standpoint of labour the authority of the capitalist and landlord is used for a corrupt end – to promote the pecuniary gain of the person in command.

Dictation of environment

Few persons who have not deliberately analysed the way in which the wage-system is organised have any adequate conception of the continuity and dictatorial character of the stream of orders by which the workman is called upon to direct his life. But this stream of orders is not the only way in which the property-owning class directs the daily life of those who are dependent on their toil. Even more dangerous, because more subtle, and less obviously an outcome of the inequality in wealth, is the power possessed by the propertied class to determine, for many years at a stretch, what shall be the physical and mental environment, not only of the manual labourer, but of all the local inhabitants. The most striking manifestation of this power is the steadily increasing 'industrialising' of a countryside, ending in the creation of an urban slum area, by the continuous pollution of the water and the atmosphere, the destruction of vegetation, the creation of nuisances, the erection of 'back to back' dwellings, in row after row of mean streets. The devastation wrought in this way, in some of the most fertile and most beautiful parts of England and Scotland, as also in the United States, is, as we now know, comparable only to that effected by a drawn-out modern war. In peace times the community as a whole fails to realise, in time, the catastrophe that is being caused by the private ownership of land and capital in the establishment and growth of an industrial centre. By the time that the evil is recognised, the health and happiness of whole generations have been vitally affected. Belated statutes and tardy by-laws may then, at best, lessen the pollution, abate the darkening of the atmosphere by noxious gases and coal smoke, perhaps even save the last surviving vegetation. But nothing can bring back the lives the dictatorship of the capitalist has wasted. The leisured rich are able to escape from the noise, the gloom, the dirt, the smoke, the smells that their power has created; but the wage-earners, the industrial brain-workers, and all their retinue of professional men and shopkeepers find themselves compelled to dwell, and to rear their families, in the graceless conditions unconsciously determined for them by the industrial and financial organisers in their pursuit of private gain. When the city dweller escapes into the still unspoilt countryside on a scanty holiday, it comes as a new insult to find himself and his children barred from the pleasant park, excluded from the forest, and warned off the mountain and the moor by the property rights of the very class of persons who have rendered his place of abode abhorrent to him. In the end he is forced in self-defence to form a perverse habit of liking grimy streets, blackened skies, and the deafening clatter of drayhorses' shoes on stone setts, on the principle that if you cannot have what you like you must like what you have.

Dictation of the mental environment

Nor is even this unconscious determination by the property-owning class of the material environment of the mass of the community, for the sake of its own private gain, the worst form taken by the inequality in personal freedom. It has been reserved to our own time for the profit-making capitalist to determine also the mental environment. Who can estimate the effect on the mind of the incessantly reiterated advertisements that hem us in on every side? It is, moreover, the capitalist who directs the character of the recreation afforded to the mass of people. It is the brewery company and the distillery that give us the public-house; other capitalists, controlling the music hall and the cinematograph, may say, with Fletcher of Saltoun, that they care not who makes the laws as long as they provide the songs and films. But the most glaring instance of the capitalist direction of our mentality, and perhaps, ultimately, the most pernicious, is the modern system of ownership of the newspaper press. Here we have even a double capitalist control, first by the millionaire proprietors of whole series of journals, daily, weekly, and monthly, under autocratic control, and secondly, by the great dispensers of lucrative advertisements to these journals. The combination of the colossal expense involved in the successful conduct of a modern daily newspaper, and the natural reluctance of the wealthy advertisers to support any publication adverse to the system, if not even to the particular business, by which they obtain their own fortunes, have made it almost impossible for the property-less wage-earners, even in co-operation with each other, to establish, either in Britain or the United States, any organ of their own at all comparable in circulation and influence with those of the millionaire proprietors. Thus, the mass of the population is quite unable to protect itself against the stream of suggestion, biassed information and corruptly selected news that is poured on them by the giant circulation of the press.[10]

Lastly, we have the control insidiously exercised by the owners and organisers of the instruments of production, by means of their wealth, over the working of municipal government and parliamentary institutions.

Dictation in government

Of this control, the direct power of the proprietors of the newspaper press – which, in Britain, goes far to make a Prime Minister, and in the United States not only to elect a President but also to go far to select his chief ministers – is only the most obvious example. The influence, not only upon elections and legislatures, but also upon national and municipal executives, of the great financial, shipping, manufacturing, and trading amalgamations and combinations, in which the power of wealth is cast defiantly into the scale as the sword of Brennus, has, in recent decades, become notorious and scandalous. It is, we suggest, to the suspicion, followed by the detection of this far-reaching coercive guidance of national and local government by the property-owners and profit-makers, large and small, more than to any other cause, that is to be ascribed the sudden and rapid decay of the confidence of the wage-earning class in these institutions, manifested not in this country alone, but throughout the Continent of Europe and North America. Unfortunately, one invidious feature of the Great War, so far as the United Kingdom is concerned, has been the extension of a similar capitalist control to the national executive, in ways not previously open. The temporary handing over of various government departments to leading representatives of the business interests concerned, and the shameless use of the influence thus acquired for the promotion of the private profits of those branches of business, represents, so it is felt by the British workman, the final degradation of the state to be the handmaid and accomplice of the profiteer.

The brain-workers in capitalist service

This control of the physical and mental environment, which, in a capitalist society, the property-owning class progressively and almost automatically accomplishes (for all those effects are mere incidents in the pursuit of private gain, and are no more consciously aimed at than the devastation caused by the trampling of a herd in pursuit of food), brings into prominence the instrument of its far-reaching dominance. The deep-seated intolerance by the more ignorant manual workers of the very existence of the professional brain-workers is not due solely to the difficulty a navvy finds in believing that a man who sits in a comfortable chair by a cheerful fire in a carefully sound-proofed room is doing any work at all, much less work that will leave him hungry and exhausted in three or four hours. Many wage-workers are sufficiently educated to know better; and others are employed in occupations quite as sedentary and even less apparently active than those of the financier or mathematician. Their share in the prejudice is explained, if not justified, by the fact that the brain-workers, in every capitalist state, find themselves attracted, and economically compelled, to take service under the property-owners. Historically the professions emerge as the hirelings of the governing class for the time being. In the modern industrial system they naturally serve the proprietors of the instruments of production, who alone can ensure to the vast majority of them a secure and ample livelihood, with some prospect of climbing up to the eminence of 'living by owning'. The lawyers, the engineers, the architects, the men of financial and administrative ability, the civil servants, the authors and journalists, the teachers of the schools beyond the elementary grade, the whole class of managers, the inventors, even the artists and the men of science – not altogether excluding, in spite of their long charitable service of the poor, the medical profession and the ministers of religion, nor yet, for all their devotion to the children of the masses, even the elementary school teachers – are almost inevitably retained, consciously or unconsciously, in the maintenance and defence of the existing social order, in which the private ownership of the instruments of production is the corner-stone. Is it surprising that the manual workers of the world should be tempted to regard, not science, art or religion (as is often ignorantly asserted), but the brain-workers who have been trained under the capitalist system, and enlisted in its service, as being as much the 'enemies of the people' as the 'idle rich'? But this is not all. The brain-workers themselves, especially those who are poorly paid and socially segregated, are beginning to rebel openly against this all-pervading coercive guidance of national policy and national culture by wealthy men and a wealthy class. As school teachers, as municipal officials, as civil servants, as scientific workers, as journalists and editors, sometimes even (notably in the United States as under the German Empire) as university lecturers and professors, they find their freedom of thought and expression strangled by the fear of dismissal, or at any rate by that of losing all chance of promotion, should they dare to oppose not merely the political party or the pecuniary interests of influential patrons, but even the current principles of social organisation to which nearly all rich men cling. Moreover, the majority of the situations of authority and affluence are still habitually reserved, in most countries, either by administrative devices or through personal influence, for persons who have qualified as brain-workers though belonging to the class of those who live by owning or organising the instruments of production, irrespective of their inferiority of attainments or inability to render, in the posts to which they are assigned, the highest service to the community. It is here that we find the fundamental cause of the prevailing unrest in all countries in practically all the brain-working professions, leading in many cases to the adherence of the younger professionals to the socialist move-ment, and nowadays even inclining some of the professional organisations to make common cause with the trade unions and the labour and socialist parties in resisting the dominance of the property-owners.

Why liberalism decayed

We may suggest that the foregoing analysis incidentally reveals the root-cause of the universal failure of the political parties styled Liberal, which were so typical of the advanced thought of European nations during the nineteenth century – notably at the zenith of unrestrained capitalism – to retain, in the twentieth century, their hold of a wage-earning class that has become con-scious of its citizenship. To the political Liberals, personal free-dom actually meant the personal power of the man of property;

just as political progress meant the abolition of feudal, ecclesiastical and syndicalist restrictions upon the right of the property-owner, small as well as large, to do what he liked 'with his own' – his own land and capital no less than his own personality. Down to the present day the unrepentant Liberal refuses to recognise – cannot even be made to understand – that, in the modern industrial state, a man who is divorced from the instruments of production cannot, as we have shown, even live his own life, let alone do what he likes with his own personality. Even to the political Liberal who is not a capitalist, such as the young barrister or doctor, artist or author, the conception that the labourer's engagement for hire is of the nature of 'wage-slavery' is unintelligible. To him it seems, on the contrary, that the typical engagement for hire of the propertyless professional, 'calling no man master' but earning his livelihood by fees from a succession of clients, upon no one of whom is he specially dependent, constitutes the very perfection of honourable service which is perfect freedom. What even this highly educated Liberal fails to understand is that, whatever may once have been the case, the industrial revolution has made anything like the freedom of professional life impossible for the artisan or the factory operative, the labourer or the clerk. The fact that the ordinary manual worker or minor clerical employee has not the ownership, and, therefore, not the control of the instruments of production, or of the complicated industrial or financial organisation by which he can earn a livelihood, and cannot support himself on a succession of fees from a multitude of clients, compels him, whether or not he desires this, to obtain his food by placing himself under a master whom he cannot call to account; whose orders he has to obey; whose interests he has to serve; who, in fact, possesses him and uses him, during the greater part of his waking life, for ends which are not his own. He cannot choose where he will live, and in what environment his children will grow up. He finds himself restricted in the amusements and even in the literature to which he has access, to that which it suits the pecuniary interests of the capitalist class to supply. He finds, as it seems to him, nearly every professional brain-worker retained against him and his class. And through this control over his working life and his leisure hours, over his physical and mental environment, the propertyless worker, by hand or by brain – though conscious that he and his fellows constitute a majority of the electorate –

discovers that even with the widest suffrage he is unable, in fact, to control the government of his state. Accordingly, once he has been admitted to voting citizenship, the liberty which Liberalism offers him seems a hypocritical pretence. He finds in the creed of Liberalism no comprehension either of the nature of the servitude in which the capitalist system has engulfed the great bulk of every industrial community, or of the need for an application to industrial organisation of the first principles of democracy. Now this comprehension is the very atmosphere of socialism. The socialist is out to destroy the dictatorship of the capitalist. And as that dictatorship is the grievance which the worker is never allowed to forget for a single working day from his cradle to his grave he naturally turns to socialism the moment he begins to connect politics with his personal affairs and perceives that his vote is an instrument of political power.

A liberal apology for capitalism

The honest defenders of capitalism admit, in substance, the truth of this criticism; but they allege, in reply, that without the potent stimulus of private profit it would have been impossible to have effected the Industrial Revolution, or to have secured the vast increase in the production of commodities and services, on which, it is suggested, modern civilisation depends. It was not merely that there was, even in the foremost nations, between the seventeenth and the nineteenth centuries, no practicable alternative to the dictatorship of the capitalist. The very inequality in riches and in personal freedom by the prospect of which he was incited and stimulated, seemed to have an economic advantage of its own which obscured its social drawbacks. As it has been well put by a contemporary economist, in the course of the nineteenth century, 'Europe was so organised socially and economically as to secure the maximum accumulation of capital. While there was some continuous improvement in the daily conditions of life of the mass of the population, society was so framed as to throw a great part of the increased income into the control of the class least likely to consume it. The new rich of the nineteenth century were not brought up to large expenditures, and preferred the power which investment gave them to the pleasures of immediate consumption. In fact, it was precisely the *inequality* of the distribution of wealth which made possible those vast accumulations of fixed wealth and of capital improvements which distinguished that age from all others. Herein lay, in fact, the main justification of the capitalist system. If the rich had spent their new wealth on their own enjoyments, the world would long ago have found such a regime intolerable. But like bees they saved and accumulated, not less to the advantage of the whole community because they themselves held narrower ends in prospect:

The immense accumulations of fixed capital which, to the great benefit of mankind, were built up during the half-century before the war, could never have come about in a society where wealth was divided equitably. The railways of the world, which that age built as a monument to posterity, were, not less than the pyramids of Egypt, the work of labour which was not free to consume in immediate enjoyment the full equivalent of its efforts.

Thus this remarkable system depended for its growth on a double bluff or deception. On the one hand the labouring classes accepted from ignorance or powerlessness, or were compelled, persuaded, or cajoled by custom, convention, authority, and the well-established order of society into accepting, a situation in which they could call their own very little of the cake, that they and nature and the capitalists were co-operating to produce. And on the other hand the capitalist classes were allowed to call the best part of the cake theirs and were theoretically free to consume it, on the tacit underlying condition that they consumed very little of it in practice. The duty of 'saving' became nine-tenths of virtue, and the growth of the cake the object of true religion. There grew round the non-consumption of the cake all those instincts of puritanism which in other ages has withdrawn itself from the world and has neglected the arts of production as well as those of enjoyment. And so the cake increased; but to what end was not clearly contemplated.[11]

We need not demur to this candidly realistic *apologia* for nineteenth-century capitalism. Of course it was not the whole, or even the bulk of their vast share of the national income that the capitalist classes abstained from consuming year by year, in order to transform it into new instruments of wealth production; but only a fraction of their share – in the United Kingdom of the nineteenth century, scarcely a quarter of it! And of this quarter, how much was invested in instruments for the production of what Ruskin called illth, of gluttony, extravagance, waste and demoralisation? For, under capitalism, wealth is counted in a false currency. But it may be freely admitted that, with all its drawbacks, the dictatorship of the capitalist scored an initial success. It delivered the goods. It created the highly efficient machinery of ever-increasing production. And, gruesome as were the accompanying social results, we may, perhaps, allow that, on balance, down to a certain date, the advantages exceeded the drawbacks.

Notes

1. 'Inequality' of income may, of course, be understood in several ways (as to which see *Some Aspects of the Inequality of Incomes in Modern Communities*, by Hugh Dalton, 1920). As for the statistics, see the estimates of various authorities quoted in Fabian Tract No. 5, *Facts for Socialists*; *Riches and Poverty*, by Sir Leo Chiozza-Money, 1905; *British Incomes and Property*, 2nd edition, 1921, and *Wealth and Taxable Capacity*, 1922, both by Sir Josiah Stamp; and *Changes in the Distribution of Income, 1880–1913, 1918, and The Division of the Product of Industry*, 1919, both by A. L. Bowley.
2. James Mackaye, *Americanised Socialism*, 1918.
3. John Adams to Thomas Jefferson, July 16, 1814; In C. F. Adams, *The Works of John Adams*, 1851–6, vol. x. p. 103.
4. James Mackaye, *Americanised Socialism*, 1918.
5. The ablest monograph on this subject has been produced in the United States (*The Theory of the Leisure Class*, by Thorstein Veblen, 1899), tracing the origin of a leisure class from ancient civilisations based on a double method of acquiring wealth, viz. the 'honorable method of seizure and conversion', *i.e.* hunting, war, predatory raids on and oppression of inferior races; and the 'dishonourable method' of personal toil (agriculture and manufacture) enforced on women and on slaves. This tradition was carried on, with modifications, through feudal civilisation, the wives and daughters of the nobles (themselves stll engaged in the honourable method of seizure and conversion) being exempt from all useful occupations, and becoming 'ladies'. 'From this point on, the characteristic feature of leisure-class life is a conspicuous exemption from all useful employment . . . Abstention from labour is the conventional evidence of wealth, and is therefore the conventional mark of social standing; and this insistence on the meritoriousness of wealth leads to a more strenuous insistence on leisure . . . Prescription ends by making labour not only disreputable in the eyes of the community, but morally impossible to the noble, freeborn man, and incompatible with a worthy life' (Veblen pp. 40–1). In modern capitalism the male pursues gain, not by manual labour, which remains dishonourable, but by direction, organisation, bargaining, and speculation – all expressions of the conqueror or exploiter – but he insists on the

vicarious leisure of his womenkind, and sometimes of his sons, as the hall-mark of his social position. The utility of conspicuous leisure, and consumption for the purpose of establishing social status lies in the element of waste – the ability to beat pecuniary loss. 'Time is consumed non-productively (1) from a sense of the unworthiness of productive work, and (2) as an evidence of pecuniary ability to afford a life of idleness' (Veblen p. 43). To this was added luxurious expenditure. 'Conspicuous consumption of valuable goods is a means of reputability to the gentleman of leisure. As wealth accumulates on his hands, his own unaided effort will not avail to sufficiently put his opulence in evidence by this method. The aid of friends and competitors is therefore brought in by resorting to the giving of valuable presents and expensive feasts and entertainments' (Veblen, p. 75). The essays on 'Conspicuous Leisure', 'Conspicuous Consumption', 'The Pecuniary Standard of Living', 'Pecuniary Canons of Taste', 'Dress as an Expression of the Pecuniary Culture', 'The Conservation of Archaic Traits', and 'Modern Survivals of Prowess' are full of significance as illustrating the culture of a leisure class in a capitalist state.

6. As has been pointed out by Veblen, the aristocratic or barbarian idea of a governing class depended on complete abstinence, not only from manual labour but more especially from the brainworking process of profit-making, whether in manufactures, commerce or speculation. If the aristcrat was idle and luxurious, he was at least free from the active pursuit of gain. On the other hand, Werner Sombart shows that the old bourgeois ideal of a governing class is seen at its best in the early stages of capitalism when idleness and extravagance are the two deadly sins, and personal industry and personal thrift are exalted as the holiest of moral virtues. ' "Take as your model the ants," wrote the father of Leonardo da Vinci (1339) – the most eminent bourgeois of his time – "who today already have a care for the needs of the morrow. Be thrifty and moderate" ' (*The Quintessence of Capitalism*, by Werner Sombart, 1915, p. 111). Benjamin Franklin, the founder of the American bourgeois ideal, writes: ' "In order to secure my credit and character as a tradesman, I took care not only to be in reality industrious and frugal but to avoid the appearance to the contrary. I dressed plain, and was seen at no places of idle diversion: I never went out a-fishing or shooting" ' (Sombart pp. 123–44). The leisure class of modern capitalism has lost the good and retained the bad features of both the aristcratic and the bourgeois ideals.

7. Matthew Arnold, 'Equality,' in *Mixed Essays*, 1879.

8. 'The Case for Equality', a lecture delivered at the National Liberal

Club, London; reported in *The Metropolitan* New York, December 1913, and also published in London in pamphlet form.

9. See E. A. Parry, *The Law and the Poor*, 1914.

10. For accounts of the manner and extent to which the newspaper press, and behind it the possessors of wealth, now control the mental environment, as well as the local and central government of the United States and Britain, the student should consult *The Press and the Organisation of Society*, by Norman Angell, 1922; and *Liberty and the News*, 1920, and *Public Opinion*, 1922, both by Walter Lippman, himself the editor of a great New York newspaper; the more lurid descriptions given from personal experience as journalists, on the one hand, by Hilaire Belloc in *The Free Press*, 1918, and by Upton Sinclair in *The Brass Check*, 1919; and, incidentally, in the technical account of how a modern newspaper is run, by G. B. Dibblee in *The Newspaper*, London, 1913, and by John La P. Given in *Making a Newspaper*, New York, 1913.

11. John M. Keynes, *The Economic Consequences of the Peace*, 1920, pp. 16–17.

Peter Bauer

The Grail of Equality

Why, in free and open societies such as those of western countries, are some people better off than others: not necessarily wiser,
nicer, happier or more virtuous, but better off? The causes of
differences in income and wealth are complex and various, and
people will always disagree on how they apply to particular
societies, groups or individuals. But, in substance, such differences result from people's wisely differing aptitudes and motivations, and also to some extent from chance circumstances. (I use
the term 'differences' rather than 'inequalities' – except in the
context of political power – for reasons I shall go into later. Also,
I use 'differences in income and wealth', or more simply 'income
differences', interchangeably with 'economic differences'.) Some
people are gifted, hard-working, ambitious and enterprising, or
had far-sighted parents, and they are therefore more likely to
become well-off.

But whatever the causes of the economic differences in an
open and free society, political action which deliberately aimed
to minimise, or even remove, these differences would entail such
extensive coercion that the society would cease to be open and
free. The successful pursuit of the unholy grail of economic
equality would exchange the promised reduction or removal of
differences in income and wealth for much greater actual
inequality of power between rulers and subjects. There is thus
an underlying contradiction in the declared objective of egalitarianism in open societies.

When social scientists talk of social problems, they usually mean
discrepancies between social reality and what they assume to be
norms. Because they are largely preoccupied with discerning,
announcing and emphasising discrepancies between the norms
they assume and reality, social scientists tend to generate social

problems rather than solve them. This way of looking at social situations and reading problems into them is evident in the persistent and extensive concern of egalitarians with economic differences.

In recent years, there has been a vast upsurge of interest in the subject of these differences: witness, in Britain, the Standing Royal Commission on the Distribution of Income and Wealth (Diamond Commission, 1975–79), and, throughout the west, the research activities and publications of academics, the contents of university curricula, and the preoccupations of journalists, broadcasters, and other popularisers.

The appeal of egalitarianism is likely to persist. As Tocqueville observed, when social differences diminish – as they have diminished in the west – those which remain appear especially irksome and objectionable; and as he also pointed out, material advance is apt to engender discontent over failure to have achieved some other objective. The contemporary predilection for numbers and quantification, and also the emphasis on material conditions, have further helped to focus attention on economic differences.

The pervasive influence of the machine and of mass production points in the same direction. The criterion of uniformity for judging the efficiency of the machines used in mass production reinforces any philosophical appeal which egalitarianism may have. An efficient lathe, mould or press is designed to turn out identical products. Even small differences give grounds for criticism. This attitude may have had a powerful, if unconscious, influence on our attitudes to social matters.

Once the moral and political case for egalitarian policies is taken for granted, the movement for egalitarianism feeds on itself. If the results of egalitarian policies are deemed favourable, it is evidence that still more could be achieved by further and sterner measures; if on the other hand the policies are deemed to have failed, it is evidence that they were not drastic enough. Such reactions are fostered when it is widely assumed that the economic position of people is properly the concern of official policy.

Political power enables rulers forcibly to restrict the choices open to their subjects. Possession of wealth, on the other hand, does not confer such coercive power in this crucial sense. Wealth can sometimes secure a degree of political influence, although the likelihood and significance of this possibility are apt to be much exaggerated. In any case, wealth as such does not imply coercive power. Indeed, those who are rich are vulnerable to envy and to criticism founded on an unreasoning presumption in favour of economic equality. These attitudes have at times led to the persecution and even destruction of productive or prosperous groups, often ethnic minorities. Possession of wealth offers no sure protection against such dangers. Moreover, the effort usually required for economic success is apt to divert the attention of the rich from political affairs; and ability to accumulate wealth is often accompanied by an indifference to political opportunities, or a failure to recognise political dangers.

In an open society, income differences normally reflect the operation of voluntary arrangements. The absence of coercive power in most forms of successful economist activity is recognised in Samuel Johnson's familiar observation that 'there are few ways in which a man can be more innocently employed than in getting money'. This conclusion is particularly evident in a modern open society. In these societies the accumulation of wealth, especially great wealth, normally results from activities which extend the choices of others, as is clear from the fortunes acquired in, say, mass retailing or the development of the motor car.

People differ in economic aptitudes as they do in artistic, intellectual, musical and athletic abilities. In particular, they differ in their ability to perceive and use economic opportunities. Readiness to take advantage of economic opportunities is of great significance in explaining economic differences in open societies. This should be evident on a little reflection. The opportunities seized by such men as Thomas Edison, Henry Ford, Lord Northcliffe or Sir Isaac Wolfson were open to most people in their countries. The same applies elsewhere; witness the many Chinese and Japanese *nouveaux riches* in the east. Income differences resulting from readiness to benefit from economic opportunities will be especially wide if there is rapid social, economic and technical change, including the development of new products and the opening up of new markets.

Chance often plays a part in economic life, and thus in the emergence and perhaps persistence of income differences. But this is no different from other fields of human endeavour. Pasteur's celebrated observation that chance visits the prepared mind applies as much to economic life as it does to scientific activity.

An unfounded belief in the basic equality of people's economic faculties has coloured the language of the discussion. If people are assumed to be equally endowed and motivated, then wide economic differences suggest that some undefined but malevolent force has perverted the course of events. Of course, people are not equally motivated or endowed in their economic attitudes and attributes, and this explains substantial economic differences between them in open societies. This discrepancy between the unfounded belief (or assumption) and reality may partly account for the almost universal practice of describing differences as inequalities. Difference is plainly the more appropriate expression since it is neutral. It does not prejudge the issue – unlike the term inequality, which clearly suggests a situation that is unjust or otherwise objectional. In recent years, inequality has come to be used interchangeably with inequity, and equality with equity. That difference is a more appropriate term than inequality is also suggested by the accepted practice of referring to people's physical characteristics, such as height and weight, as differences rather than inequalities, and under no circumstances as inequities.

On the other hand, the term inequality is appropriate in discussing political power because that power implies a relationship of command between rulers and subjects. As I suggested above, those who have political power can coerce others by restricting their choices, while wealth does not by itself confer such powers on the rich.

In contemporary parlance, social justice has come to mean substantially equal incomes. Why should this be so? It is not obvious why it should be just to penalise those who are most productive and contribute more to output, and to favour those who produce less. This conclusion is reinforced when it is remembered that relatively well-off people have often given up leisure, enjoyment and consumption, and that these past sacrifices have significantly contributed to their higher incomes. This is but one instance of a wider issue. Income differences or changes in income and the nature of poverty cannot be discussed seriously without examining how they have come about. Although this matter is central to an analysis of egalitarian ideas and proposals, further discussion of it is left until other matters which are more prominent in the espousal and presentation of egalitarianism have been considered.

Advocates of redistribution propose that results of economic processes should be separated from the processes themselves, that people should share the fruits of economic activities in which they have not participated. The idea of equality over the past two centuries has progressed, or declined, from equality before the law, through equality of opportunity, to equality of result (or even equality of one quantifiable aspect of the result).

The demands to divorce the results of economic activity from the processes leading up to them are one facet of the contributory preoccupation with situations and the neglect of the antecedent sequences. Such practices reflect the unhistorical approach of much contemporary discussion of social issues, the amputation of the time dimension from our culture, to borrow from Sir Ernst Gombrich.

A given degree of concentration of income and wealth at a particular time has a very different meaning if the societies are fluid, such as, say, those of Malaysia or Western Europe, or more nearly stable or static as, for example, that of rural India. This rather basic consideration rarely enters into egalitarian rhetoric. Moreover, for a rounded view of income differences, incomes have to be considered beyond one generation. Economic differences may be extended or reduced, or rankings of individuals or families maintained or reversed, over a span of a generation or two.[1] Again, this consideration is rarely reflected in discussion of income differences.

Egalitarians often suggest that the incomes of the rich, or property incomes, have been received at the expense of other people, rather than earned by supplying valuable resources. A familiar instance is the use of the term unearned income, when in fact such income is no less earned than is any other income.

Incomes, including those of the relatively prosperous or the owners of property, are not taken from other people. Normally they are produced by their recipients and the resources they own; they are not misappropriated from others; they do not deprive others of what those others had, or could have had, or should have had. (Certain specific exceptions which do not affect the substance of the argument are noted later.)

The misconception that the incomes of the well-off are some-

213

how obtained by exploitation rather than earned has often had disastrous consequences: for instance, it has led to spurious justification of the expropriation, and even destruction, of economically productive groups to which I have already referred. The same misconception is behind the familiar references to shares (usually unequal shares) of different groups in the national cake, and behind assertions that certain groups have not shared in national or international prosperity – assertions which do not ask how much these groups may have contributed to it.

The terminology of the economic theory of distribution has a long history and a reputable ancestry. It has come to be accepted so generally that it is almost impossible not to use it. Nevertheless, the terminology is misleading. Distribution of income suggests a pre-existing income which somehow is parcelled out. But, as I have just noted, recipients of income normally produce their incomes: there is no distribution of income divorced from its production. Distribution also has a technical meaning in statistics (as, for instance, a normal distribution), which is quite different from the meaning of the term both in the theory of income and in egalitarian discourse. These different uses of the term should not be confused.

In a market economy, the production and distribution of income are two sides of the same process. Income will be equally distributed when people's contribution to it will be equal. The term redistribution is especially misleading because what is being 'redistributed' is not a pre-existing income. What happens in fact is that part of the income is removed from those who have produced it, and transferred to other groups.

The general proposition that incomes, including those of the well to do or of producers of services, are generated, produced and not taken from others, is subject to partial qualification. The incomes of some groups are often augmented by the exercise of monopoly power, which in most instances reflects barriers to entry, or other forms of restriction, erected or supported by the state. It has even been argued that state-supported restrictions have contributed materially to the extent of income differences in some western societies, a contribution which would be eliminated if market forces were allowed freer play.

It is difficult to tell just how important a factor this is. In any event, it does not mean that the incomes of these favoured groups (other than the recipients of straight state subsidies) are not generated by their members; what it means is that restrictions enable these groups to charge more for their services than they could otherwise. But such a situation does not mean that high incomes are usually achieved at the expense of the rest of the community. The levels of income of particular groups do not by themselves indicate the presence or absence of restriction on entry. Successful businessmen, entertainers and athletes, for instance, can earn very high incomes even when they do not curtail their output, and when there are no contrived barriers to entry into their activities. Similarly, an expansion of demand can greatly increase the incomes of certain groups even when, again, there are no such barriers. On the other hand, even modest incomes of professional people, trade unionists, or farmers may be inflated by barriers to entry.

The policy termed redistribution benefits some people by confiscating part of the incomes of others. The beneficiaries may be poor, but this is by no means always so. Major beneficiaries of redistribution include its advocates, organisers and administrators, notably politicians and civil servants. This outcome promotes the self-perpetuation of the process. And once the notion is accepted that economic differences are somehow reprehensible, the door is opened to forcible intervention on any number of different and shifting grounds and criteria; these include differences in income or wealth, differences in their rate of change, and many others besides.

On the national level, the operation of the welfare state comprises two quite different forms of redistribution: wealth transfers between groups, and redistribution of responsibility between the agents of the state and private citizens. Welfare state policies do not always redistribute income between the rich and the poor. They do not necessarily redistribute income even among individuals. The same people may be taxed at some times and subsidised at others.

The substantial taxes, including direct taxes, paid by the poor in the welfare states of the west make clear that, contrary to what is widely believed, the welfare state is not simply an agency of redistribution from rich to poor. In Britain in 1978 a single man earning £25 a week (less than one-half of the average unskilled wage) paid direct taxes. Those who earn the average wage of manual workers and have two children pay substantial direct taxes. Both categories also pay heavy indirect taxes.

The substantial taxation of the poor in countries which have extensive provision of social services is one facet of the confusion of redistribution of income with redistribution of responsibility just noted. By now, egalitarians and other supporters of social services often recognise explicitly that state-financed old-age pensions, health care, education, subsidised housing and food, welfare and unemployment payments and other social services do not represent solely or even primarily transfers from rich to poor. Heavy taxation of the poor, together with extensive provision of welfare services, reflects the self-perpetuating character of redistributive policies. The case for these continues to be taken for granted, even after it has become plain that to a considerable extent they benefit people other than the supposed beneficiaries.

Old age, ill-health, the bringing-up of children, housing, interruption of earnings, these are contingencies of life to be paid for out of one's income, and for which adults can be expected to provide by saving or insurance. In many western countries, provision for these contingencies has come to be taken over largely by the state. Because the provision cannot be adjusted to the widely differing circumstances of individuals and families, it is apt to be both expensive and unsatisfactory. Such provision is necessarily financed by taxation. As a result, many people's post-tax income becomes like pocket-money, which is not required for major necessities and hazards of life, because these are paid for by taxes largely levied on themselves. This policy treats adults as if they were children. Adults manage incomes: children receive pocket-money. The redistribution of responsibilities implied in the operation of the welfare state means the reduction of the status of adults to that of children.

There is a further result of large-scale redistribution of responsibility between the agents of the state and private individuals, a result which acts as an anomalous and even ominous force for perpetuating and extending the policy. Prudent people, even if poor, can normally provide for the contingencies of life by saving and insurance, but only if the value of money is stable. They are unable to do so when this condition does not hold. The heavy state spending on the welfare state promotes inflation, the erosion of the value of money, a risk against which many people cannot protect themselves, certainly not by saving and insurance.

The difficulty, or impossibility, of protecting themselves effectively leads them to accept or to demand that tax-financed provision for these contingencies should be maintained or extended, even if this is recognised to be unsatisfactory. The result greatly reinforces political, administrative and other sectional interests in perpetuating and extending the welfare system.

Many people receive in subsidies or government services broadly the same amount as they pay in taxes. But the two transfers do not simply cancel out, leaving things unchanged. People subject to them are still unable to escape certain adverse consequences of redistributive policies. First, taxation usually has some disincentive effects, and so may eligibility for subsidies. Second, people's ability to dispose of their incomes has been shifted from themselves to the politicians and officials who design and carry out such policies, and this reduces their range of choice in the disposal of their income.

Proposals for redistribution, supposedly in order to reduce differences in incomes, are also often pretexts for measures for the political or economic benefit of some persons or groups at the expense of others, with no certainty, or even presumption, of a reduction in conventionally measured differences in income. That they do not ensure even approximate economic equality is suggested by the experience of communist countries. International comparisons of the distribution of incomes are fraught with conceptual and statistical problems, some of them intractable. But there are evident wide differences in income in communist countries after decades of communist rule. And in the Soviet Union (a country often thought to be dedicated to the removal of economic differences), the differences in income and living standards are quite as pronounced as in some more market-oriented societies – and this after more than half a century of mass coercion.

Equality of opportunity was until recently the principal theme of egalitarian ideology. For example, many Fabians, notably Tawney, thought that equality of opportunity would result in substantial equality of income; that any remaining differences would reflect merit, and would therefore be widely respected and readily accepted. These ideas by-pass the fundamental and intractable problem behind the central dilemma of egalitarianism: granted that equals should be treated equally, how shall we treat those who are unequally endowed, motivated or placed? For instance, loving parents and a cultivated background benefit those fortunate enough to possess them. Good looks and other such advantages result in unequal opportunities.

An open society, one with *la carrière ouverte aux talents*, is the most familiar interpretation of the ambiguous concept of equality of opportunity. The concept is then certainly and obviously incompatible with substantial equality of income and wealth. This is so because individuals and groups differ in economic aptitudes and motivations. These differences are evident in the rise from poverty to prosperity of countless individuals and groups the world over. They are evident also in the wide and persistent differences in prosperity between religious and ethnic groups in different areas and societies. Instructive examples include the economic success of certain communities in the face of adverse official discrimination, such as Nonconformists, Huguenots and Jews in the west, and the Chinese communities in South-East Asia. An open society may well bring about greater economic and social equality than a closed or caste society, but wide economic differences are bound to emerge and persist in it.

Only the belief that everybody's aptitudes and motivations are the same – a belief which can have sinister consequences – supports the notion that an open society is practically synonymous with economic equality, or at any rate promotes or ensures it. It is extraordinary that this notion should have been entertained for so long, and is often still entertained, when the evidence to the contrary is both overwhelming and obvious.

The idea that the economic aptitudes and motivation of all people are the same derives from the doctrine of the natural equality of man. According to this idea, we are all the same except for differences in money and education; the poor are like the rich except for having less money; and the peoples of the Third World, themselves are all much the same, differ from those of the west only in being poorer.

This scheme of things envisages economic differences between people as being the only difference of any significance. At the same time, it is assumed that the differences can be removed without changing people's behaviour and without affecting their economic performance significantly. The continued belief that the persistence of economic differences in open societies is abnormal or accidental then leads to proposals and measures which go counter to equality before the law or to the maintenance of equality of opportunity – witness educational quotas on a racial basis in the United States and elsewhere.

The champions of equality in the sense of *la carrière ouverte aux talents* used to argue that income differences would be readily accepted once it became clear that they reflected achievement. This assumption, too, is facile. Lack of economic success is apt to be keenly felt and resented when economic achievement is thought to be important, and when failure is thought to result from inadequacy rather than from, say, an accident of birth. When faced with differences of economic achievement in an open society, many people react by denying that success reflects a contribution to society, let alone that it reflects merit. Such reactions have contributed to the denigration of market economies in open societies, because economic differences have persisted in them.

The adverse effects of redistributive policies on economic performance are implied in such expressions as trade-off between efficiency and equity, or between social justice and efficiency. These formulations recognise to some extent that economic activity is not a zero-sum game. But they still disguise the extent to which the outcome of economic processes depends on the performance of people – performance which can be promoted or obstructed by official policy.

I have already noted that it is by no means obvious why it should be unjust that those who produce more should enjoy higher incomes. And attempts to prevent them from doing so will affect adversely the average level of income. It will do so cumulatively because if everybody can expect to receive only something like an average of all incomes, this average itself will fall. A neat example of this process emerged from an experiment designed a few years ago by a teacher in an American university. The students demanded much greater equality in all walks of life, including the grading of their papers. In response to these demands, the teacher announced that from a given date the students would be given equal grades for their weekly papers, and that the grades would be based on the average performance of the class. The experiment brought about a rapid decline in average performance and thus in average grade, because the incentive to work declined greatly.

Because wide income differences have not disappeared in open societies, pressures for their further reduction or elimination have also continued. Hence the demands for increasing the scope and level of what is misleadingly termed redistributive taxation. It is misleading because, as I have noted earlier, it is not a pre-existing income that is being redistributed; rather, part of the incomes produced by some people is confiscated for the benefit of other people, including those who derive political or personal advantage from advocating or administering these arrangements. This last point, that the organisers and administrators of redistribution benefit from it, deserves attention. These beneficiaries are not poor and are indeed often prosperous, so that here also redistribution works in a fashion very different from what is usually assumed.

The imposition of more specific disabilities (additional to progressive taxation) on groups and individuals with cultural and personal characteristics favourable to economic success is now widely advocated and even practised. Special taxation of talented persons has been proposed on the argument that their talents should be regarded as communal property. Such proposals mean conscription of abilities, which is to some extent implicit in progressive taxation as well. The removal of children from their parents, and even attempted manipulation of the genetic code, have also been suggested as instruments for the promotion of equality, though dismissed at any rate for the time being. Quotas handicapping the ambitious and the gifted have already been widely adopted in higher education and in certain areas of economic activity in the United States.

There may be a further reason for the attempts to control and standardise the social and personal determinants of economic differences, as distinct from the attempts to equalise net incomes. An income serves two functions. First, it enables its recipient to buy goods and services. Second, it is an indicator of achievement, and a mark of recognition and status. The former rôle depends on net income. If differences in recognition or status are considered objectionable, this sets up pressure for equalising incomes before tax, and thus for controlling and standardising the factors behind them.

Attempts to minimise economic differences in an open and free society necessarily involve the use of coercive power. They politicise economic life: economic activity comes to depend largely on political decisions, and the incomes of people and their economic *modus vivendi* come increasingly under the control of politicians and civil servants. The extent of these consequences will depend on the degree of economic equality the rulers wish to achieve; and also on the capacities, ambitions and circumstances of the groups and individuals between whom economic differences are to be curtailed or abolished.

Extensive politicisation of life enhances the prizes of political power and thus the stakes in the fight for it. This outcome in turn intensifies political tension, at least until opposition is effectively demoralised, or forcibly suppressed. And because people's economic fortunes come to depend so much on political and administrative decisions, their talents and energies are diverted from economic activity to political life, sometimes from choice and often from necessity. These consequences are manifest in many societies, especially in multiracial societies.

In numerous countries, politicisation of life, often pursued in the name of equality, now means that the question of who are the rulers has become a matter of the greatest importance. The effect on people's fears, feelings and conduct is observable in many countries where there is some ethnic diversity, including the United Kingdom. It stands out starkly in the heterogeneous societies of the Third World, where the conduct of the rulers is often a matter of life and death for millions of people. The ferocity of the political struggle in many Third World countries cannot be understood without an awareness of the politicisation of life there. This process has been helped along by the slogans of equality, and reinforced by the idea that high incomes, especially of minorities, have not been earned but have been taken by them from other people.

When the inequality in political power between rulers and subjects is pronounced, conventional measurements of incomes and living standards cannot even remotely convey the substance of the situation. Such measurements greatly understate the realities of inequality in the society, in which the rulers can command the resources available practically at will. They may use their power to secure for themselves large incomes; or they may choose austere forms of life. They still have vast power over the lives of their subjects, which they can use to secure higher living standards for themselves whenever they wish. Dzerzhinski, Nasser and Nyerere have been among rulers whose relatively simple mode of life has elicited sycophantic adulation from their admirers. But their simple mode of life has not prevented them from combining it with the ruthless exercise of their virtually unlimited power over their subjects.

It is now widely urged that differences in income and living standards should be reduced or eliminated not only within countries but between them, and indeed even globally. There are the proposals for a New International Economic Order approved by the General Assembly of the United Nations. Because of the enormous and stubborn differences between peoples, policies designed to equalise their living standards would require world government with totalitarian powers. Such a government, to be equal to its ambitions, would be even more coercive and brutal than the totalitarian governments of individual countries.

The various adverse and often sinister consequences of the politicisation of life promoted by egalitarianism are widely ignored or swept under the carpet, even when they are both pronounced and evident. A major reason for this neglect is that egalitarians, including many academics, are more interested in advocating the removal of economic differences than in enquiring what is behind them; that is, how they have come about. Yet the background is indispensable for an understanding of the situations to which egalitarians address themselves, and for an assessment of the implications and results of egalitarian policies.

Economic differences are largely the result of people's capacities and motivations. This is evident in open societies, and also where societies are not open, nor yet completely closed or caste-bound. A disproportionate number of the poor lack the capabilities and inclination for economic achievement, and often for cultural achievement as well. Weak members of a society need to be helped. But large-scale penalisation of productive groups for the benefit of the materially and culturally less productive, and for the benefit of those who administer wealth transfers, impairs the prospects of a society. This outcome is especially likely when the less productive receive support without stigma and, indeed, as of right; and even more so when those who are more productive are made to feel guilty on that account. These are precisely the stances and attitudes prominent in the advocacy and practices of redistribution.

The terminology of the negative income tax reflects the acceptance of the principle of support without stigma. The payment of income tax is a statutory obligation. A negative income tax is the inverse: the right to an income regardless of performance, simply by virtue of being alive and poor.

Personal and group differences in economic aptitudes and motivations are likely to disappoint the expectation that guarantee of a cash income would make it possible to abolish specific welfare services. These services will still have to be supplied to the many recipients of cash payments who will nevertheless fail to provide for the contingencies of life. Such people are likely to be disproportionately represented among the recipients of negative income tax. In Britain this is suggested, for instance, by the prevalence of avoidable ill-health and dental decay among children of unskilled workers who own television sets.

Many recipients of both domestic and international wealth transfers are paupers, in the traditional sense of persons dependent on official charity. But because the support is given as of right and even envisaged as restitution for past wrongs, the paupers can not only insist on these transfers, but can attempt also to prescribe the political conduct of the donors. This is evident in the advocacy of international wealth transfers from the west to the Third World.

Some modern egalitarians seem readier than their predecessors to recognise personal and group differences in economic endowment and in motivation. This acknowledgement brings into the open previously ignored dilemmas. The recognition of such differences has also induced these egalitarians to advocate the elimination not only of economic differences but also of differences in aptitudes and motivations; that is, the causes of economic differences. Hence some of the policies and drastic proposals noted above.

Although acknowledgement of the determinants of economic differences has helped to clarify some central issues and dilemmas of egalitarian policies, in other ways the level of discourse has remained unsatisfactory. Indeed, in recent decades the standard may even have deteriorated.

The uncritical reliance on statistics in egalitarian discourse and policies provides a major illustration. There is, for instance, the familiar practice of expressing the income or wealth of a small proportion of the population of a country as a percentage of the income or wealth of the whole population. The misleading, even meaningless, nature of this practice should be evident. Thus children have no incomes, or very low incomes; people normally cannot make appreciable savings until well into middle age; and many married women have no cash incomes or only low cash incomes. Income differences need to be expressed on a basis which separates the different age groups, and also men from women. In technical language, the differences have to be expressed on an age or sex-standardised basis.

Further complexities and ambiguities ensue if we compare family incomes. A childless couple is likely to have a higher per capita income than a family with children. But it does not follow that the former is better off. The conventional method of calculating the national income implies that children are simply an unavoidable cost or burden, and assumes that people do not enjoy the generation and possession of children sufficiently to outweigh any differences in income per capita. It also results in paradoxes, such as the recording in many conventional national income calculations of the birth of a calf or the survival of a cow as an increase in per capita income, while the birth or survival of a child is registered as a diminution. Further problems arise over the definition of 'capita'. For example, should a child be treated as equivalent to half an adult? Moreover, conventional income comparisons do not distinguish adequately between income and the cost of securing income, for instance in such contexts as the cost of training, or of enjoyment foregone in training, or in long hours of work, or in the cost of travel to and from work. And professional people who have invested heavily in training which has enabled them to earn high incomes are disadvantaged in terms of real income compared with those who have used their time to learn to do things such as household repairs for themselves – a consideration of some significance when direct taxation and the cost of labour-intensive services are high.

State-provided or guaranteed pensions represent another

example of the intractable conceptual difficulties behind assessment of economic differences. Such pensions can be very valuable to particular individuals, and they represent the equivalent of large capital sums, notably when they are index-linked. But they are unmarketable and thus cannot be turned into capital. And their value depends on the ability and willingness of future governments to honour them.

Finally, we come to a wide issue, mentioned briefly earlier in this essay, which is crucial to an examination of income differences and changes. Even when income statistics are free of problems of concept and measurement, which is unusual, by themselves they tell us nothing about the background of the situation they reflect. It is indispensable for sensible assessment and policy to know why people are poor and how income differences have arisen. For instance, those who are poor through crippling disease or unavoidable or uninsurable accident, or erosion of savings through inflation, need to be treated differently from those people whose poverty has resulted from persistent overspending of large incomes. Again, incomes can become more equal as a result of more people dying or being forcibly sterilised. Yet conventional terminology describes the result as an 'improvement in income distribution'. Conversely, if more very poor people live longer, this registers as a so-called worsening of income distribution.

Some policies, popular beliefs and mores affect income differences between societies so greatly that they are central to any sensible discussion on such differences. The many obvious examples include the persecution of productive groups in Asia and Africa; the subordination of economic advance to egalitarian objectives as in Britain; the refusal to take animal life as in South Asia; or to let women work outside the home as in many Muslim countries. These pertinent matters are freely ignored by advocates of global redistribution who focus entirely on conventionally measured income differences. Altogether, we have become so preoccupied with quantifiable matters that even such an obvious distinction (and one formerly well-recognised) as that between sturdy beggars and needy poor has come to be neglected or even derided by egalitarians.

Disregard of such basic matters reflects the naive belief that statistics denote facts more effectively and more exactly than does qualitative description, or even that statistics alone objectively depict social facts. These habits of mind are of a piece with Mr Gradgrind's attitude in Dickens's *Hard Times*.[2]

Neglect of the time dimension of historical processes frequent in contemporary discourse (which I have briefly mentioned earlier) in references to international income differences is another highly misleading practice. Incomes and living standards in the west are the outcome of many centuries of cultural and economic progress; they have not come about in one or two generations. It is therefore not surprising, abnormal or reprehensible that many Third World countries (notably in Africa) which do not have centuries of progress behind them should have much lower incomes than the twentieth-century west. The pertinence of this long period of antecedent development is ignored in the advocacy of global redistribution. It is ignored also in the insistence that Third World countries should promptly reach western levels of income by a process of virtually instant development. This insistence is apt to issue in coercive policies in these countries, which not only inhibit a rise in living standards but also provoke social tension, or even upheaval, as well as political conflict.

Redistribution of income and reduction of poverty are often thought to be interchangeable concepts. Indeed, it is often taken for granted that egalitarian policies necessarily improve the condition of the poor. This is not so. The promotion of economic equality and the alleviation of poverty are distinct and often conflicting. To make the rich poorer does not make the poor richer.

The advocates of egalitarian policies focus on relative income differences, or the relative positions of different groups. They thereby divert attention from the causes of poverty, especially the causes which underlie real hardship; and from the possibilities of effective remedial measures. Relief of poverty, especially the improvement in the position of the very poor, has nothing to do with the pursuit of equality. Egalitarian policies often ignore the poor, especially those who are self-reliant and enterprising.

Except perhaps over very short periods, redistributive policies are much more likely to depress the living standards of the poor than to raise them. The extensive politicisation brought about by large-scale redistribution diverts people's energies and ambitions

from productive economic activity to politics and public administration, and also to attempts to benefit from politically-organised
redistribution, or to escape its consequences. An even more evident result is that these policies systematically transfer resources
from people who are economically productive to others who are
less so. Thus, such policies inhibit the rise in incomes and living
standards, including those of the poor.

Besides these results of wide egalitarian policies, many specific
measures thought to be egalitarian often benefit middle income
groups at the expense both of the rich and the poor. This is the
likely result of such policies as, for instance, the granting of
privileges to trade unions, official prescription of minimal wages,
the imposition of rent controls, restrictive licensing of enterprises,
legislation for the promotion of so-called equal opportunities,
and heavy direct taxation of persons and of enterprises.

In sum, the pursuit of economic equality is more likely to
harm than to benefit the living standards of the very poor by
politicising life, by restricting the accumulation and effective
deployment of capital, by obstructing social and economic
mobility at all levels, and by inhibiting enterprise in many different ways. Continued poverty, whether resulting from *soi-disant*
egalitarian measures or from other causes, then serves as plausible argument or rationalisation for further and more stringent
egalitarianism. These repercussions are necessarily ignored when
the promotion of equality and the alleviation of poverty are
regarded as identical.

Disregard of the restriction of the opportunities of the poor
brought about by such policies is promoted by a curious asym-
metrical application of that environmental determinism which
underlies so much contemporary discourse of social affairs. The
poor are seen as helpless victims of their environment, as people
at the mercy of external forces and without wills of their own.
The implication is that they are without the primary human
characteristic of responsibility. This determinism, however, does
not extend to the rich. They are seen as having wills of their own
which are, however, deployed for selfish and even villainous
ends. Poverty is thus a condition caused by external forces and
not by personal conduct. Wealth, on the other hand, is the result

of conduct which is purposeful but reprehensible. The poor are seen as passive but virtuous, the rich as active but wicked.

This picture is painted by certain groups who regard themselves as standing apart from rich and poor, and perhaps as above both. They are, in the main, politicians, social reformers, welfare administrators, social scientists, writers, artists, media people, churchmen and even entertainers. They now form much of what was once called the political nation. In the advocacy of redistribution and its altogether misleading identification with the relief of poverty, a significant section of this new political nation operates in a manner which has been termed (I believe, by Dr R. M. Hartwell of Oxford University) the redistribution industry.

Many members of these groups, especially politicians, academics and media men, have in recent decades done much to articulate, institutionalise and organise envy and resentment against economically effective people. Envy and resentment may be as old as mankind;[3] but especially in the west and in westernised Third World countries, these sentiments seem nowadays more insistent, persistent and extensive than they had been formerly. Politicians and intellectuals have supplied articulation and a veneer of intellectual respectability to envy and resentment. They have argued that economic differences are abnormal and reprehensible, and also that they result from exploitation. And they have also advanced the cause of more esoteric arguments such as that of the diminishing marginal utility of money, and also by encouraging preoccupation with quantifiable matters, especially conventionally measured income differences. Also, the confirmation of spurious legitimacy on envy and resentment has been made easier by the wide-spread feeling of guilt. Unless arguments and rationalisations, which have played such a part in the articulation of envy and resentment in the name of equality, are exposed effectively, they may do irreparable damage to the prospects of a free and open society.

Notes

1. A full assessment of changes in income differences over time is a complex exercise which requires examination of inter-generation as well as intra-generation changes, that is, changes in income differences between generations as well as those within a generation. The

introduction of more than one generation into the analysis also implies that the income-receiving group must be thought of as extending beyond the family. (Otherwise consideration of more than one generation would imply marriages between brothers and sisters.) Take the case where group A and group B are drawn from the same generation, and let us assume that, whatever the relative position of A and B in any single year, the aggregated lifetime income of A exceeds that of B. In other words, there is a clear intra-generation difference. Now let us contrast two opposing situations: in the first, group A descendants have larger incomes than group B descendants but in the second the reverse is the case. We need not concern ourselves at this stage with the reasons why differences in incomes between specified groups may continue between generations or be reversed. But we can already note certain consequences. Taking first and second generation circumstances together, we clearly have a far less unequal income situation in the second case than in the first. Or, putting the same argument in another way, it is not sufficient to confine oneself to lifetime income comparisons: one needs also to know whether such differences are perpetuated or reversed over generations if we are to have a fully rounded view of income differences or inequalities in a society. (In the same way, unemployment statistics mean very different things if they relate to two people being out of work for short periods rather than to one for a long period.

2. 'Now, what I want is Facts. Teach these boys and girls nothing but Facts. Facts alone are wanted in life. Plant nothing else, and root out everything else. You can only form the minds of reasoning animals upon Facts, nothing else will ever be of any service to them. This is the principle on which I bring up my own children, and this is the principle on which I bring up these children. Stick to Facts, sir!'

3. The antiquity and ubiquity of envy is the major theme of Helmut Schoek's massive treatise, *Envy: A Theory of Social Behaviour* (London, 1970; New York, 1970).

Hugh Dalton

Some Aspects of the Inequality of Incomes in Modern Communities

'The problem of poverty' is an economic commonplace. On its existence and importance, though not upon its solution, all thoughtful persons are agreed.

The word poverty, as commonly used, implies a contrast. It signifies a failure, through insufficiency of income, to reach a certain standard of economic welfare. This standard may be either a standard which *is in fact reached* by certain communities, or sections of communities, or a standard which, it is thought, *should be reached*, if life, from an economic point of view, is to be worth living.

Thus, on the one hand, we speak of the poverty of the inhabitants of India, as compared with those of Great Britain, or of the worst paid workers in Great Britain, as compared with the working classes in general, or of the working classes in general as compared with 'the rich'; or, on the other hand, we speak of the poverty of certain sections of the population, as compared with a standard which is held to be 'reasonable', or with a standard measured by the purchasing power of a 'living wage', however defined.

Further, it accords with common knowledge and common usage to say that, in almost all modern communities, there exists great poverty side by side with great wealth. In the United Kingdom, for example, it was estimated before the war that half the total income of the community went to about 12 per cent, and a third of the total income to about 3 per cent, of the population.[1]

The contrast between wealth and poverty, based upon the size of incomes, is heightened by the contrast between different methods of obtaining income and, in particular, between active work and passive ownership. It is again a commonplace that, while the great majority of incomes, and especially of small incomes, are only obtained by hard work, many of the larger incomes are obtained with little or no work on the part of their recipients. It results, in the words of an Italian economist, that in modern communities 'some live without working and others work without living'.[2]

The degree of acquiescence with which these facts have generally been regarded may surprise the philosopher, as it would assuredly surprise a visitor from some happier planet, where such strong contrasts were unknown. The acquiescence of the more fortunate classes does not, perhaps, need much explanation. It is common to find even reflective men of good will regarding the economic arrangements under which they prosper as being better than any practicable alternative, and attributing a great part of their own prosperity to their own merits. To others acquiescence comes even more easily, though it may sometimes be tinged with a sense of insecurity. 'The shallow rich,' says Bagshot, who was a shrewd observer but no revolutionary, 'talk much of the turbulence of the poor and their tendency to agitate. But it is the patience of the poor that most strikes those who know them'.[3] Yet what seems like conscious patience is often the almost unconscious acquiescence of habit, that 'enormous flywheel of society, its most precious conservative agent, which alone keeps us within the bounds of ordinance, and saves the children of fortune from the envious uprisings of the poor'.[4] Nor is this all. 'One must remember the stuff of which life is made. One must consider what an overwhelming preponderance of the most tenacious energies and most concentrated interests of a society must be absorbed between material cares and the solicitude of the affections . . . Men and women have to live. The task for most of them is arduous enough to make them well pleased with even such imperfect shelter as they find in the use and wont of daily existence'.[5] The more arduous the task, the less the opportunity for discontent, or even for reflection. Only when men have a surplus of energy over and above that necessary for earning a living, have they the time, or the power, or the spirit, to take stock of their condition and to ponder large projects of improvement.

The majority of mankind have always been poor,[6] and nearly always acquiescent in their poverty.[7] Such is the general evidence of history. But recent years have seen in many countries a perceptible and widespread change, a stirring of the mud of acquiescence, if nothing more. The general causes of this 'unrest', as it is vaguely called, cannot be adequately discussed here, but certain aspects of the modern movement of opinion, of which this unrest is a symbol, may be shortly noticed.

In the first place, the thought of ordinary people concerning the economic structure of society is becoming both more comprehensive and more critical. The kindred forces of education and 'agitation' are powerful, and their power is increased by the growth of great cities, where intercourse and the circulation of ideas are easy. And, as common thought becomes more comprehensive, the larger economic contrasts are more clearly realised, and, as it becomes more critical, these contrasts are more sharply called in question. Modern social classes are chiefly defined by differences of income, and modern sentiment is increasingly opposed to large inequalities between classes. There is, indeed, an appreciable movement of adults from class to class, and a still more appreciable movement of children into other classes than those of their parents. Such mobility does something no doubt to weaken resentment at the inequalities between classes. But the mobility will need to grow much greater, and the inequalities much smaller, before such resentment can be expected to disappear.

At the present time the opinion steadily gains ground that there is at least a presumption against all economic inequality. Inequality, according to this view, is not necessarily, nor in all cases, an evil, and even where it is admittedly an evil, it may none the less be the least of alternative evils. But 'inequality is always on the defensive, and the greater and more lasting it is, the more difficult is its defence'.[8] The possessors of abnormally swollen incomes are coming more and more to be regarded as somewhat unwholesome economic freaks.

In the second place, we may notice the growth of a spirit, which those who dislike it call 'materialist'. A heavier and more deliberate stress is laid upon the importance of economic conditions. He, upon whom the economic forces of this world press hardly, is less satisfied than of old with the promise of better times beyond the grave. He wants to enjoy them now.

In the third place, in proportion as forms of government grow more democratic, the poor are liable to experience more acutely a sense of divided personality. Political equality, but economic inequality; political sovereignty, some would say, but economic subjection! The wide diffusion of political power acts, no doubt, as a check on counsels of violence. But it acts no less strongly, in the long run, as a stimulus to levelling policies, to be achieved by political means.

Finally, it is no longer believed, if indeed it ever was, except by a few, that great economic inequalities tend to disappear 'of themselves', that any 'invisible hand' removes them, while human hands are folded in passive expectation, that any 'economic harmonies' dissolve them, while men go plodding along the beaten tracks of their fathers. On the contrary, it is constantly asserted and widely believed that 'the rich are growing richer and the poor poorer',[9] and the development of modern society seems to be marked, in many directions, by increasing disharmonies, both economic and psychological, between man and his environment.[10]

And thus it could be truly said eight years ago that 'today we are in a temper to reconstruct economic society, as we were once in a temper to reconstruct political society.'[11] Upon that temper came the impact of four years of war, shattering, agonising, embittering, disillusioning beyond the possibility of estimate. The full effects of that impact will gradually unfold themselves. But some things are clear now. In some countries the survivors of the fighting have been promised 'a land fit for heroes', and are busily searching for it. In others the old economic structure of society has collapsed already and the new structure, which will eventually replace it, is likely to differ widely from the old. In no country, it may safely be said, has the war failed to quicken men's criticism of the social order, and to strengthen their intolerance of all sharp economic contrasts, which appear to them to lack justification. Rather does it seem that throughout the world 'there is a great tide flowing in the hearts of men', which will wash against the foundations of inequality, wherever they may be found, and may flow so strongly as to carry away many familiar landmarks.[12] In such a situation there is both great promise of good and great danger of evil and, in order to realise the former and avoid the latter, each member of the community should make the contribution of thought and effort, of which he is most capable. Among the contributions which a student of economic science can best make is an attempt to solve some of those outstanding problems of economic cause and effect, which are relevant to the contrast of wealth and poverty, but for which complete solutions have not yet been found. This essay is an attempt of this kind.

Human welfare is divisible into economic, or material, welfare on the one hand and, on the other hand, various kinds of welfare which are not economic. This division will be sufficiently intelligible without further discussion, though by the nature of things the dividing line is not clear cut.[13]

The relative importance which should be attached to economic and non-economic welfare, and the probable effects of changes in economic welfare upon welfare as a whole, have been much disputed. But modern opinion, in the civilised countries of the western world at any rate, seems to hold with increasing strength that economic welfare is of very great importance, both for its own sake and as a means to other sorts of welfare, which may often be of even greater intrinsic importance, and further that an increase in economic welfare is generally likely to cause an increase in human welfare as a whole. Man does not live by bread alone, but without bread he cannot live at all, and without a sufficiency of bread he cannot even hope to live worthily. Moreover, the burden of proof rests upon those who assert that, in any particular case, an increase of economic welfare diminishes welfare in the widest sense. With this view of things I personally have no quarrel, and I shall adopt it in what follows.

Income consists of the means of economic welfare,[14] and great inequality of incomes in any community implies great inequality in the economic welfare attained by different individuals. But this is not all. For it implies also considerable waste of potential economic welfare. Put broadly, and in the language of common sense, the case against large inequalities of income is that the less urgent needs of the rich are satisfied, while the more urgent needs of the poor are left unsatisfied. The rich are more than amply fed, while the poor go hungry. This is merely an application of the economists' law of diminishing marginal utility, which states that, other things being equal, as the quantity of any commodity or, more generally, of purchasing power, increases, its total utility increases, but its marginal utility diminishes. An unequal distribution of a given amount of purchasing power among a given number of people is, therefore, likely to be a wasteful distribution from the point of view of economic welfare, and the more unequal the distribution the greater the waste. Up to a certain point, the more equal the distribution, the further a given amount is likely to go in satisfying economic needs, and hence in increasing economic welfare.

Where, however, is this point? An absolutely equal division of a given income, whether between individuals or between families, will obviously fall a long way short of making the economic welfare derivable from this given income a maximum. The ideal distribution would rather be a distribution according to the capacity of individuals, or families, to make a good use of income. This ideal is very far from realisation in the actual world. To mention two obvious details only, it requires not only that many of the young should be richer, and some of the old poorer, than they now are, but that those who have the power of making money should have also, far more than now, the gift of spending it well. Furthermore, the capacity to make good use of income can only be developed, in any high degree, by the habitual handling of an income larger than that to which a considerable part of mankind ever attain throughout their lives. It is only through opportunities of spending income as they will that people can learn to spend income well. It is clear, however, without labouring the matter further, that a large reduction in the existing inequality could be made, which would result in bringing us considerably nearer to the ideal.

So far we have been considering the ideal distribution of a given income among a given number of people, and it has appeared that, though absolute equality of incomes is not desirable, yet a large reduction in the inequality found in modern communities would increase economic welfare. This conclusion may obviously need qualification, if such a reduction of inequality causes either a reduction of the total income to be divided, or an increase in the number of people relatively to the total income to be divided among them. The fear that an increase in the incomes of the poorer classes would stimulate the growth of their numbers and lead to 'over population' and a consequent reduction of these incomes of their old, or even to a lower, level was much in the minds of the early Victorian economists.[15] But in the civilised countries of the western world at the present time this fear seems groundless, though among Eastern peoples it may still be otherwise. In the modern communities of the west, however, the evidence available seems to show conclusively that an increase in the economic welfare of any class tends to lower rather than to raise its rate of numerical increase.[16]

The danger that certain methods of reducing inequality might check production is very much more serious, and is the chief objection to many far-reaching projects of economic change. Thus Sidgwick tersely observed, 'I object to socialism, not because it would divide the produce of industry badly, but because it would have so much less to divide.'[17] The effects upon production of any change which would reduce inequality must be considered in each particular case upon their merits before we can decide whether or not such a change would increase economic welfare. It may safely be asserted, however, that many changes, which would reduce inequality, would also stimulate production. Further, economic welfare may sometimes be increased by changes which, while reducing inequality, tend to check production, provided that the check is not severe, and still more, provided that it is only temporary. In Marshall's words, 'a slight and temporary check to the accumulation of material wealth need not necessarily be an evil, even from a purely economic point of view, if, being made quietly and without disturbance, it provided better opportunities for the great mass of the people, increased their efficiency, and developed in them such habits of self-respect as to result in the growth of a much more efficient race of producers in the next generation. For then it might do more in the long run to promote the growth of even material wealth than great additions to our stock of factories and steam-engines'.[18]

The proposition that economic welfare is increased by an increase in production per head is subject to a further qualification, which is often insufficiently recognised. The economic ideal here is evidently not maximum production, but such a relation between product on the one hand and the efforts and sacrifices involved in production on the other, as to yield a maximum of economic welfare.[19] As the productive power of a community grows, the importance of reducing the subjective cost of production increases relatively to the importance of increasing the product. Further, the distribution of the total subjective cost in modern communities is, like the distribution of income, exceedingly unequal, and just as economic welfare will be increased, other things being equal, by a reduction in the inequality of incomes, so it will be increased by a reduction in the inequality of subjective cost borne by different individuals.[20] This inequality of subjective cost is specially great in modern communities, owing to the fact that incomes derived from property involve practically no subjective cost when the property has been received by inheritance or gift, and often comparatively little when the property is based upon savings made by the recipient, while, of course, the subjective cost of obtaining incomes from work bears no regular relation to their size, but is often exceedingly heavy for some of the smallest incomes, and is reduced for many of the larger by the intrinsic interest of the work and the comparative independence of the worker. One method of diminishing subjective costs is to increase leisure, provided that work is not more than proportionately speeded up during the shorter working hours. And of leisure, as of income, it may be laid down that the ideal distribution is according to the capacity of individuals to make a good use of it. From which it follows that, other things being equal, both an increase in leisure and a decrease in the inequality of its distribution will increase economic welfare.

The comparative importance of a further increase in production, of a diminution in the inequality of incomes, of a diminution in the subjective cost involved in production, and of a diminution in the inequality of subjective cost borne by different individuals, will vary in different stages of a community's economic development and will always depend to some extent upon individual opinion.[21] In even the wealthiest communities a considerable increase in productive power is still necessary before a point will be reached, at which an approximately equal distribution of income and a large general reduction of subjective costs will provide, according to modern standards, a reasonably high level of economic welfare.[22] For a while, though not, we may hope, for ever, a serious check to production would be a high price to pay for an improvement in the other main factors of economic welfare. This consideration makes it all the more important to discover methods of improvement in these other factors, which shall actually stimulate production.[23]

It remains to notice that among certain sections of the workers in modern communities, there is growing up, alongside of the resentment at the contrasts of wealth and poverty, a resentment at the contrasts of economic function which are found in the modern industrial system.[24] Objection is taken, not only to the fact that large numbers of workers receive a comparatively small share of the total product of industry, but also to the fact that they exercise comparatively little control over the management of the industries in which they are employed. These two objections are sometimes combined in the objection, not indeed very happily phrased, to working 'in order to make unlimited profits for private capitalists'. Of this resentment at contrasts of economic function Mr Justice Sankey in the Second Report of the Coal Commission of 1919 wrote: 'Half a century of education has produced in the workers of the coalfields far more than a desire for the material advantages of higher wages and shorter hours. They have now, in many cases and to an ever increasing extent, a higher ambition of taking their due share and interest in the direction of the industry to the success of which they, too, are contributing'.[25] And this ambition is not confined to workers in the coalfields.

The idea of increased 'control of industry' by the workers employed in each industry takes various forms, and has been worked out in various ways. It is one of the dynamic ideas of this generation and raises important issues, in relation both to economic and to non-economic welfare. No modern student of economic science can afford to neglect it. But it does not fall within the scope of this essay. It has been claimed by enthusiastic advocates of this idea that 'the question of poverty has now given place to the question of status', but this is an exaggeration. The problem of poverty will continue to exercise men's thoughts, as long as the fact of poverty remains a reality, and the idea of a more equal distribution of an increasing income obtained with diminishing effort will not easily be surpassed in practical importance or in vividness of appeal to modern minds.

In the last section the inequality of incomes was considered in relation to economic welfare. In this section it will be considered in relation to the idea of justice. This division corresponds to Professor Cannan's distinction between considerations of economy and considerations of equity.[25]

The conception of justice has been the subject of agelong dispute, and the statement of ideals, and especially of economic ideals, in terms of justice seldom leads to clear practical conclusions.[26] More often it leads to moral indignation without reflection, to the enthusiastic assertion of inconsistencies, or to such absurd bravado as that of the old Roman who cried *'fiat justitia, ruat cœlum!'* – 'Let justice be done, though it should bring down the sky upon our heads!' But if the sky *had* fallen and had proved as heavy as the physicists of those days imagined it to be, just and unjust Romans would have been overwhelmed together, and the just might plausibly have complained of the injustice of their fate.

For the purpose of our present enquiry, it is important to answer two questions. First, how far, if at all, are current canons of economic justice regarding the distribution of incomes in conflict with the canons of economic welfare discussed in the last section, and second, in so far as there is no such conflict, does the idea of economic justice lead us to any important practical conclusions in addition to those reached in the last section?

Essay V of Mill's *Utilitarianism*, 'On the Connection between Justice and Utility', suggests a clue to the answers we are seeking. 'People find it difficult to see in justice,' says Mill, 'only a particular kind or branch of utility',[27] but in truth justice is no more than 'a name for certain moral requirements, which, regarded collectively, stand higher in the scale of social utility, and are of more paramount obligation than any others'.[28] According to this view, the sphere of justice is included within the sphere of social utility, or, as some would prefer to say, of social welfare. Nothing is just which does not increase welfare, but, out of the aggregate of actions which increase welfare, some, which increase it in a specially high degree, may be classed together as just.

Thus Mill distinguishes justice from mere beneficence or generosity. 'Justice implies something which it is not only right to do, and wrong not to do, but which some individual person can claim from us as his moral right'.[29] The practical question at issue might, therefore, be restated in this form. What classes of actions which increase welfare may justly be demanded by individuals as their moral rights and, in particular, what public policies which increase welfare may be justly demanded by individuals from society? This view of justice is fatal to the formula *'fiat justitia ruat cœlum'*, except on the assumption that, if the sky were to fall, welfare would be increased.

We may now consider, in the light of their probable effects upon economic welfare, various current ideas of justice, which bear on the problem of the ideal distribution of income. These ideas fall into two groups, according as they do, or do not, offer a complete solution of this problem. Among those that offer only an incomplete solution, we may here notice two, namely the positive idea that it is just that all workers should receive a 'living wage', and the negative idea that it is unjust to 'disappoint legitimate expectations'.

In common usage a living wage means a wage which will enable a worker to live and bring up a family at the lowest standard of comfort which modern opinion regards as 'reasonable' or 'tolerable for human beings'. This is a very vague and fragmentary conception. It is vague, because it is defined by reference to a standard of reasonableness, which is itself not only vague, but liable to arbitrary change. It is fragmentary, because it takes account of wages only and not of other factors in the worker's standard of life, such as leisure and healthy conditions of employment and housing. Further it only offers an incomplete solution of the problem of ideal distribution of income, assuming that all workers have at least a living wage, it is just that great inequalities of income, due to the inheritance of property and other causes, should continue.

The principle of the living wage, as commonly interpreted, is not inconsistent with the canons of economic welfare. But it is less comprehensive and less easy to apply. The principle of the National Minimum, which is conceived with reference to economic welfare as a whole, includes it and much more besides, and is to be preferred as a guide to practical policy.

The disappointment of legitimate expectations is often said to be unjust. It was this conception of justice which led the Rugby schoolboy to say of Temple that he was 'a beast, but a just beast'. It is, of course, often very difficult to decide what expectations *are* legitimate.[30] But it is obvious that, in normal times, any large and sudden interference with economic expectations, which, whether legitimate or not, have become firmly established in men's minds, creates a sense of insecurity, which tends to check production and thus to diminish economic welfare.[31] Considerations of economic welfare carry us thus far, and the doctrine of legitimate expectations carries us no further, in the pursuit of practical conclusions.

This doctrine is, in any case, purely negative and cannot furnish any positive solution of the problem of ideal distribution. In practice, this and similar notions of justice act only as slowly yielding obstacles to new ideas, as somewhat undiscriminating 'brakes upon the wheels of change'. They supply no positive guidance as to the form which change should take.

We may now go on to consider various competing principles of economic justice, which do offer complete solutions of our problem. The two main principles here are 'distribution according to deserts' and 'distribution according to needs'. But at least three rival interpretations of 'distribution according to deserts' are commonly met with. The first is absolute equality of incomes, the second is distribution according to the value of work done, provided that 'equality of opportunity' is first secured, the third is distribution according to the value of work done in the existing state of society.[32]

Absolute equality of incomes, as an ideal of economic justice, has found few weighty advocates. It requires no lengthy argument to prove that an absolutely equal distribution, whether among families or among individuals, is in fact quite impracticable, and that, even if it could be realised in the modern world, it would inflict vast damage on economic welfare. It would, indeed, be a typical application of the shallow precept *'fiat justitia, ruat cœlum!'* 'Perfect equality,' as Bentham says, 'is a chimera, all we can do is to diminish inequality.'

The rejection of crude equalitarianism does not, however, take us far, though there are some who seem to think that, when they have disposed of the argument for absolute equality, they have disposed also of all arguments for reducing existing inequalities.[33]

Given equality of opportunity, distribution according to the value of work done appears to many to be just. Many, therefore, hold that equality of opportunity is just. 'The firm basis of government,' said President Wilson in his Inaugural Address to the people of the United States in 1913, 'is justice, not pity; and equality of opportunity is the first essential of justice in the body politic.'

If we are to use words strictly, it is obvious that absolute equality of economic opportunity is no more attainable in the real world than absolute equality of incomes.

'A logical individualism requires a fair start and an equal opportunity for each individual *within the period of his own life*, whereas the actual unit, the family, is all the time doing its utmost to abolish the boundaries between life and death and to give its own members, with the aid of the dead hand as well as the living, a long lead and a safe retreat.'[34] To alter this state of things, so as to secure absolute equality of opportunity, we should need effectively to prohibit all inheritances and bequests, all gifts from one person to another, and all expenditure, in excess of a small prescribed maximum, by parents on the education and upbringing of their children. Indeed we should need to go further, and to take all children away from their parents as soon as possible after birth and lodge them in public institutions. For a child's opportunity in life depends intimately upon the conditions and surroundings in which its early years are spent. Such policies are, of course, fantastic. If it were practicable to carry them into effect, which obviously it is not, nearly all motives for saving and many motives for exertion would disappear, and economic welfare would gravely suffer. Fantastic, therefore, would be an unconditional demand, in the name of justice, for equality of opportunity. It would once more be a cry of *'fiat justitia, ruat cœlum.'*

But, though the establishment of perfect equality of opportunity is impracticable, there are many practicable policies which will make opportunities far more nearly equal than they are to-day in most modern communities.[35] Wisely carried out, such policies will increase economic welfare both by diminishing the inequality of incomes and by increasing production.

Equality of opportunity, then, is defensible conditionally by reference to considerations of economic welfare. It is not defensible unconditionally be reference to considerations of justice. But the greater the approach towards equality of opportunity, the more reasonable the contention that a distribution according to the value of work done is just.

In communities where rough equality of opportunities prevails, and where men recognise that it prevails, economic contrasts are likely to cause less resentment than elsewhere. Such rough equality is found at certain stages in the development of new countries, when nearly all large incomes are due, not to inheritance, nor to a superior education, but to the labour and fortunate enterprise of their possessors, and when all men have an almost equal chance to make their way. But no community has hitherto succeeded in maintaining such a state of things for long.

The justice of distribution according to the value of work done in the existing state of society in an old country is a doctrine which it is hard to render plausible. For inequalities in the value of work done are here largely due to unequal opportunities of doing work that is valuable, and a social order which permits great inequalities of opportunity is, as we have seen, widely held to be itself essentially unjust.

Further, in most interpretations of this doctrine, 'work done' is taken to include all economic services rendered to society, and all owners of property are held to render services in proportion to the income which society permits them to receive. Such an interpretation is necessary, if the doctrine is to cover incomes from property. Now, though it is clear enough that he who saves renders a service to society by adding to the stock of existing capital and hence to society's productive power, it is by no means clear that he who inherits property, or he who merely happens to own property, which, through no action of his own, increases in value, necessarily renders any service at all. Many thoughtful people find it hard to believe that merely to permit one's land to be used, or merely to refrain from consuming one's capital, is to render any positive service,[36] or that income from inherited property can be seriously regarded as payment for service rendered by the present owner. It is also very hard to believe that, if competing sellers of any commodity cease to compete and enter into a combination, as a result of which their output is deliberately restricted, the price of the commodity raised and their incomes largely increased by monopoly profits, these increased incomes represent increased services rendered to society.

Suggestions of this kind, though capable of being so 'interpreted' as to be logically flawless, strain language to the breaking point. If made by rich men, poor men might be pardoned for thinking them disingenuous. When made by professional economists, they tend to discredit economic science in the eyes of the simple.

The proposition that justice requires that the distribution of income *should be* according to the value of services rendered in the existing state of society is logically distinct from the proposition that distribution in the existing state of society *is in fact* according to the value of services rendered.[37] But, in practice, those who maintain the former generally maintain the latter also.[38]

Having examined various interpretations of the doctrine that justice requires distribution according to deserts, we may now pass on to examine the doctrine that justice requires distribution according to needs. The meaning of 'needs' is not altogether clear, but if we understand by an individual's needs his capacity for making good use of income, this doctrine is identical in practical effect with the principle suggested in the last essay for securing an ideal distribution from the point of view of economic welfare, provided that its application does not react unfavourably upon production and other relevant factors. Thus, as Professor Cannan points out, the principle of distribution according to need 'is adopted in besieged cities, in ships short of provisions at sea, in hospitals and between members of the family unable to support themselves in every well conducted home. It is not adopted by 'nations', not because it is not a good principle, but because the amount to be distributed . . . would be immediately affected by the change in distribution and that in a very disastrous manner'.[39] It may be added that attempts have recently been made by various nations, both during and after the war, to adopt this principle to some extent by means of 'rationing' various commodities and fixing maximum prices. For the condition of many nations during the past few years has closely resembled that of 'besieged cities' or of 'ships short of provisions at sea.' The principle of distribution according to need is, in fact, yet another example of a principle, which may be defended conditionally by reference to considerations of economic welfare, but not unconditionally by reference to considerations of justice.

It is a principle which, within the limits of prudence, may profitably be adopted by nations even in normal times. Much modern legislation, which creates what is spoken of later in this essay as 'income from civil rights',[40] in effect transfers a certain amount of income from the general body of taxpayers to particular groups of persons, and this income is distributed, and is meant to be distributed, in rough accordance with the needs of those who receive it. Its distribution on this principle may increase economic welfare both by diminishing the inequality of incomes and by increasing production.[41] An important question, which needs further investigation, is how far, if at all, the principle of rationing and fixing maximum prices for necessaries can be profitably applied in time of peace.

In any case, 'It is certain,' as Professor Cannan says, 'that as a general rule approximations towards greater equality of income mean at the same time approximations towards distribution according to need, and should therefore be welcomed, whenever the advantage thus gained is not offset by an equal or greater loss resulting from damage to production.'[42]

The results reached in this essay may be thus summed up. The current canons of economic justice, which we have examined, are seen to be largely inconsistent with one another, and this is specially the case with those which offer complete solutions of the problem of ideal distribution. 'Who,' as Mill asks, 'shall decide between these appeals to conflicting principles of justice?' Thus, in the conflict between the ideals of distribution according to the value of work done and of distribution according to needs, 'justice has two sides to it, which it is impossible to bring into harmony, and the two disputants have chosen opposite sides; the one looks to what it is just that the individual should receive, the other to what it is just that the community should give. Each, from its own point of view, is unanswerable; and any choice between them, on grounds of justice, must be perfectly arbitrary. Social utility alone can decide the preference'.[43]

But, while the canons of economic justice are highly disputable, the canons of economic welfare are, by comparison, matters of general agreement. There is comparatively little ground for dispute in the propositions that economic welfare will be increased, other things in each case being equal, by a more equal distribution of income, by an increase in production per head, by an increase, and by a more equal distribution, of leisure. It is probable that all these propositions would be accepted by a large majority among reflective and reasonable people. There is certainly no such majority unconditionally in favour of any one of the rival canons of economic justice.

We have seen, further, that some of the current canons of economic justice, such as equality of opportunity and distribution according to need, are defensible conditionally, by reference to considerations of economic welfare, but that, if applied unconditionally to the real world, with which alone we need concern ourselves, they would diminish economic welfare to a disastrous extent.

Although, however, certain canons of economic justice, if prudently and partially applied, may increase economic welfare, such prudent and partial applications are from another point of view only applications of the canons of economic welfare. Mill's saying that justice is included within the sphere of social utility is thus illustrated.

In view of these conclusions, it is not surprising to find that most modern economists, in so far as they enter upon the discussion of economic ideals, base their arguments upon the ideal of social utility or economic welfare, rather than upon the ideal of economic justice. Sidgwick is driven, by the grave economic objections to the realisation of 'distributive justice', to a direct discussion of 'economic distribution'.[44] Marshall points out that 'the tendency of careful economic study is to base the rights of private property, not on any abstract principle, but on the observation that in the past they have been inseparable from solid progress'.[45] Professor Pigou in his *Wealth and Welfare* is content to investigate 'the general relations that subsist between economic welfare on the one hand, and, on the other hand, the magnitude, the distribution among people, and the distribution in time, of the national dividend'.[46] Finally, Professor Cannan has thus contrasted 'the principles of equity and economy', in so far as they are in conflict with one another. It is indeed true, that 'no government can afford to disregard the ideas of equity entertained by its subjects at any particular time. It is no use to try to forget the fact that men are generally prepared to sacrifice their economic interests on many altars, one of which is dedicated to justice. But of the two principles, Equity and Economy, Equity is ultimately the weaker. History, and indeed the recollection of every middle-aged man, provide instances which go to show that the judgment of mankind about what is equitable is liable to change, and that one of the forces which cause it to change is mankind's discovery from time to time that what was supposed to be quite just and equitable in some particular matter has become, or perhaps always was, uneconomical'.[47]

But the saying that equity should give way to economy, and that the ideal of economic welfare is a better guide to practice than the ideal of justice, must not be misunderstood. The ideal of human welfare, of which economic welfare is a fundamental and seldom a disharmonious part, is not less high than the ideal of human justice. The first demands for mankind the highest good which the conditions of an imperfect world allow, and the second can demand no more. The appearance of disharmony between these two ideals for the most part disappears, when words are clearly defined and the effects of given causes coolly traced.

Notes

1. These are Sir L. Chiozza Money's figures (*Riches and Poverty*, 1910. Essay III), which are admitted by other experts to be substantially accurate. Compare Bowley, *Division of the Product of Industry*. It is not yet possible to speak with any precision of the effects of the war on distribution.
2. Loria, *Basi Economiche della Società*, p. 1.
3. J. A. Spender, *Comments of Bagshot*, I, p. 38.
4. William James, *Principles of Psychology*, I, p. 121.
5. Morley, *On Compromise*, p. 203.
6. Poor by comparison not only with the wealthier classes of their day and nation, but with the lowest standard of economic welfare, which can be deemed to permit of a civilised existence.
7. Compare Maine, (*Ancient Law*, p. 68) who remarks that at every point of past time 'by far the greater part of mankind' has been without any conscious desire for 'progress'.
8. Taussig, *Principles of Economics*, I, p. 137.
9. This form of words, though very common, is not free from ambiguity.
10. Compare Graham Wallas, *The Great Society*, Essays I and IV.
11. Woodrow Wilson, *The New Freedom*, p. 26. Compare Taussig, *Principles of Economics.*, I, p. 137.
12. Mr Keynes in the second essay of his *Economic Consequences of the Peace* has brilliantly pictured the pre-war psychology of modern capitalistic societies and their inherent instability.
13. Compare Cannan, *Wealth*, Essay I.
14. Compare Part III, Essay II.
15. See, for example, Mill's argument (*Principles*, pp. 361–6) on the probable effects of a legal minimum wage.
16. Compare Pigou, *Wealth and Welfare*, pp. 28–31.
17. *Principles of Political Economy*, p. 516.
18. *Principles.* p. 230
19. This is obvious, but many economists have failed to emphasise it. Historically, economic science has been built up chiefly on what may be called its positive side; stress has been laid on the conditions under which wealth is produced, rather than on the limits within which the production of wealth is worth while. Compare the comments of Mr. Robertson (*Study of Industrial Fluctuation*, pp. 208–9), on 'the didactic and somewhat priggish attitude of the other classes'

towards those manual workers, who decide to take part of their share of increased prosperity in the form of increased leisure.

20. The analogy is tolerably close, though not exact. To the law of diminishing marginal utility of income roughly corresponds the law of increasing marginal 'disutility of labour'. Compare Jevons, *Theory of Political Economy,* Essay V. Mr J. A. Hobson in his *Work and Wealth* recognises more clearly than most economists the importance of what I have called subjective cost.

21. Compare Marshall, *Industry and Trade,* p. 659, and the problem as stated by Robertson, *Industrial Fluctuation,* pp. 253–4.

22. Compare Dr Stamp's pre-war estimates of *The Wealth and Income of the Chief Powers, Journal of the Royal Statistical Society.* July 1919.

23. Mr Keynes, *Economic Consequences of the Peace,* pp 16 ff, argues that inequality was a dominant cause of accumulation during the nineteenth and early twentieth century. This no doubt is true, though it seems an obvious exaggeration to say that during this period 'Europe was so organised as to secure the maximum accumulation of capital.' (p. 16). But the circumstances of the future are likely to differ markedly from those of the past and the problem of diminishing inequality, without diminishing production, will need a solution appropriate to the changed circumstances. The development of the habit of collective, as distinct from individual saving will be a necessary condition of the successful abandonment of the capitalist system.

24. Compare de Maeztu, *Authority, Liberty and Function,* pp. 197–9.

25. *Report* p. 11.

25. See, for example, his *History of Local Rates,* Essays VII and VIII and his *Economic Outlook,* pp. 299 ff.

26. 'Blessed,' it is said, 'are they that hunger and thirst after justice!' But perhaps it is more easy to hunger and thirst after it than to define precisely what it means.' Mackenzie, *Manual of Ethics,* p. 310.

27. *Utilitarianism.* p. 63.

28. Mill, p. 95.

29. Mill, p. 75.

30. Compare Cannan, *History of Local Rates,* pp. 162–3.

31. In abnormal times, when a strong sense of insecurity is already present, this objection to drastic changes loses much of its force. In Russia, for example, a strong case can be made out, on grounds of economic expediency, for the recent expropriation of large landowners and other capitalists without compensation and for the repudiation of the internal, though not perhaps of the external, debt.

32. 'Value of work done' in both cases is generally taken to mean exchange value. Attempts are sometimes made to interpret value as 'social value', but this idea, on closer examination, is too vague to

permit of wide practical application. Value, therefore, in the discussion which follows is taken to mean exchange value, as elsewhere in economics.

33. See, for example, Smart, *Distribution of Income*, pp. 100–2, and the writings of Mr Mallock, *passim*.
34. Spender, *Comments of Bagshot*, II, pp. 15–16.
35. Compare Part IV. Essays II, III, IV and X.
36. It might be thought more reasonable to regard the consumption of capital as a positive disservice to society, for which a diminution of income in the future is an inadequate penalty.
37. The identification of what should be with what is, or at any rate with what 'is evolving', is the leading fallacy of Herbert Spencer's 'Evolutionary Ethics', which was exposed by Huxley in his Romanes Lecture in 1893 (reprinted in his *Essays Ethical and Political*). But his fallacy seems to have trapped so eminent an economist as Principal Hadley (*Economics*, pp. 18–19).
38. For example, Smart and Professor J. B. Clark.
39. *Economic Outlook*, p. 309.
40. See Part III, Essay III and Part IV, Essay II.
41. Whether or not such transfers of income tend to increase production largely depends on how far they increase the health and efficiency of the recipients. This question is discussed further in Part III, Essay II. Such transfers may increase economic welfare not only by diminishing the inequality of incomes of different individuals during any given period, but also by diminishing the inequality of the incomes of given individuals during different periods. Compare Pigou, *Wealth and Welfare*, Part IV.
42. *Economic Outlook*, p. 310.
43. *Utilitarianism*, pp. 86–7.
44. *Principles of Political Economy*, pp. 515 ff.
45. *Principles of Economics*, p. 48.
46. *Wealth and Welfare* p. 487.
47. *History of Local Rates*, p. 173.

Lionel Robbins

The Significance of Economic Science

It is sometimes thought that certain developments in modern economic theory furnish *by themselves* a set of norms capable of providing a basis for political practice. The law of diminishing marginal utility is held to provide a criterion of all forms of political and social activity affecting distribution. Anything conducive to greater equality, which does not adversely affect production, is said to be justified by this law; anything conducive to inequality, condemned. These propositions have received the support of very high authority. They are the basis of much that is written on the theory of public finance.[1] No less an authority than Professor Cannan has invoked them, to justify the ways of economists to Fabian socialists.[2] They have received the widest countenance in numberless works on applied economics. It is safe to say that the great majority of English economists accept them as axiomatic. Yet with great diffidence I venture to suggest that they are in fact entirely unwarranted by any doctrine of scientific economics, and that outside this country they have very largely ceased to hold sway.

The argument by which these propositions are supported is familiar. But it is worth while repeating it explicitly in order to show the exact points at which it is defective. The law of diminishing marginal utility implies that the more one has of anything the less one values additional units thereof. Therefore, it is said, the more real income one has, the less one values additional units of income. Therefore the marginal utility of a rich man's income is less than the marginal utility of a poor man's income. Therefore, if transfers are made, and these transfers do not appreciably affect production, total utility will be increased. Therefore, such transfers are 'economically justified'. *Quod erat demonstrandum.*

At first sight the plausibility of the argument is overwhelming. But on closer inspection it is seen to be merely specious. It rests upon an extension of the conception of diminishing marginal utility into a field in which it is entirely illegitimate. The law of diminishing marginal utility here invoked does not follow in the least from the fundamental conception of economic goods; and it makes assumptions which, whether they are true or false, can never be verified by observation or introspection. The proposition we are examining begs the great metaphysical question of the scientific comparability of different individual experiences. This deserves further examination.

The law of diminishing marginal utility, as we have seen, is derived from the conception of a scarcity of means in relation to the ends which they serve. It assumes that, for each individual, goods can be ranged in order of their significance for conduct; and that, in the sense that it will be preferred, we can say that one use of a good is more important than another. Proceeding on this basis, we can compare the order in which one individual may be supposed to prefer certain alternatives with the order in which they are preferred by another individual. In this way it is possible to build up a complete theory of exchange.[3]

But it is one thing to assume that scales can be drawn up showing the *order* in which an individual will prefer a series of alternatives, and to compare the arrangement of one such individual scale with another. It is quite a different thing to assume that behind such arrangements lie magnitudes which themselves can be compared. This is not an assumption which need anywhere be made in modern economic analysis, and it is an assumption which is of an entirely different kind from the assumption of individual scales of relative valuation. The theory of exchange assumes that *I* can compare the importance *to me* of bread at sixpence per loaf and sixpence spent on other alternatives presented by the opportunities of the market. And it assumes that the order of my preferences thus exhibited can be compared with the order of preferences of the baker. But it does not assume that, at any point, it is necessary to compare the satisfaction which I get from the spending of sixpence on bread with the satisfaction which the baker gets by receiving it. That comparison is a comparison of an entirely different nature. It is a comparison which is never needed in the theory of equilibrium and which is never implied by the assumptions of that theory. It is a comparison which necessarily falls outside the scope of any positive science. To state that A's preference stands above

B's in order of importance is entirely different from stating that A prefers n to m and B prefers n and m in a different order. It involves an element of conventional valuation. Hence it is essentially normative. It has no place in pure science.

If this is still obscure, the following considerations should be decisive. Suppose that a difference of opinion were to arise about A's preferences. Suppose that I thought that, at certain prices, he preferred n to m, and you thought that, at the same prices, he preferred m to n. It would be easy to settle our differences in a purely scientific manner. Either we could ask A to tell us. Or, if we refused to believe that introspection on A's part was possible, we could expose him to the stimuli in question and observe his behaviour. Either test would be such as to provide the basis for a settlement of the difference of opinion.

But suppose that we differed about the satisfaction derived by A from an income of £1,000, and the satisfaction derived by B from an income of twice that magnitude. Asking them would provide no solution. Supposing they differed. A might urge that he had more satisfaction than B at the margin. While B might urge that, on the contrary, he had more satisfaction than A. We do not need to be slavish behaviourists to realise that here is no scientific evidence. *There is no means of testing the magnitude of A's satisfaction as compared with B's.* If we tested the state of their blood-streams, that would be a test of blood, not satisfaction. Introspection does not enable A to measure what is going on in B's mind, nor B to measure what is going on in A's. There is no way of comparing the satisfactions of different people.

Now, of course, in daily life we do continually assume that the comparison can be made. But the very diversity of the assumptions actually made at different times and in different places is evidence of their conventional nature. In western democracies we assume for certain purposes that men in similar circumstances are capable of equal satisfactions. Just as for purposes of justice we assume equality of responsibility in similar situations as between legal subjects, so for purposes of public finance we agree to assume equality of capacity for experiencing satisfaction from equal incomes in similar circumstances as between economic subjects. But, although it may be convenient to assume this, there is no way of proving that the assumption rests on ascertainable fact. And, indeed, if the representative of some other civilisation were to assure us that we were wrong, that members of his caste (or his race) were capable of experiencing ten times as much satisfaction from given incomes as members of an inferior caste (or an 'inferior' race), we could not refute him. We might poke fun at him. We might flare up with indignation, and say that his valuation was hateful, that it led to civil strife, unhappiness, unjust privilege, and so on and so forth. But we could not show that he was wrong in any objective sense, any more than we could show that we were right. And since in our hearts we do not regard different men's satisfactions from similar means as equally valuable, it would really be rather silly if we continued to pretend that the justification for our scheme of things was in any way *scientific*. It can be justified on grounds of general convenience. Or it can be justified by appeal to ultimate standards of obligation. But it cannot be justified by appeal to any kind of positive science.

Hence the extension of the law of diminishing marginal utility, postulated in the propositions we are examining, is illegitimate. And the arguments based upon it therefore are lacking in scientific foundation. Recognition of this no doubt involves a substantial curtailment of the claims of much of what now assumes the status of scientific generalisation in current discussions of applied Economics. The conception of diminishing relative utility (the convexity downwards of the indifference curve) does not justify the inference that transferences from the rich to the poor will increase total satisfaction. It does not tell us that a graduated income tax is less injurious to the social dividend than a nongraduated poll tax. Indeed, all that part of the theory of public finance which deals with 'social utility' must assume a different significance. Interesting as a development of an ethical postulate, it does not at all follow from the positive assumptions of pure theory. It is simply the accidental deposit of the historical association of English economics with utilitarianism: and both the utilitarian postulates from which it derives and the analytical economics with which it has been associated will be the better and the more convincing if this is clearly recognised.[4]

But supposing this were not so. Suppose that we could bring ourselves to believe in the positive status of these conventional assumptions, the commensurability of different experiences, the equality of capacity for satisfaction, etc. And suppose that, proceeding on this basis, we had succeeded in showing that certain policies *had the effect* of increasing 'social utility', even so it would be totally illegitimate to argue that such a conclusion by itself warranted the inference that these policies *ought* to be carried out. For such an inference would beg the whole question whether the increase of satisfaction in this sense was socially obligatory.[5] And there is nothing within the body of economic generalisations, even thus enlarged by the inclusion of elements of conventional valuation, which affords any means of deciding this question. Propositions involving 'ought' are on an entirely different plane from propositions involving 'is'. But more of this later.

Exactly the same type of stricture may be applied to any attempt to make the criteria of free equilibrium in the price system at the same time the criteria of 'economic justification'. The pure theory of equilibrium enables us to understand how, given the valuations of the various economic subjects and the facts of the legal and technical environment, a system of relationships can be conceived from which there would be no tendency to variation. It enables us to describe that distribution of resources which, given the valuations of the individual concerned, satisfies demand most fully. But it does not by itself provide any ethical sanctions. To show that, under certain conditions, demand is satisfied more adequately than under any alternative set of conditions, does not prove that that set of conditions is desirable. There is no penumbra of approbation round the theory of equilibrium. Equilibrium is just equilibrium.

Now, of course, it is of the essence of the conception of equilibrium that, given his initial resources, each individual secures a range of free choice, bounded only by the limitations of the material environment and the exercise of a similar freedom on the part of the other economic subjects. In equilibrium each individual is free to move to a different point on his lines of preference, but he does not move, for, in the circumstances postulated, any other point would be less preferred. Given certain norms of political philosophy, this conception may throw an important light upon the types of social institutions necessary to achieve them.[6] But freedom to choose may not be regarded as an ultimate good. The creation of a state of affairs offering the maximum freedom of choice may not be thought desirable, having regard to other social ends. To show that, in certain conditions, the maximum freedom of this sort is achieved is not to show that those conditions should be sought after.

Moreover, there are certain obvious limitations on the possibility of formulating ends in price offers. To secure the conditions within which the equilibrating tendencies may emerge there must exist a certain legal apparatus, not capable of being elicited by price bids, yet essential for their orderly execution.[7] The negative condition of health, immunity from infectious disease, is not an end which can be wholly achieved by individual action. In urban conditions the failure of one individual to conform to certain sanitary requirements may involve all the others in an epidemic. The securing of ends of this sort must necessarily involve the using of factors of production in a way not fully compatible with complete freedom in the expenditure of given individual resources. And it is clear that society, acting as a body of political citizens, may formulate ends which interfere much more drastically than this with the free choices of the individuals composing it. There is nothing in the corpus of economic analysis which in itself affords any justification for regarding these ends as good or bad. Economic analysis can simply point out the implications as regards the disposal of means of production of the various patterns of ends which may be chosen.

For this reason, the use of the adjectives 'economical' and 'uneconomical' to describe certain policies is apt to be very misleading. The criterion of economy which follows from our original definitions is the securing of given ends with least means. It is, therefore, perfectly intelligible to say of a certain policy that it is uneconomical, if, in order to achieve certain ends, it uses more scarce means than are necessary. Once the ends by which they are valued are given as regards the disposition of means, the terms 'economical' and 'uneconomical' can be used with complete intelligibility.

But it is not intelligible to use them as regards ends themselves. As we have seen already, there are no economic ends. There are only economical and uneconomical ways of achieving given ends. We cannot say that the pursuit of given ends is uneconomical because the ends are uneconomical; we can only say it is uneconomical if the ends are pursued with an unnecessary expenditure of means.

Thus it is not legitimate to say that going to war is uneconomical, if, having regard to all the issues and all the sacrifices necessarily involved, it is decided that the anticipated result is worth the sacrifice. It is only legitimate so to describe it if it is attempted to secure this end with an unnecessary degree of sacrifice.

It is the same with measures more specifically 'economic' – to use the term in its confused popular sense. If we assume that the ends of public policy are the safeguarding of conditions under which individual demands, as reflected in the price system, are satisfied as amply as possible under given conditions, then, save in very special circumstances which are certainly not generally known to those who impose such measures, it is legitimate to say that a protective tariff on wheat is uneconomical in that it imposes obstacles to the achievement of this end. This follows clearly from purely neutral analysis. But if the object in view transcends these ends – if the tariff is designed to bring about an end not formulated in consumers' price offers – the safeguarding of food supply against the danger of war, for instance – it is not legitimate to say that it is uneconomical just because it results in the impoverishment of consumers. In such circumstances the only justification for describing it as uneconomical would be a demonstration that it achieved this end also with an unnecessary sacrifice of means.[8]

Again, we may examine the case of minimum wage regulation. It is a well-known generalisation of theoretical economics that a wage which is held above the equilibrium level necessarily involves unemployment and a diminution of the value of capital. This is one of the most elementary deductions from the theory of economic equilibrium. The history of this country since the war is one long vindication of its accuracy.[9] The popular view that the validity of these 'static' deductions is vitiated by the probability of 'dynamic improvements' induced by wage pressure, depends upon an oversight of the fact that these 'improvements' are themselves one of the manifestations of capital wastage.[10] But such a policy is not *necessarily* to be described as uneconomical. If, in the society imposing such a policy, it is generally thought that the gain of the absence of wage payments below a certain rate more than compensates for the unemployment and losses it involves, the policy cannot be described as uneconomical. As private individuals we may think that such a system of preferences sacrifices tangible increments of the ingredients of real happiness for the false end of a mere diminution of inequality. We may suspect that those who cherish such preferences are deficient in imagination. But there is nothing in scientific economics which warrants us in passing these judgments. Economics is neutral as between ends. Economics cannot pronounce on the validity of ultimate judgments of value.

In recent years, certain economists, realising this inability of economics, thus conceived, to provide within itself a series of principles binding upon practice, have urged that the boundaries of the subject should be extended to include normative studies. Mr Hawtrey and Mr J. A. Hobson, for instance, have argued that economics should not only take account of valuations and ethical standards as given data in the manner explained above, but that also it should pronounce upon the ultimate validity of these valuations and standards. 'Economics', says Mr Hawtrey, 'cannot be dissociated from ethics'.[11]

Unfortunately it does not seem logically possible to associate the two studies in any form but mere juxtaposition. Economics deals with ascertainable facts; ethics with valuations and obligations. The two fields of enquiry are not on the same plane of discourse. Between the generalisations of positive and normative studies there is a logical gulf fixed which no ingenuity can disguise and no juxtaposition in space or time bridge over. The proposition that the price of pork fluctuates with variations in supply and demand follows from a conception of the relation of pork to human impulses which, in the last resort, is verifiable by introspection and observation. We can ask people whether they are prepared to buy pork and how much they are prepared to buy at different prices. Or we can watch how they behave when equipped with currency and exposed to the stimuli of the pig-meat markets.[12] But the proposition that it is *wrong* that pork should be valued, although it is a proposition which has greatly influenced the conduct of different races, is a proposition which we cannot conceive being verified at all in this manner. Propositions involving the verb 'ought' are different in kind from propositions involving the verb 'is'. And it is difficult to see what possible good can be served by not keeping them separate, or failing to recognise their essential difference.[13]

All this is not to say that economists may not assume as postulates different judgments of value, and then on the assumption that these are valid enquire what judgment is to be passed upon particular proposals for action. On the contrary, as we shall see, it is just in the light that it casts upon the significance and consistency of different ultimate valuations that the utility of economics consists. Applied economics consists of propositions of the form, 'If you want to do this, then you must do that.' 'If such and such is to be regarded as the ultimate good, then this is clearly incompatible with it.' All that is implied in the distinction here emphasised is that the validity of assumptions relating to the value of what exists or what may exist is not a matter of scientific verification, as is the validity of assumptions relating to mere existence.

Nor is it in the least implied that economists should not deliver themselves on ethical questions, any more than an argument that botany is not æsthetics is to say that botanists should not have views of their own on the lay-out of gardens. On the contrary, it is greatly to be desired that economists should have speculated long and widely on these matters, since only in this way will they be in a position to appreciate the implications of *given* ends of problems which are put to them for solution. We may not agree with J. S. Mill that 'a man is not likely to be a good economist if he is nothing else'. But we may at least agree that he may not be as useful as he otherwise might be. Our methodological axioms involve no prohibition of outside interests. All that is contended is that there is no logical connection between the two types of generalisation, and that there is nothing to be gained by invoking the sanctions of one to reinforce the conclusions of the other.

And, quite apart from all questions of methodology, there is a very practical justification for such a procedure. In the rough and tumble of political struggle, differences of opinion may arise either as a result of differences about ends or as a result of differences about the means of attaining ends. Now, as for the first type of difference, neither economics nor any other science can provide any solvent. If we disagree about ends it is a case of thy blood or mine – or live, and let live, according to the importance of the difference, or the relative strength of our opponents. But, if we disagree about means, then scientific analysis can often help us to resolve our differences. If we disagree about the morality of the taking of interest (and we understand what we are talking about), then there is no room for argument. But if we disagree about the objective implications of fluctuations in the rate of interest, then economic analysis should enable us to settle our dispute. Shut Mr Hawtrey in a room as secretary of a committee composed of Bentham, Buddha, Lenin and the head of the United States Steel Corporation, set up to decide upon the ethics of usury, and it is improbable that he could produce an 'agreed document'. Set the same committee to determine the objective results of state regulation of the rate of discount, and it ought not to be beyond human ingenuity to produce unanimity – or at any rate a majority report, with Lenin perhaps dissenting. Surely, for the sake of securing what agreement we can in a world in which avoidable differences of opinion are all too common, it is worth while carefully delimiting those fields of enquiry where this kind of settlement is possible from those where it is not to be hoped for[14] – it is worth while delimiting the neutral area of science from the more disputable area of moral and political philosophy.

But what, then, is the significance of economic science? We have seen that it provides, within its own structure of generalisations, no norms which are binding in practice. It is incapable of deciding as between the desirability of different ends. It is fundamentally distinct from ethics. Wherein, then, does its unquestionable significance consist?

Surely it consists in just this, that, when we are faced with a choice between ultimates, it enables us to choose with full awareness of the implications of what we are choosing. Faced with the problem of deciding between this and that, we are not entitled to look to economics for the ultimate decision. There is nothing in economics which relieves *us* of the obligation to choose. There is nothing in any kind of science which can decide the ultimate problem of preference. But, to be completely rational, we must know what it is we prefer. We must be aware of the implications of the alternatives. For rationality in choice is nothing more and nothing less than choice with complete awareness of the alternatives rejected. And it is just here that economics acquires its practical significance. It can make clear to us the implications of the different ends we may choose. It makes it possible for us to will with knowledge of what it is we are willing. It makes it possible for us to select a system of ends which are mutually consistent with each other.[15]

An example or two should make this quite clear. Let us start with a case in which the implications of one act of choice are elucidated. We may revert once more to an example we have already considered – the imposition of a protective tariff. We have seen already that there is nothing in scientific economics which warrants our describing such a policy as good or bad. We have decided that, if such a policy is decided upon with full consciousness of the sacrifices involved, there is no justification for describing it as uneconomical. The deliberate choice by a body of citizens acting collectively to frustrate, in the interests of ends such as defence, the preservation of the countryside, and so on, their several choices as consumers, cannot be described as uneconomical or irrational, if it is done with full awareness of what is being done. But this will not be the case unless the citizens in question are fully conscious of the objective implications of the step they are taking. And in an extensive modern society it is only as a result of intricate economic analysis that they may be placed in possession of this knowledge. The great majority, even of educated people, called upon to decide upon the desirability of, let us say, protection for agriculture, think only of the effects of such measures on the protected industry. They see that such measures are likely to benefit the industry, and hence they argue that the measures are good. But, of course, as every first year student knows, it is only here that the problem begins. To judge the further repercussions of the tariff an analytical technique is necessary. This is why in countries where the level of education in economics is not high, there is a constant tendency to the approval of more and more protective tariffs.

Nor is the utility of such analysis to be regarded as confined to decisions on isolated measures such as the imposition of a single tariff. It enables us to judge more complicated systems of policy. It enables us to see what *sets* of ends are compatible with each other and what are not, and upon what conditions such compatibility is dependent. And, indeed, it is just here that the possession of some such technique becomes quite indispensable if policy is to be rational. It may be just possible to will rationally the achievement of particular social ends overriding individual valuations without much assistance from analysis. The case of a subsidy to protect essential food supplies is a case in point. It is almost impossible to conceive the carrying through of more elaborate policies without the aid of such an instrument.[16]

We may take an example from the sphere of monetary policy. It is an unescapable deduction from the first principles of monetary theory that, in a world in which conditions are changing at different rates in different monetary areas, it is impossible to achieve at once stable prices and stable exchanges.[17] The two ends – in this case the 'ends' are quite obviously subordinate to other major norms of policy – are logically incompatible. You may try for one or you may try for the other – it is not certain that price stability is either permanently attainable or conducive to equilibrium generally – but you cannot rationally try for both. If you do, there must be a breakdown. These conclusions are well known to all economists. Yet without some analytical apparatus how few of us would perceive the incompatibility of the ends in question!

And even this is a narrow example. Without economic analysis it is not possible rationally to choose between alternative *systems* of society. We have seen already that if we regard a society which permits inequality of incomes as an evil in itself, and an equalitarian society as presenting an end to be pursued above all other things, then it is illegitimate to regard such a preference as uneconomic. But it is not possible to regard it as rational unless it is formulated with a full consciousness of the nature of the sacrifice which is thereby involved. And we cannot do this unless we understand, not only the essential nature of the capitalistic mechanism, but also the necessary conditions and limitations to which the type of society proposed as a substitute would be subject. It is not rational to will a certain end if one is not conscious of what sacrifice the achievement of that end involves. And, in this supreme weighing of alternatives, only a complete awareness of the implications of modern economic analysis can confer the capacity to judge rationally.

But, if this is so, what need is there to claim any larger status for economic science? Is it not the burden of our time that we do not realise what we are doing? Are not most of our difficulties due to just this fact, that we will have ends which are incompatible, not because we wish for deadlock, but because we do not realise their incompatibility. It may well be that there may exist differences as regards ultimate ends in modern society which render some conflict inevitable. But it is clear that many of our most pressing difficulties arise, not for this reason, but because our aims are not co-ordinated. As consumers we will cheapness, as producers we choose security. We value one distribution of factors of production as private spenders and savers. As public citizens we sanction arrangements which frustrate the achievement of this distribution. We call for cheap money and lower prices, fewer imports and a larger volume of trade.[18] The different 'will-organisations' in society, although composed of the same individuals, formulate different preferences. Everywhere our difficulties seem to arise, not so much from divisions between the different members of the body politic, as from, as it were, split personalities on the part of each one of them.[19]

To such a situation, economics brings the solvent of knowledge. It enables us to conceive the far-reaching implications of alternative possibilities of policy. It does not, and it cannot, enable us to evade the necessity of choosing between alternatives. But it does make it possible for us to bring our different choices into harmony. It cannot remove the ultimate limitations on human action. But it does make it possible within these limitations to act consistently. It serves for the inhabitant of the modern world with its endless interconnections and relationships as an extension of his perceptive apparatus. It provides a technique of rational action.

This, then, is a further sense in which economics can be truly said to assume rationality in human society. It makes no pretence, as has been alleged so often, that action is necessarily rational in the sense that the ends pursued are not mutually inconsistent. There is nothing in its generalisations which necessarily implies reflective deliberation in ultimate valuation. It relies upon no assumption that individuals will always act rationally. But it does depend for its practical *raison d'être* upon the assumption that it is desirable that they should do so. It does assume that, within the bounds of necessity, it is desirable to choose ends which can be achieved harmoniously.

And thus in the last analysis economics does depend, if not for its existence, at least for its significance, on an ultimate valuation – the affirmation that rationality and ability to choose with knowledge is desirable. If irrationality, if the surrender to the blind force of external stimuli and uncoordinated impulse at every moment is a good to be preferred above all others, then it is true the *raison d'être* of economics disappears. And it is the tragedy of our generation, red with fratricidal strife and betrayed almost beyond belief by those who should have been its intellectual leaders, that there have arisen those who would uphold this ultimate negation, this escape from the tragic necessities of choice which has become conscious. With all such there can be no argument. The revolt against reason is essentially a revolt against life itself. But for all those who still affirm more positive values, that branch of knowledge which, above all others, is the symbol and safeguard of rationality in social arrangements, must, in the anxious days which are to come, by very reason of this menace to that for which it stands, possess a peculiar and a heightened significance.

Notes

1. See, for example, Edgeworth, *The Pure Theory of Taxation*, Papers relating to Political Economy, vol. ii, p. 63.
2. See *Economics and Socialism, The Economical Outlook*, pp. 59–62.
3. So many have been the misconceptions based upon an imperfect understanding of this generalisation that Dr Hicks has suggested that its present name be discarded altogether and the title Law of Increasing Rate of Substitution be adopted in its place. Personally, I prefer the established terminology, but it is clear that there is much to be said for the suggestion.
4. See Davenport, *Value and Distribution*, pp. 301 and 571; Benham, *Economic Welfare, Economica*, June 1930, pp. 173–187; M. St Braun, *Theorie der staatlichen Wirtschaftspolitik*, pp. 41–4. Even Professor Irving Fisher, anxious to provide a justification for his statistical method for measuring 'marginal utility', can find no better apology for his procedure than that 'Philosophic doubt is right and proper, but the problems of life cannot and do not wait' (*Economic Essays in Honour of John Bates Clark*, p. 180). It does not seem to me that the problem of measuring marginal utility as between individuals is a particularly pressing problem. But whether this is so or not, the fact remains that Professor Fisher solves his problem only by making a conventional assumption. And it does not seem that it anywhere aids the solution of practical problems to pretend that conventional assumptions have scientific justification. It does not make me a more docile democrat to be told that I am equally capable of experiencing satisfaction as my neighbour; it fills me with indignation. But I am perfectly willing to accept the statement that it is *convenient* to assume that this is the case. I am quite willing to accept the argument – indeed, as distinct from believers in the racial or proletarian myths, I very firmly believe – that, in modern conditions, societies which proceed on any other assumption have an inherent instability. But we are past the days when democracy could be made acceptable by the pretence that judgments of value are judgments of scientific fact. I am afraid that the same strictures apply to the highly ingenious *Methods for Measuring Marginal Utility* of Professor Ragnar Frisch.
5. Psychological hedonism in so far as it went beyond the individual

may have involved a non-scientific assumption, but it was not by itself a necessary justification for ethical hedonism.

6. See two very important papers by Professor Plant, 'Co-ordination and Competition in Transport' *Journal of the Institute of Transport*, vol. xiii, pp. 127–136; 'Trends in Business Administration', *Economica*, No. 35, pp. 45–62.

7. On the place of the legal framework of economic activity, the 'organisation' of the economy as he calls it, Dr Strigl's work cited above is very illuminating. See Strigl, pp. 85–121.

8. See a paper by the present author on *The Case of Agriculture* in *Tariffs: The Case Examined* (edited by Sir William Beveridge).

9. Hicks, *The Theory of Wages*, chs ix and x. On the evidence of post-War history, Dr Benham's *Wages, Prices and Unemployment (Economist* June 20, 1931) should be consulted.

10. It is curious that this should not have been more generally realised, for it is usually the most enthusiastic exponents of this view who also denounce most vigorously the unemployment 'caused' by rationalisation. It is, of course, the necessity of the conversion of capital into forms which are profitable at the higher wage level which is responsible both for a shrinkage in social capital and the creation of an industrial structure incapable of affording full employment to the whole working population. There is no reason to expect permanent unemployment as a result of rationalisation *not* induced by wages above the equilibrium level.

11. See Hawtrey, *The Economic Problem*, especially pp. 184 and 203–15, and Hobson, *Wealth and Life*, pp. 112–40. I have examine Mr Hawtrey's contentions in some detail in an article entitled, *Mr Hawtrey on the Scope of Economics* (*Economica*, No. 20, pp. 172–178). But in that article I made certain statements with regard to the claims of 'welfare economics' which I should now wish to formulate rather differently. Moreover, at that time I did not understand the nature of the idea of *precision* in economic generalisations, and my argument contains one entirely unnecessary concession to the critics of economics. On the main point under discussion, however, I have nothing to retract, and in what follows I have borrowed one or two sentences from the last few paragraphs of the article.

12. On all this it seems to me that the elucidations of Max Weber are quite definitive. Indeed, I confess that I am quite unable to understand how it can be conceived to be possible to call this part of Max Weber's methodology in question. (See *Der Sinn der 'Wertfreiheit' der Soziologischen und Ökonomischen Wissenschaften, Gesammelte Aufsätze zur Wissenschaftslehre*, pp. 451–502.)

13. Mr J. A. Hobson, commenting on a passage in my criticism of Mr Hawtrey which was couched in somewhat similar terms, protests

that 'this is a refusal to recognise any empirical *modus vivendi* or contact between economic values and human values' (Hobson p. 129). Precisely, but why should Mr Hobson, of all men, complain? My procedure simply empties out of economics – what Mr Hobson himself has never ceased to proclaim to be an illegitimate intrusion – any 'economic' presumption that the valuations of the marketplace are ethically respectable. I cannot help feeling that a great many of Mr Hobson's strictures on the procedure of economic science fall to the ground if the view of the scope of its subject-matter suggested above be explicitly adopted.

14. In fact, of course, such has been the practice of economists of the 'orthodox' tradition ever since the emergence of scientific economics. See, for example, Cantillon, *Essai sur la Nature du Commerce* (Higgs ed., p. 85): 'It is also a question outside of my subject whether it is better to have a great multitude of inhabitants poor and badly provided, than a smaller number much more at their ease'. See also Ricardo, *Notes on Malthus*, p. 188: 'It has been well said by M. Say that it is not the province of the Political Economist to advise – he is to tell you how you may become rich, but he is not to advise you to prefer riches to indolence or indolence to riches.' Of course, occasionally among those economists who have worked with a hedonistic bias, there has been confusion of the two kinds of proposition. But this has not happened to anything like the extent commonly suggested. Most of the allegations of bias spring from unwillingness to believe the facts that economic analysis brings to light. The proposition that real wages above the equilibrium point involve unemployment is a perfectly neutral inference from one of the most elementary propositions in theoretical economics. But it is difficult to mention it in some circles without being accused, if not of sinister interest, at least of a hopeless bias against the poor and the unfortunate. Similarly at the present day it is difficult to enunciate the platitude that a general tariff on imports will affect foreign demand for our exports without being thought a traitor to one's country.

15. It is perhaps desirable to emphasise that the consistency which is made possible is a consistency of achievement, not a consistency of ends. The achievement of one end may be held to be inconsistent with the achievement of another, either on the plane of valuation, or on the plane of objective possibility. Thus it may be held to be ethically inconsistent to serve two masters at once. It is objectively inconsistent to arrange to be with each of them at the same time, at different places. It is the latter kind of inconsistency in the sphere of social policy which scientific economics should make it possible to eliminate.

16. All this should be a sufficient answer to those who continually lay it down that 'social life is too complex a matter to be judged by economic analysis'. It is because social life is so complicated that economic analysis is necessary if we are to understand even a part of it. It is usually those who talk most about the complexity of life and the insusceptibility of human behaviour to any kind of logical analysis who prove to have the most *simpliste* intellectual and emotional make-up. He who has really glimpsed the irrational in the springs of human action will have no 'fear' that it can ever be killed by logic.

17. See Keynes, *A Tract on Monetary Reform*, pp. 154–55; also an interesting paper by D. H. Robertson, 'How do We Want Gold to Behave?' reprinted in the *International Gold Problem*, pp. 18–46.

18. Compare with M. S. Braun, *Theorie der Staatlichen Wirtschaftspolitik*, p. 5.

19. In this way economic analysis reveals still further examples of a phenomenon to which attention has often been drawn in recent discussion of the theory of sovereignty in public law. See Figgis, *Churches in the Modern State*; Maitland, Introduction to Gierke's *Political Theories of the Middle Ages*; Laski, *The Problem of Sovereignty. Authority in the Modern State*.

James Woodburn

Egalitarian Societies[1]

Greater equality of wealth, of power and of prestige has been achieved in *certain* hunting and gathering societies than in any other human societies. These societies, which have economies based on immediate rather than delayed return, are assertively egalitarian. Equality is achieved through direct, individual access to resources; through direct, individual access to means of coercion and means of mobility which limit the imposition of control; through procedures which prevent saving and accumulation and impose sharing; through mechanisms which allow goods to circulate without making people dependent upon one another. People are systematically disengaged from property and therefore from the potentiality in property for creating dependency. A comparison is made between these societies and certain other egalitarian societies in which there is profound intergenerational inequality and in which the equality between people of senior generation is only a starting point for strenuous competition resulting in inequality. The value systems of non-competitive, egalitarian hunter-gatherers limit the development of agriculture because rules of sharing restrict the investment and savings necessary for agriculture; they may limit the care provided for the incapacitated because of the controls on dependency; they may, in principle, extend equality to all mankind.

In a work published after his death, Malinowski made the splendidly forthright declaration that 'authority is the very essence of social organisation'.[2] I am going to talk about a type of social organisation, not understood in Malinowski's day, in which individuals have no real authority over each other. This essay is about certain societies in which there is the closest approximation to equality known in any human societies and about the basis for that equality. I have chosen to use the term egalitarian to describe these societies of near-equals because the term directly suggests that the equality that is present is not neutral, the mere absence of inequality or hierarchy, but is *asserted*. The term egality, from which egalitarian is derived, was introduced into English with its present meaning in a poem by Tennyson in 1864 to suggest politically assertive equality of the French variety.[3] Even today egalitarian carries with it echoes of revolution, of fervour for equality in opposition to elaborate structures of inequality. But politically assertive egalitarianism is, of course, not found only in hierarchical systems under challenge and in their successor regimes. It is equally characteristic of many systems without direct experience of elaborate instituted hierarchy. Yet it may still seem surprising at first that equality should be asserted in certain very simply organised contemporary hunting and gathering societies which I am going to talk about, and in which, one might think, equality would simply be taken for granted.

In these societies equalities of power, equalities of wealth and equalities of prestige or rank are not merely sought but are, with certain limited exceptions, genuinely realised. But, the evidence suggests, they are never unchallenged. People are well aware of the possibility that individuals or groups within their own egalitarian societies may try to acquire more wealth, to assert more power or to claim more status than other people, and are vigilant in seeking to prevent or to limit this. The verbal rhetoric of equality may or may not be elaborated but actions speak loudly: equality is repeatedly acted out, publicly demonstrated, in opposition to possible inequality.

It is noteworthy that although very many societies are in some sense egalitarian, those in which inequalities are at their minimum depend on hunting and gathering for their subsistence. For reasons which I shall seek to explain, only the hunting and gathering way of life permits so great an emphasis on equality. But there is, of course, no question of the equality being a simple product of the hunting and gathering way of life. Many hunter-gatherers have social systems in which there is very marked inequality of one sort or another, sometimes far more marked than the inequalities in certain simple agricultural or nomadic pastoral societies.

In a number of recent papers,[4] I have sought to classify hunting and gathering societies – that is societies in which people obtain their food from wild products by hunting wild animals, by fishing and by gathering wild roots, fruits and the honey of wild bees[5] – into two major categories, those with immediate-return systems and those with delayed-return systems.

Immediate-return systems have the following basic characteristics. People obtain a direct and immediate return from their labour. They go out hunting or gathering and eat the food obtained the same day or casually over the days that follow. Food is neither elaborately processed nor stored. They use relatively simple, portable, utilitarian, easily acquired, replaceable tools and weapons made with real skill but not involving a great deal of labour.

Delayed-return systems, in contrast, have the following characteristics. People hold rights over valued assets of some sort, which either represent a yield, a return for labour applied over time or, if not, are held and managed in a way which resembles and has similar social implications to delayed yields on labour. In delayed-return hunting and gathering systems these assets are of four main types, which may occur separately but are more commonly found in combination with one another and are mutually reinforcing:

- Valuable technical facilities used in production: boats, nets, artificial weirs, stockades, pit-traps, beehives and other such artefacts which are a product of considerable labour and from which a food yield is obtained gradually over a period of months or years.
- Processed and stored food or materials usually in fixed dwellings.
- Wild products which have themselves been improved or increased by human labour: wild herds which are culled selectively, wild food-producing plants which have been tended, and so on.
- Assets in the form of rights held by men over their female kin who are then bestowed in marriage on other men.

In principle all farming systems, unless based on wage or slave labour, must be delayed-return for those doing the work, since the yield on the labour put into crop-growing or herding domestic animals is only obtained months or years later. Of course, in all delayed-return systems there is some immediate-return activity, but it is usually rather restricted and may be treated as low-status activity. Among hunting and gathering societies, the available information suggests that both immediate-return systems and delayed-return systems are common. Most are surprisingly easily classified into one or the other category, but there are some which cause difficulties, as is inevitable with any simple binary distinction.[6]

Delayed-return systems in all their variety (for almost all human societies are of this type) have basic implications for social relationships and social groupings: they depend for their effective operation on a set of ordered, differentiated, jurally defined relationships through which crucial goods and services are transmitted. They imply binding commitments and dependencies between people. For an individual to secure the yield from his labour or to manage his assets, he depends on others. The farmer, for example, will almost invariably pool his labour with others – at least with a spouse and usually during the labour peaks of the agricultural cycle with several others – but, equally important, he depends on others for the protection of his growing crops, of his use of and rights to the land on which they are growing and of the yield when he obtains and stores it.[7] While it would, in principle, be possible to imagine situations in which individuals invested substantial amounts of labour over time *on their own*, protected the asset in which the labour was invested *on their own*, and then secured and managed the yields *on their own*, in practice this seems almost never to occur.

Until quite recently most anthropological research has been conducted in relatively small-scale, delayed-return, pastoral, agricultural and hunting and gathering societies and here we find the familiar kinship commitments and dependencies; lineages, clans and other kinship groups; marriages in which women are bestowed in marriage by men on other men; marriage alliances between groups. Immediate-return systems have only recently begun to be properly investigated and hence their social arrangements are still relatively unfamiliar. Societies which fall into this category include the Mbuti Pygmies of Zaire;[8] the !Kung Bushmen of Botswana and Namibia;[9] the Pandaram and Paliyan of south India;[10] the Batek Negritos of Malaysia[11] and the Hadza of Tanzania[12] among whom my own fieldwork was conducted and about whom I can talk with most confidence.[13] Most of my illustrations will be drawn from material on the Hadza and the !Kung.

The characteristics of these immediate-return systems I have spelt out in some detail elsewhere. Here all I intend is an outline sufficient to provide a background for my discussion of how these societies promote equality. The social organisation of these societies has the following basic characteristics:

- Social groupings are flexible and constantly changing in composition.
- Individuals have a choice of whom they associate with in residence, in the food quest, in trade and exchange, in ritual contexts.
- People are not dependent on *specific* other people for access to basic requirements.
- Relationships between people, whether relationships of kinship or other relationships, stress sharing and mutuality but do not involve long-term binding commitments and dependencies of the sort that are so familiar in delayed-return systems.

I should stress, as I have before,[14] that I am not seeking to reduce social organisation in hunter-gatherer or other societies to no more than a mere epiphenomenon of technology, the work process and the rules governing the control of assets. All I am saying is this: in a delayed-return system there must be organisation having the very general characteristics I have outlined. The *particular* form the organisation will take cannot be predicted, nor can one say that the organisation exists in order to control and apportion these assets because, once in existence, the organisation will be used in a variety of ways, which will include the control and apportionment of assets, but which are not otherwise determined. In societies without delayed yields and assets, we do not find delayed-return social organisation.

All the six immediate-return systems listed are egalitarian, profoundly egalitarian, though not all quite in the same way or to the same extent; delayed-return systems are far more variable, but to the best of my knowledge not one of them is egalitarian to nearly the same extent as any one of the immediate-return systems. There is no doubt that, whatever else I may be defining by these categories, I certainly am marking off one set of societies that resemble one another in their realisation of a remarkable degree of equality.

What is perhaps surprising is that these societies systematically eliminate distinctions – other than those between the sexes – of wealth, of power and of status. There is here no disconnection between wealth, power and status, no tolerance of inequalities in one of these dimensions any more than in the others. I have exempted relations between men and women from this sweeping assertion. In fact formal relationships between men and women are quite variable in these societies, although in all of them women have far more independence than is usual in delayed-return systems. But since I have talked specifically about male-female relations (1978), I have decided to leave them out of the discussion in this essay. All the general statements I make about relationships here should be taken unless otherwise stated as referring only to adult males.

Let us now see how these systems operate in practice.

Mobility and flexibility

In all these six societies nomadism is fundamental. There are no fixed dwellings, fixed base camps, fixed stores, fixed hunting or fishing apparatus – such as stockades or weirs – or fixed ritual sites to constrain movements. People live in small camp units containing usually a dozen or two people and moving frequently.

These small nomadic camp units are associated with particular areas, usually described in the literature as territories, large enough to provide for subsistence requirements during the annual cycle. Each area at any one time will usually contain one or more camps: camp size and the number of camps vary seasonally. In some cases rights are asserted over its natural resources by the people most closely associated with the area. There is variation between these societies in the extent to which such rights are asserted, but what seems clear is that in every case individuals have full rights of access to camps in several of these areas and there is no question of tightly defined groups monopolising the resources of their areas and excluding out-siders. People can and do move from one camp to another and from one area to another, either temporarily or permanently and without economic penalty. Lee describes how the compo-sition of !Kung camps, which usually contain between ten and thirty individuals, changes from day to day. Intercamp visiting is, he says, the main source of this fluctuation, but each year about 13 per cent of the population makes a permanent residen-tial shift from one camp to another. Another 35 per cent divides its period of residence equally among two or three different camps which may or may not be within the same area.[15]

For the Hadza the situation is relatively simple. Like the !Kung, individual Hadza identify strongly with particular areas but, unlike the !Kung, Hazda do not assert rights to the areas with which they are associated. Anyone may live, hunt and gather wherever he or she likes without restriction – both within the area with which he or she is mainly associated and anywhere else in Hadza country. The camp units in which people live are not fixed entities: there is constant movement in and out while a camp remains at one site: when the site is changed people may move together to one or more new sites or all or some may choose to move to an existing camp elsewhere. There are continuities in the composition of these local groupings but none which seriously limit individual freedom of movement.[16]

In all these societies nomadic movement of all types, both within and outside the local area, is apparently not seen as a burdensome necessity but positively as something healthy and desirable in itself. I have discussed elsewhere how neither the frequency nor the spatial patterning of Hadza moves can be interpreted in terms of ecological factors alone, although probably such flexible movement does, among other things, rapidly accomplish a rational distribution of people in relation to resources available at any particular time.[17] What it also does is to allow people to segregate themselves easily from those with whom they are in conflict, without economic penalty and without sacrificing any other vital interests. Most important of all for this discussion is the way that such arrangements are subversive for the development of authority. Individuals are not bound to fixed areas, to fixed assets or to fixed resources. They are able to move away without difficulty and at a moment's notice from constraint which others may seek to impose on them and such possibility of movement is a powerful levelling mechanism, positively valued like other levelling mechanisms in these societies.

Access to means of coercion

Another important factor in this context is the access which all males have to weapons among the !Kung, Hadza, Mbuti and Batek. Hunting weapons are lethal not just for game animals but also for people. There are serious dangers in antagonising someone: he might choose simply to move away, but if he feels a strong sense of grievance that his rights have been encroached upon he could respond with violence. Lee gives a number of important case histories of !Kung murders showing clearly that there are contexts in which individuals are prepared to use their poisoned arrows.[18] Hadza recognise not just the danger of open public violence, where at least retaliation may be possible, but also the hazard of being shot when asleep in camp at night or being ambushed when out hunting alone in the bush.[19] Effective protection against ambush is impossible. Those of you who have seen the film about the Hadza which I was involved in making may remember Salida, the successful hunter of an impala in the film and of very many other animals in ordinary life.[20] He is now dead and is believed by the Hadza to have died in such an ambush. Only his bones were found. The Hadza had theories about who the murderer might be, but there was much uncertainty; the cause of the conflict is said to have been a dispute over a woman.[21] No action was taken. The important point in all that is that, with such lethal weapons available to all men, with the possibility of using them for murder undetected, with the likelihood that even if detected no action will be taken,[22] with the knowledge that such weapons have indeed been used for murder in the past, the dangers of conflict between men over claims not only to women but more generally to wealth, to power or to prestige are well understood.

Yet there have been instances over the years of Hadza men who have, in spite of the apparent risks, demonstrated that they are not averse to attempting to dominate other Hadza, to order them about, to take their wives or to plunder their possessions. What is striking is that these instances are typically backed by coercive powers derived *from outside Hadza society* and have only been effective to the extent that such men have been able to override the crucial limiting mechanisms – the mobility of the victims and their individual capacity to retaliate – which would in normal circumstances be sufficient to prevent such predation.[23]

In normal circumstances the possession by all men, however physically weak, cowardly, unskilled or socially inept, of the means to kill secretly anyone perceived as a threat to their own well-being not only limits predation and exploitation; it also acts directly as a powerful levelling mechanism. Inequalities of wealth, power and prestige are a potential source of envy and resentment and can be dangerous for holders where means of effective protection are lacking.

What we have here is direct and immediate access to social control, access which is not mediated through formal institutions or through relationships with other people. It is directly analogous to, and matched by, the direct and immediate access, again not normally mediated through formal institutions or through relationships with other people, which people have to food and other resources.

Access to food and other resources

I have already discussed how, within the general pattern of nomadic movement, individuals are able to avoid constraint by their freedom to detach themselves from others at a moment's notice without economic or other penalty. But let us now look more closely at the rights which individuals enjoy without which such action would not be practicable. What are an individual's entitlements to food and other resources and how are these entitlements taken up?

In all these societies individuals have direct access, limited by the division of labour between the sexes, to the ungarnered resources of their country. Whatever the system of territorial rights, in practice in their own areas and in other areas with which they have ties, people have free and equal access to wild foods and water; to all the various raw materials they need for making shelters, tools, weapons and ornaments; to whatever wild resources they use, processed or unprocessed, for trade.

Among the !Kung each area and its resources are used both by a core of men and women with long-standing associations with the area, who identify with it rather than with other areas, and by a wide range of other people who have come from other areas, some temporarily and some more permanently, and who are in most cases linked to one or more of the core members or other residents by a kinship or affinal tie.[24] Anyone with such a link who comes to live with the people of the area cannot, in practice, be refused full access to its resources provided that he or she observes certain minimal rules of politeness. As Marshall explains, newcomers share equally while they live there. No core member or anyone else has the right to withhold resources from the newcomer or to take a larger share.[25]

Among the !Kung, this relative freedom of access operates in spite of the fact that people long associated with an area claim to be 'owners' (*k"ausi*) of it and in particular of its plant and water resources. The !Kung notion of 'ownership' is clearly a broad one and seems here to mean association with, involvement in, identification with the area rather than narrow possession of it. Lee tells us that the usual term for a hunter in !Kung is *!gaik"au*, for which he gives the literal translation 'hunt owner'.[26] This suggests that the term *k"au* ('owner') can indicate association and not just possession. In general in these societies, and even among the !Kung where land rights might at first sight appear to be important in constraining movement and access, what association with a particular locality seems usually to provide is a means of identifying oneself and others, a way of mapping out social relations spatially, rather than a set of exclusive rights. Among the Hadza, people identify strongly with their own areas but place far more emphasis than the !Kung do on an individual's rights of access to resources everywhere, both in his own area and elsewhere.

The boundaries of Hadza areas are, as one would expect from what has already been said, undefined: in effect there are no boundaries.[27] According to Marshall, !Kung boundaries between areas are rather closely defined in localities where important wild plants can be gathered (1976: 187–8).[28] Lee subsequently suggests that, at least in the region where he worked, territories are not clearly defined or bounded even in relation to plant foods: he tells us that he believes 'the !Kung *consciously* strive to maintain a boundaryless universe because this is the best way to operate as hunter-gatherers in a world where group size and resources vary from year to year'.[29] If there were a rather rigid principle of recruitment to local groups combined with rather rigid boundaries between the areas used by local groups, material inequalities between local groups would inevitably develop as populations and resources fluctuated through time. Double flexibility – over group boundaries and territorial boundaries – obviously limits, in a bad year, the dangers of local food shortages or of destructive over-exploitation of sources of wild food. But given the low population density and the limited pressure on resources even in bad years I think it would be appropriate to give less attention to the nutritional benefits of all this flexibility in very rare times of crisis and to stress its day to day significance as a levelling mechanism.

Not just among the !Kung but generally in these societies, this double flexibility directly limits the development of local variation in wealth or in standard of living. If in one area people are eating better than in another, or obtaining food more easily than in another, then, other things being equal, movement of people, coupled perhaps with adjustment of boundaries, is likely over time to tend to even out such unacceptable discrepancies.

The direct and immediate access to food and to other resources which people enjoy is important in other ways. Without seeking permission, obtaining instructions, or being recognised as qualified (except by sex), individuals in these societies can set about obtaining their own requirements as they think fit. They need considerable knowledge and skill but this is freely available to all who are of the appropriate sex and is not, in general, transmitted by formal (or even informal) instruction: rather it is learnt by participation and emulation. In most, but not all, of these societies neither kinship status nor age is used as a qualification to obtain access to particular hunting and gathering skills or equipment.[30] A Hadza boy who wishes to try to hunt large game with bow and poisoned arrows can do so without restriction as soon as he wishes to do so and is able to make or obtain the necessary arrows. More important still, any person – man, woman or child – who seeks to obtain his or her requirements either individually or in association with others can do so without entering into commitments to and dependencies on kin, affines or contractual partners. Adults of either sex can readily, if they choose, obtain enough food to feed themselves adequately and are, in spite of the rules of the division of labour, *potentially* autonomous. It is not rare, at least among the Hadza, to find individuals, usually males, living entirely on their own as hermits for long periods. Of course in practice people living within the community do not live simply on self-acquired food: there are pooling and sharing practices, some of them very important, which I shall describe separately. What matters here is the lack of *dependence* on sharing or pooling of resources: a Hadza woman out gathering with other women will consume much of the proceeds on the spot and, out of what she brings back to camp, little, if any, may go to her husband. Similarly a Hadza man out hunting will expect to feed himself by picking and eating berries and by consuming any small animal he may kill. Only food surpluses cross the sexual boundary. The Hadza are perhaps an extreme instance: in some other immediate-return societies much more food is used socially – is brought back to camp and consumed jointly by people of both sexes. Only among the net-hunting Mbuti (as distinct from the archer Mbuti) does co-ordinated activity provide a substantial amount of food and even in this instance many sources of food are available to and obtained by individuals.

The net-hunting Mbuti apparently gather wild fruits and roots in a manner not very different from the Hadza.[31] But hunting is a co-operative venture: women and children drive game animals, large and small, into a semi-circle of nets set up by the men. The yield is shared out among the various participants as soon as they return to camp.[32] I must stress that this co-operation in the hunt is of a very specific sort. Within the rather broad limits set by the optimal numbers for an efficient hunt,[33] anyone who is present may participate according to his or her sex role and is entitled to a proportion of the yield. There is no commitment to participate and no basis for exclusion from participation. Each hunt is complete in itself and participation today apparently carries no obligation to participate tomorrow. This is fundamentally different from co-operation in any agricultural system where the members of the productive group are not an *ad hoc* aggregation but are a set of people bound by more enduring ties of kinship or of contract.

What I want to stress here, in this lack of dependence on specific others, is the implication for authority and, most obviously, for domestic authority. The process of production is not in general controlled and directed by the household head or, if it is, the control is not authoritarian and is better described as limited co-ordination by consent. Indeed among the Hadza I would say there are no household heads.[34] Older children and young unmarried adults in these societies are not dependent on the senior generation for access to property, to food or to resources though they may receive some property, food and resources from them. Among both Hadza and !Kung, children do relatively little work and what they do is done at their choice rather than under parental direction. Neither the parent-child nexus, nor the relationship between generations more generally, provide either a model or a training ground for relationships of authority and dependency; indeed they provide an alternative model for and training in personal decision-making and in the possibilities of self-reliance, in sharing but not dependency on sharing.

The point can perhaps be made most clear if a simple contrast is drawn with some agricultural and pastoral societies living in south eastern Africa. Using detailed ethnographic evidence on the Southern Bantu, Richards long ago drew attention to the importance of access to food and other resources for an understanding of inequality: she stressed how, in the absence of other valuables, possession or control of food is singularity important as a means of differentiating one member of the community from another and as a source of power.[35] The authority of a man as household head over his unmarried sons, both immature and adult, his right to direct their labour and to demand obedience and respect from them is linked with

the father's possession and control over the food supply – the cattle-herd and their produce, and in general, the grain supply too. The head of the family is . . . bound to support his sons . . . The receipt of food marks the dependence of the child on the father . . . Unless he can earn money [in employment] . . . he simply cannot acquire food except from his parents' hands . . . one woman alone – his mother, or her substitute – must cook [it for him]. His dependence is thus displayed concretely by the receipt of actual food . . . [36]

In immediate-return hunting and gathering societies the household head has no comparable role as real or symbolic provider, as the source of most good things. It is, I am sure, not accidental that neither !Kung nor Hadza usually place much emphasis on formal meal times. A great deal of food is eaten informally throughout the day.[37] Marshall records that 'Meat is not habitually cooked and eaten as a family meal among the !Kung . . . The men, women, and children may cook their pieces when and as they wish, often roasting bits in the coals and hot ashes and eating them alone at odd times.'[38]

Sharing

The genuine equality of opportunity that individuals enjoy in their access to resources, limited only by the division of labour between the sexes, does not, of course, ensure equality of yield.

The quantities of all the various items which individuals obtain, either on their own or jointly with other people, vary greatly depending on skill, on luck, on persistence, on capacity to work and on other factors. It is at this point that the most crucial controls on the development of inequality come into action.

The principal occasions in which individuals in these societies are brought into association with valued assets which could be accumulated or distributed to build status are when large game animals are killed. And it is then that the most elaborate formal rules dissociating the hunter from his kill and denying him the privileges of ownership are brought to bear. Levelling mechanisms come into operation precisely at the point where the potential for the development of inequalities of wealth, power and prestige is greatest. Among the Hadza and the !Kung hunting success among adult men seems to be very variable. A high proportion of animals are killed by a small proportion of men.[39] Techniques for drying meat and converting it into relatively lightweight stores of biltong are known. Yet successful individual hunters are specifically denied the opportunity to make effective use of their kills to build wealth and prestige or to attract dependents. Lee has reported how !Kung are expected to be self-deprecating about their hunting successes; boasting is met with scorn.[40] Turnbull tells us that 'some [Mbuti] men, because of exceptional hunting skill, may come to resent it when their views are disregarded, but if they try to force those views they are very promptly subjected to ridicule'.[41] A Hadza returning to camp having shot a large animal is expected to exercise restraint. He sits down quietly with the other men and allows the blood on his arrow shaft to speak for him. If the animal has only been wounded, the name of the species may not be mentioned directly: the effect of uttering its name would, Hadza believe, allow it to recover from the arrow poison and escape. Special respectful terms must be used and there should be a minimum of comment. Similarly, to talk of a dead animal before it has been dismembered is believed to put at risk the animal's fat which the Hadza value more highly than lean meat. One effect of these rules is, certainly, to deny to the hunter praise which he might otherwise expect to receive.[42]

For the !Kung, the owner of the first arrow to hit the animal effectively is the owner of the kill with the right to distribute it. Arrow-lending is common and the owner of the arrow is often someone other than the hunter himself. Lee explains that meat distribution brings prestige but it also brings the risk of accusations of stinginess or improper behaviour if the distribution is not to everybody's liking.[43] So hunters are not reluctant to hunt sometimes with someone else's arrow and to pass over the responsibility for distributing the kill to him. When discussing this practice, Marshall suggests that 'the society seems to want to extinguish in every way possible the concept of the meat belonging to the hunter'.[44]

The meat of the kill is widely shared within the camp unit. Among the Hadza the best portions (which differ depending on which species has been killed) belong to the initiated men and may not under any circumstances be eaten by the hunter on his own. For the Hadza this would be a particularly heinous offence which would be likely to result in violence towards the hunter; it would also, Hadza believe, cause him to become seriously ill and perhaps even die. The hunter's rights to the initiated men's meat are identical to those of each of the other initiated men: the meat must be eaten in secret by the initiated men as a group until it is finished. The rest of the meat is described as people's meat and is distributed first at the kill site among those who have come to carry in the meat, then back at camp it is distributed among those who remained behind and then, finally, when it is cooked, it is consumed by those who happen to be present and not simply by the person or the family grouping to whom the meat was allocated. The hunter himself will often not be involved in dismembering the carcass and in distributing the meat but he and his wife's mother and father, if they are present, will receive substantial shares. Among the !Kung the meat is distributed and redistributed in waves of sharing through the camp: everyone receives a share.

It has often been suggested that meat-sharing is simply a labour-saving form of storage. The hunter surrenders his rights to much of his kill in order to secure rights over parts of the kills of other hunters in future. There are problems with this formulation: as I have already mentioned, hunting success is unequal. Donors often remain on balance donors and may not receive anything like an equivalent return. Entitlement does not depend in any way on donation. Some men who are regular recipients never themselves contribute. Instead of seeing the arrangement as being in the interest of the donor, I think we should be clear that it is imposed on the donor by the community. Instead of seeing the transaction as a form of reciprocal exchange, I would suggest we treat it as analogous to taxation on incomes of the successful in our own society. The successful pay more than the less successful and are obliged to do so. They are not able to establish greater claims in future through having paid more tax and do not derive much prestige from having contributed more to the tax pool than they have withdrawn from it in benefits. The analogy may sound rather crude: certainly the hunter derives more prestige from contributing an animal than any taxpayer does from paying his taxes, but it does bring out the important fact that we are dealing here with a socially imposed levelling mechanism and not a mere practical convenience for the hunter.

Vegetable foods, which are less highly valued and which are obtained more easily and more predictably and in amounts which correspond more closely to the needs of the gatherers, are less widely shared but are not narrowly reserved for each gatherer and her immediate family. Among the Hadza it would be out of the question for a woman to hoard food while others are hungry. Sharing rights for pregnant women are particularly emphasised by the Hadza: they have the right to ask anyone for food at any time and are believed to be at risk if they are refused.

Sanctions on the accumulation of personal possessions

Clothing, tools, weapons, smoking pipes, bead ornaments and other similar objects are personally held and owned. At least in the case of the three African societies, they are in general *relatively* simple objects, made with skill, not elaborately styled or decorated and not vested with any special significance. They can be made or obtained without great difficulty. Rules of inheritance are flexible and no one depends on receiving such objects either by inheritance or by formal transmission from close kin of the previous generation during their lifetime.

Everywhere we find that there are sanctions against accumulation. This cannot be explained, as so many writers have mistakenly suggested, simply in practical terms: nomadic peoples who have to carry everything they possess are concerned that their possessions should be readily portable so that they can be carried with ease when the time comes to move camp, but sanc-

tions against accumulation go far beyond meeting this requirement and apply even to the lightest objects such as beads,
arrowheads or supplies of arrow poison.

The transmission of possessions between people

Hadza use a distinctive method for transmitting such personally
owned objects between people which has profound consequences for their relationships. In any large camp men spend
most of their time gambling with one another, far more time
than is spent obtaining food. They gamble mainly for metal-
headed hunting arrows, both poisoned and non-poisoned, but
are also able to stake knives, axes, beads, smoking pipes, cloth
and even occasionally a container of honey, which can be used in
trade. A few personally owned objects cannot be staked, because,
Hadza say, they are not sufficiently valuable. These are a man's
hunting bow, his non-poisoned arrows without metal heads used
for hunting birds and small animals, and his leather bag used for
carrying his pipes and tobacco, arrowheads and other odds and
ends. These objects excluded from gambling share two characteristics: first, they maintain a man's capacity to feed and protect
himself and secondly, they are made from materials available in
every part of the country. In contrast many of the objects used
in gambling are made, at least in part, of materials not available in every part of the country. For example, poisoned arrows
incorporate a head made from scrap metal obtained in trade
from non-Hadza, poison which is made from the sap of one tree
or the seeds of another which are local in their distribution and
entirely absent from large areas of the country, and, if possible,
a lightweight shaft of a particular species of shrub even more
restricted in its range. Stone smoking pipes are made from a type
of soapstone which is again only found in certain localities.

The game involves tossing a handful of bark discs against a
tree and reading the result which depends on which way up the
various discs fall. Basically it is a game of chance, and players
have relatively little opportunity of influencing the result. Skill
in throwing does play some part, but the effect is reduced by
banning the winner of the previous throw from acting as thrower
next time.

In the course of a day, in a large dry-season camp, there will
usually be hundreds of contests each one involving the transfer

of a piece of property from the loser or losers to the winner. During the day, many objects pass through competitors' hands, but as the game is a game of chance the randomising effect means that they will usually end the day without a substantial net gain or loss. If the player ends the day with some winnings, usually they will include some objects he wants to keep and use. He restakes objects he does not want and keeps back, as far as he can, objects he wants. From time to time people do gain substantial winnings and are then subject to great pressure to continue to compete so that other competitors can win back their lost possessions. Often winners, in an attempt to keep their winnings intact for longer than would otherwise be possible, move to another camp, but they are then usually followed by some of the other competitors. I can recall only one instance of a man who succeeded in keeping most of his winnings for a period of as long as a few weeks, and he was a quite exceptional person who withstood the pressures on him and rationed his subsequent play whenever he won.

I have discussed Hadza gambling at greater length than might at first seem justified because its effects are so important. It is the major means by which scarce and local objects are circulated throughout the country: much inter-camp visiting is stimulated by gambling and winnings are constantly on the move. Objects such as stone pipes which are made in one part of the country circulate out to other areas where they are withdrawn from the game and put to use.

This circulation is accomplished, then, not through some form of exchange which would bind participants to one another in potentially unequal relationships of kinship or contract. The transactions are neutralised and depersonalised by being passed through the game. Even close kin and affines gamble with each other and the game acts against any development of one-way flows and dependency in relationships between them.

Individual effort, craft skill and, particularly, the skill of trading with outsiders are quite variable. The attraction of gambling mobilises effort and skill but distributes its proceeds at random in a way which subverts the accumulation of individual wealth by the hard-working or by the skilled. It further subverts any tendency to regional differentiation within Hadza country based on valuable local resources which are in demand in other areas. It is paradoxical that a game based on the desire to win and, in a sense, to accumulate should operate so directly against the possibility of systematic accumulation. Its levelling effect is very powerful.

!Kung transmit personal possessions in a quite different way, which has far less levelling potential. Each !Kung enters into formal exchange partnerships, known as *hxaro*, with a number of other people with whom systematic exchanges of personal possessions and of hospitality take place. Far from subverting relationships as Hadza gambling does, these exchanges create ties involving some mutual commitment. They seem, however, to be organised in ways which stress the equal relationship between partners and provide little opportunity for property accumulation or the development of patron-client type relations between partners.[45] Marshall shows how the gifts are simple tokens of generosity and friendly intent. The trivial debts incurred are quite unlike the binding jural obligations at the centre of delayed-return systems. And as Marshall says 'no one was dependent on obtaining objects by gift giving'.[46]

Both among the !Kung and among the Hadza, individuals with any objects for which they appear to have no immediate need are under the greatest pressure to give them up and many possessions are given away almost as soon as they are obtained and usually, I think, without any expectation of return.[47] Among the Hadza the attitude to property often seems very casual. I well remember early on in my fieldwork being pressed very strongly to give people hoop iron to make arrowheads: I obtained the iron with some difficulty, gave out a piece to each man in the camp and was rather affronted when I discovered that, because I had given out more than could immediately be used, some of it had simply been thrown away. Limitations on the uses to which property can be put, especially if no gambling is going on at the time, in a context in which saving and accumulation are so actively discouraged and pressure for *de facto* equality of wealth is so great, mean that people often seem to place surprisingly little value both on their own and on other people's possessions.

Leadership and decision-making

In these societies there are either no leaders at all or leaders who are very elaborately constrained to prevent them from exercising

authority or using their influence to acquire wealth or prestige.[48]
A Hadza camp at any particular time is often known by the
name of a well-known man then living in it (for example, /ets'a
ma Durugida – Durugida's camp). But this indicates only that the
man is well enough known for his name to be a useful label,
and not that he acts as either a leader or a representative of the
camp.[49] Hadza decisions are essentially individual ones: even
when matters such as the timing of a camp move or the choice
of a new site are to be decided, there are no leaders whose
responsibility it is to take the decisions or to guide people
towards some general agreement. Sporadic discussion about
moving does occur, but usually it takes the form of announce-
ments by some individual men that they are going to move and
where they are going to move to. Other men will often defer a
decision about whether to stay, whether to accompany those
who are moving, or whether to move elsewhere, until the move
actually begins. Certainly some, particularly older men with
large families who are often those after whom camps are named,
are likely to have more influence on the outcome than others
and to precipitate by their individual decisions the movement of
an entire camp or a segment of a camp. But I would not describe
them as leaders.[50]

The !Kung also name camps after individuals, whom Lee
describes as leaders but leaders with a very limited role. 'In
group discussions these people may speak out more than others,
may be deferred to by others, and one gets the feeling that their
opinions hold a bit more weight than the opinions of other
discussants'.[51] What is particularly striking is that personal qualities suggesting that a !Kung individual is ambitious for power or
wealth exclude such a person from the possibility of leadership:

None is arrogant, overbearing, boastful, or aloof. In !Kung terms these traits
absolutely disqualify a person as a leader and may engender even stronger
forms of ostracism . . . Another trait emphatically not found among traditional camp leaders is a desire for wealth or acquisitiveness . . . Whatever
their personal influence over group decisions, they never translate this into
more wealth or more leisure time than other group members have[52] . . . Their
accumulation of material goods is never more, and is often much less, than
the average accumulation of the other households in their camp.[53]

Leaders should ideally be 'modest in demeanor, generous to a
fault, and egalitarian . . .'[54] Leaders such as these pose no threat

to egalitarian values and indeed could be said to display and reinforce egalitarianism.

These are, of course, not the only contexts in which equality is expressed and levelling mechanisms operate: to do justice to the subject it would be necessary to go much further and in particular to explore the expression of egalitarianism in religious belief and practice. But I think I have said enough to show that we have here the application of a rigorously systematic principle: in these societies the ability of individuals to attach and to detach themselves at will from groupings and from relationships, to resist the imposition of authority by force, to use resources freely without reference to other people, to share as equals in game meat brought into camp, to obtain personal possessions without entering into dependent relationships – all these bring out one central aspect of this specific form of egalitarianism. *What it above all does is to disengage people from property, from the potentiality in property rights for creating dependency.* I think it is probable that this specialised development can only be realised without impoverishment in societies with a simple hunting and gathering economy because elsewhere this degree of disengagement from property would damage the operation of the economy. Indeed the indications are that this development is intrinsic, a necessary component of immediate-return economies which occurs only in such economies.

It is time that I discussed very briefly how these societies compare with others that have been described as egalitarian. We are all familiar with the application of the term to those modern complex societies, including our own, in which egalitarian sentiments are commonly expressed in political discourse. But let us leave these aside. Anthropologists, at least those conducting research outside Europe, have more commonly used the term as a simple synonym for acephalous societies, societies without rulers, societies without formal political offices. Delayed-return systems within this category, in contrast to the immediate-return systems which I have been discussing in some detail, are egalitarian in a very different sense. To generalise about so wide and variable a category is not really satisfactory but a few obvious points can be made: first, the community of political equals is usually a community of property-holding household heads whose relations with their wives and female kin and with their junior male kinsmen within the household are far from equal. Intergenerational inequality and especially the inequality of holder and heir is usually stressed. The household head has the right and the duty to maintain and control the assets held by the household and to direct the labour of its members.

Equality between household heads is in many of these systems only a starting-point, a qualification to compete in a strenuous competition for wealth, power and prestige. Writing about Papua New Guinea, Forge tells us that 'to be equal and stay equal is an extremely onerous task requiring continual vigilance and effort. Keeping up with the Joneses may be hard work, but keeping up with all other adult males of a community is incomparably harder. The principal mechanism by which equality is maintained is equal exchange of things of the same class or of identical things. Basically all presentations of this type are challenges to prove equality'.[55] The outcome of such challenges is striking inequality. Writing about the same area Burridge tells us what happens to the casualties. 'Rubbish-men', as impoverished people are called:

were men who had either opted out of the status competition, or who habitually failed to meet their obligations. Often, they lived on the fringes of a settlement, between the village proper and the forest or bush outside: a placement which reflected their position in the moral order. Because they had failed to meet their obligations, or were unable or had chosen not to participate in the process whereby proper men were supposed to demonstrate their moral nature, they hardly rated as men, were not fully moral beings in the locally recognised sense. Treated with a charitable contempt which they accepted with resigned equanimity, rubbish-men were generally left to their own devices, working by and for themselves at a markedly lower level of subsistence than others.[56]

This type of competitive equality contrasts dramatically with the non-competitive equality of the systems I have been describing. There equality does not have to be earned or displayed, in fact should not be displayed, but is intrinsically present as an entitlement of all men. There are no casualties of the principle of equality among the Hadza[57] or the !Kung, none of whose moral worth is destroyed by poor economic performance or lack of personal competitiveness. Egalitarianism is asserted as an automatic entitlement which does not have to be validated.

New Guinea is something of an extreme instance, but even the less aggressive egalitarianism of East African pastoral societies, whose members do not engage in the competitive displays of wealth so characteristic of New Guinea, are still highly competitive in comparison with the !Kung and the Hadza and have far more in common socially with New Guinea than they do with these hunter-gatherers. There are marked differences in wealth in cattle and in standard of living. They too have casualties. Household heads who through bad management or bad luck lose all or most of their herd, lose at the same time the essential qualification for equality with herdowners. They have then to work as low-status clients or else move out of the pastoral economy.

Burnham has recently discussed what he describes as the structural conservatism of nomadic pastoral societies.[58] In a valuable paper he argues that fluidity of local grouping and spatial mobility are remarkably resistant to change. They promote egalitarianism and greatly inhibit the development of both political centralisation and class stratification. Within sub-Saharan African nomadic pastoral societies such centralisation and stratification have emerged only in situations of conquest and/or substantial sedentarisation.

I would argue that the nomadic hunting and gathering societies I have discussed are even more profoundly conservative. Fluidity of local grouping and spatial mobility, here combined with and reinforced by a set of distinctive egalitarian practices which disengage people from property, inhibit not only political change but any form of intensification of the economy. There is no easy transition from non-competitive egalitarianism to competitive egalitarianism.

Lee has described the difficulties some !Kung have encountered in their efforts to live by agriculture and by keeping domestic animals.[59] The difficulties are not technical ones: some individual !Kung have for years worked for neighbouring farmers and have become knowledgeable about farming techniques. The overwhelming difficulties lie in the egalitarian levelling mechanisms. There is no way that farming can be carried on without some accumulation, without stores of grain and of agricultural tools, and the major difficulty for the few individual !Kung who wish to make a real effort to farm is not that they themselves are unable to exercise self-restraint and to build up their stocks but that they are unable to restrain their kin and affines from coming to eat the harvested grain. Exactly the same has occurred again and again in the Hadza government-run settlements. Almost everybody understands the basic agricultural techniques and almost everybody is prepared to carry out some cultivation. But those few who apply their labour systematically and skilfully and obtain a good crop have found that their fields are raided by other Hadza even before the grain is harvested, and once it has been harvested those with grain in store are under relentless pressure to share it with other Hadza rather than to ration its use so that it will last until the next harvest is obtained. In the face of such obstacles, even the successful farmer is likely to give up. If it is so difficult for these egalitarian hunter-gatherers to take up agriculture nowadays with so many pressures on them to settle, it is even less likely that they would have been able to convert to agriculture in the past.[60] I have suggested elsewhere that if we are to understand the development of agriculture from hunting and gathering, we ought to look at delayed-return hunter-gatherers who have the values and the organisation to facilitate the transition.

To end I would like to return briefly again to the nature of equality in these systems and its association with certain other values. Are people in these societies, who are relatively free from want and free from many of the forms of competition which are so evident in other societies, humane, altruistic and caring towards those who are not able to care for themselves? The answer is not simple, but it is possible to say a little. In delayed-return systems people are bound to their close kin and to certain other associates in relationships which commonly involve the constant exchange of goods and services in fulfilment of obligations of one sort or another. People are committed to one another both in the sense that they have material obligations to one another and in the wider sense that they accept a measure of responsibility for one another. The potentiality for autonomy and the limitation of obligations to *specific* other people – as opposed to the generalised obligation to share – certainly seem to reduce the sense of commitment that people feel to others, at least in the Hadza instance where the movement of goods between people is so often depersonalised by the gambling game. There are instances in which the Hadza have abandoned the seriously ill when they moved camp, leaving them with their possessions and with food and water but knowing that they were unlikely to be able to provide for themselves. I was very surprised by the neglect of a previously popular grandmother in one of the settlements when she became senile, and I think it less likely that this would have occurred within a household of one of the neighbouring agricultural societies. I have to allow, though, for the fact that the total number of instances of neglect or abandonment that have come to my attention is small and that such instances are more public among the Hadza than they are in societies where they can occur behind closed doors.

In another respect I can report with more confidence. Hadza society is open. People who are able to associate themselves at will with whatever area and whatever camp they choose do not impose social boundaries between themselves and others. There is no basis for exclusion. I think this is best brought out by their treatment of lepers. Among neighbouring sedentary societies lepers are not able to participate effectively in social life and are commonly ostracised or even expelled (these days usually to a leprosarium). There are a very small number of Hadza lepers who appear to be treated exactly like everyone else although the Hadza are very well aware of the dire consequences of the disease and the fact that it can be transmitted from one person to another. The principle is entirely clear. It is not that the Hadza are particularly sympathetic or humane towards lepers, who may well be mercilessly teased about their clumsiness: the principle is that Hadza society is open and there is simply no basis for exclusion. Equality is, in a sense, generalised by them to all mankind but, sadly, few of the rest of mankind, so enmeshed in property relations, would be willing to extend parity of esteem to hunter-gatherers who treat property with such a lack of seriousness.

Notes

1. Malinowski Memorial Lecture for 1981, given at the London School of Economics and Political Science on 5 May 1981.
2. B. Malinowski, *A Scientific Theory of Culture*. New York: Oxford University Press, 1960, p. 61.
3. The term was used earlier with a different meaning (J. A. H. Murray *et al.* (eds), *The Oxford English Dictionary*. Oxford: Clarendon Press, 1970).
4. J. C. Woodburn, 'Sex Roles and the Division of Labour in Hunting

and Gathering Societies'. Paper presented at the first international conference on hunting and gathering societies. Paris, June 1978; J. C. Woodburn, 'Minimal Politics: The Political Organisation of the Hadza of North Tanzania. In *Politics in Leadership: A Comparative Perspective* (eds) W. A. Shack & P. S. Cohen, Oxford: Clarendon Press, 1979; J. C. Woodburn, Hunters and gatherers today and reconstruction of the past. In *Soviet and Western Anthropology* (ed.) E. Gellner, London: Duckworth, 1980.

5. In some, people obtain part of their food from wild products and part directly in exchange for wild products.

6. In using this simple, indeed over-simplified, dichotomous categorisation into immediate-return and delayed-return systems, I should stress that it is designed as an initial, rough-and-ready basis for looking at what seem to be crucial variables for understanding social organisations. The job of specifying them more precisely and of disentangling their implications is still to come if it is accepted that the timing of yields on labour is significant for social organisation. I recognise, of course, that the four types of assets listed for delayed-return systems are qualitatively different and certainly do not have identical implications for social organisation though they do, it seems to me, have enough in common for it to be useful to group them together initially. I recognise too that some yields are part-immediate and part-delayed, that some immediate yields are much more immediate than others and that some delayed yields are much more delayed than others. I also recognise not only that there is always some immediate-return activity in delayed-return systems (most strikingly in the case of Australian Aboriginal societies) but also that there is some delayed-return activity in immediate-return systems. In taking the matter further, the valuable comments of the following colleagues will be taken into account: J. Andrade, The economic, social and cosmological dimensions of the preoccupation with short-term ends in three hunting and gathering societies: the Mbuti Pygmies of Zaire, the !Kung San of Namibia and Botswana, and the Netsilik Eskimos of Northern Canada. Thesis, University of London, 1979; R. Dodd, 'Ritual and the Maintenance of Internal Co-operation among the Baka Hunters and Gatherers. In *Second International Conference on Hunting and Gathering Societies, 19 to 24 September 1980*. Quebec: Université Laval, Départment d'Anthropologie, 1980; Firth personal communication 1981; T. Ingold, 'The Principle of Individual Autonomy and the Collective Appropriation of Nature'. In *Second International Conference on Hunting and Gathering Societies, 19 to 24 September 1980*. Quebec: Université Laval, Département d'Anthropologie, 1980; Ndagala personal communication 1981; P. Wiessner, History and continuity in !Kung San reciprocal

relationships. In *Second International Conference on Hunting and Gathering Societies, 19 to 24 September 1980*. Quebec: Université Laval, Département d'Anthropologie, 1980.

7. If some undemanding agricultural crop is grown in an area where land is plentiful, if it does not require systematic application of labour over time and if it is unsuitable for storage, then this dependency may be small and the organisational requirements more limited.

8. C. M. Turnbull, *The Mbuti Pygmies: An Ethnographic Survey* (Anthrop. Papers Am. Mus. Nat. Hist. 50: 3. New York: American Museum of Natural History, 1965; C. M. Turnbull, *Wayward Servants: the Two Worlds of the African Pygmies*. London: Eyre & Spottiswoode, 1966.

9. R. B. Lee, *The !Kung San: Men, Women, and Work in a Foraging Society*. Cambridge: Cambridge University Press, 1979; L. Marshall, *The !Kung of Nyae Nyae*. Cambridge, Mass.: Harvard University Press, 1976; R. B. Lee and I. DeVore (eds), *Kalahari Hunter-gatherers: Studies of the !Kung San and their Neighbors*. Cambridge, Mass.: Harvard University Press, 1976; P. Wiessner, Hxaro: a regional system of reciprocity for reducing risk among the !Kung San. Thesis, University of Michigan, 1977.

10. B. Morris, An analysis of the economy and social organisation of the Malapantaram, a South Indian hunting and gathering people. Thesis, University of London, 1975; P. M. Gardner, 'The Paliyans'. In *Hunters and Gatherers Today* (ed.) M. G. Bicchieri. New York: Holt, Rinehart & Winston, 1972.

11. K. L. Endicott, Batek Negrito economy and social organisation. Thesis, Harvard University; K. L. Endicott, Batek Negrito sex roles. Thesis, Canberra: Australian National University, 1979.

12. J. C. Woodburn, 'An Introduction to Hadza Ecology'. In *Man the Hunter* (eds) R. B. Lee and I. DeVore. Chicago: Aldine, 1968; J. C. Woodburn, 'Stability and Flexibility in Hadza Residential Groupings'. In *Man the Hunter* (eds) R. B. Lee and I. DeVore. Chicago: Aldine, 1968; J. C. Woodburn, *Hunters and Gatherers: The Material Culture of the Nomadic Hadza*. London: The British Museum, 1970; J. C. Woodburn, 'Ecology. Nomadic Movement and the Composition of the Local Group among Hunters and Gatherers: An East African Example and its Implications'. In *Man, Settlement and Urbanism* (eds) P. J. Ucko, R. Tringham & G. W. Dimbleby. London: Duckworth, 1972.

13. I have listed here only a few of the more relevant references. Additional references to these societies are given in J. C. Woodburn, 'Hunters and Gatherers Today and Reconstruction of the Past'. In *Soviet and Western Anthropology* (ed.) E. Gellner. London: Duckworth, 1980.

14. Woodburn, 'Minimal Politics', p. 111.
15. Lee, *The !Kung San*, p. 54.
16. Woodburn, 'Stability and Flexibility'; Woodburn, 'Ecology'.
17. Woodburn, 'Ecology'.
18. Lee, *The !Kung San*, pp. 370–400.
19. Woodburn, 'Minimal Politics'. Out of the twenty-two !Kung homicides which Lee records, seventeen occurred during spontaneous open public violence while five were the result of premeditated sneak attacks (R. B. Lee, *The !Kung San: Men, Women, and Work in a Foraging Society*. Cambridge: Cambridge University Press, p. 382). Ambushes are possibly less likely to occur among the !Kung where 'a person's footprints are as well known as his face' (L. Marshall, *The !Kung of Nyae Nyae*. Cambridge, Mass.: Harvard University Press, 1976, p. 188). Hadza are expert trackers but are usually not able to recognise one another's footprints.
20. J. C. Woodburn and S. Hudson, *The Hadza: The Food Quest of an East African Hunting and Gathering Tribe* (16 mm film), 1966.
21. The murdered man was a rather aggressive character and had in the past been involved in disputes about women. Years earlier he himself had made threats in my presence that he would kill a man – not his suspected assailant – whom he accused of committing adultery with his wife.
22. Among the !Kung some killings lead to retaliatory killings, others do not. According to Lee's figures, four killings led to retaliatory killings (some of them multiple) while seven did not (Lee, p. 389).
23. Woodburn, 'Minimal Politics', pp. 262–4.
24. L. Marshall, *The !Kung of Nyae Nyae*. Cambridge, Mass.: Harvard University Press, 1976; R. B. Lee, *The !Kung San: Men, Women, and Work in a Foraging Society*. Cambridge: Cambridge University Press, 1979.
25. Marshall, p. 189.
26. Lee, *The !Kung San*, p. 206.
27. Woodburn, 'Stability and Flexibility', p. 104.
28. Marshall, *The !Kung of Nyae Nyae*, pp. 187–8.
29. Lee, *The !Kung San*, p. 335.
30. Mbuti are an exception here: for them age distinctions are of some importance in the work process (C. M. Turnbull, *Wayward Servants: the Two Worlds of the African Pygmies*. London: Eyre & Spottiswoode, 1966).
31. Turnbull, *Wayward Servants*, pp. 166–8.
32. Turnbull, pp. 157–8.
33. Turnbull, p. 154.
34. J. C. Woodburn, 'Stability and flexibility in Hadza Residential Groupings', p. 109.

35. A. I. Richards, *Hunger and Work in a Savage Tribe; A Functional Study of Nutrition among the Southern Bantu.* London: Routledge, 1932, p. 89.
36. Richards, *Hunger and Work in a Savage Tribe*, p. 77.
37. Lee, *The !Kung San*, p. 199.
38. Marshall, *The !Kung of Nyae Nyae*, p. 302.
39. Lee, *The !Kung San*, pp. 242–4.
40. Lee, pp. 243–6.
41. Turnbull, *Wayward Servants*, p. 183.
42. I am not, of course, suggesting that this is the main significance of such rules.
43. Lee, *The !Kung San*, pp. 247–8.
44. Marshall, *The !Kung of Nyae Nyae*, p. 297.
45. P. Wiessner, Hxaro: a regional system of reciprocity for reducing risk among the !Kung San. Thesis, University of Michigan, 1977.
46. Marshall, *The !Kung of Nyae Nyae*, p. 308.
47. The unremitting demands Hadza make on one another are highly conspicuous and often go beyond asking for things for which the owner has no immediate need. A man who obtains a ball of tobacco, a shirt or a cloth by trading with or begging from non-Hadza is unlikely to keep it for long unless he is very determined and willing to make himself unpopular. He will be asked for it endlessly. The pressures on outsiders (including anthropologists) to give away their possessions is equally great. Lee writes of how he was repelled by the !Kung's 'nagging demands for gifts, demands that grow more insistent the more we give' (Lee, p. 458).
48. I leave aside leaders imposed on these societies by outsiders or who derive their power from links with outsiders (Lee, pp. 348–50; Woodburn, 1979, pp. 261–4).
49. Woodburn, 'Stability and Flexibility', p. 105.
50. Woodburn, 'Minimal Politics'.
51. Lee, *The !Kung San*, p. 343.
52. Lee, p. 345.
53. Lee, p. 457.
54. Lee, p. 350.
55. A. Forge, 'The Golden Fleece', *Man* (N.S.) 7, pp. 527–40, 1972.
56. K. O. L. Burridge, 'The Melanesian Manager'. In *Studies in Social Anthropology: Essays in Memory of E. E. Evans-Pritchard by his Former Oxford Colleagues* (eds) J. H. M. Beattie & R. G. Lienhardt. Oxford: Clarendon Press, 1975.
57. As I mention at the end of this essay, there are casualties of one sort: the seriously ill, the senile and others unable to care for themselves and to claim equality, may not be well treated.
58. P. Burnham, 'Spatial Mobility and Political Centralisation in Pastoral

Societies'. In *Pastoral Production and Society: Proceedings of the International Meeting on Nomadic Pastoralism, Paris 1–3 December 1976*. Cambridge University Press, 1979, pp. 349–60.

59. Lee, *The !Kung San*, pp. 409–14.
60. In an important recent article Cashdan discusses the contrast between equality among the !Kung and inequality (especially in wealth) among the //Gana, a Central Kalahari population derived from mixed marriages between immigrant Bakgalagadi men and San (Bushman) women. The //Gana supplement their basic hunting and gathering subsistence with some farming. They are nomadic but from a home base. She attributes //Gana inequality not to the development of any formal organisation of inequality but to 'the inevitable result of the *lifting* of the constraints that produce strict egalitarianism among other Kalahari hunter-gatherers' (E. A. Cashdan, 'Egalitarianism among Hunters and Gatherers', Am. Anthrop, 82, pp. 116–20). I differ from her in believing that egalitarian values, so deeply built into traditional hunting and gathering systems in the area, would be unlikely to be so easily shed were it not for the fact that the community is of mixed origin and drew part of its membership from people with experience of farming and delayed-return.

Edwin Cannan

Inequality Between the Sexes

Whether a child is born to parents who are well to do or to parents who are poor, it is an economic advantage to be born a boy rather than a girl. It is commonly observed that women's earnings are considerably lower than men's; it is often said that they do not average more than about half.

Now if there was only one occupation, and that occupation required heavy muscular exertion and none of those qualities in which women excel, we should have no hesitation in explaining the difference of earnings by the smaller output of the women. To many men, and perhaps to some women, this appears a sufficient explanation of things as they are. They see that in many occupations in which men and women compete the women's output is measurably less than the men's, and in regard to others, in which the output cannot be measured by the ounce or the yard, they argue that the very fact that men continue to be employed along with women, although the men earn more money, shows that the men are somehow worth more to the employers than the women, which must mean that at any rate their net produce is greater. This is quite sound as far as it goes, but it by no means covers the whole ground. There are, no doubt, many occupations in which men are superior to women. If the less well-paid women's work came cheaper to the employer than the men's work, women would rapidly, or at least slowly, drive out men, just as men would drive out women if men's work were the cheaper: the employers who declined to move would be driven out by those who did. But there are also employments in which women are superior to men – to take an example about which no one has any doubt, we may give as an instance the care of children. In such occupations men do not compete, and if they tried to do so they would get few situations, even if they offered themselves at rates immensely below those at present earned by the women. The reason obviously is that in these

297

occupations the men's output would be much inferior to the women's.

Yet here, too, we find women's earnings low as compared with men's. We cannot compare them with the non-existent men's earnings in the same occupation; we must compare them with the earnings of men employed in occupations of the same class, in the sense of occupations which were open to the particular women in question (both men and women being employed), or which would have been open to their choice if they had been born boys (men only being employed). It would be absurd, for example, to compare the earnings of the average children's nurse with the earnings which we might suppose her brother might make as a nurse, and consequently to declare her earnings high. What we must do is to compare her earnings with the actual earnings of her brother in his occupation of, say, carting coal, and then we find that her earnings are low – at any rate when hours, loss of freedom, and other considerations are taken into account. Now, it is clearly no use to say that the woman earns less than her brother because she cannot heave as much coal; we might just as well say that he should earn less than his sister because he cannot wash as much baby.

The true explanation of the general inferiority of women's earnings, like every true explanation of any earnings, must combine the consideration of amount of output with the consideration of the value of a unit of output. The real reason why women's earnings are low in occupations in which the ultimate judge, the consumer, finds their output superior to men's, is to be found in the fact of the restricted area of employment offered by these occupations in comparison with the number of girls choosing them, which of course brings down the value of the output. The value of work being thus depressed in these occupations, not only are men driven out or kept out of them, but many girls find they can do as well for themselves by going into occupations in which men are superior, although they have to take earnings inferior to those of the men. This, of course, throws us back on the question why the area in which women are superior is so restricted. Like women, men are only superior within a certain area, but they have no need to invade the women's field, whereas the women do need to invade theirs. The number of women is certainly appreciably greater than that of men in the 'old' countries from which there is migration, but the difference in the world at large, the real market, cannot be great enough to make much difference. It seems clear that the field within which women show themselves superior to men must be smaller than that in which men show themselves superior to women.

Believers in the generally smaller capacity of women may attribute this, in part at any rate, simply to that smaller capacity. If women are, for productive purposes as a whole, inferior editions of men, it is only natural that there should be a smaller field of occupation in which they excel, although it includes the very large occupation of motherhood. But even if this be, in part, the explanation, it certainly is not the whole explanation. The pressure of competition in the occupations in which women are superior would be less than it is if it were not for restrictions which prevent women from entering many occupations in which they could, if allowed to compete, succeed better than they do at present in occupations in which they are allowed. If these forbidden occupations, of which railway clerical work in this country is a very obvious and important example, were unlocked for women, the women who entered them would be withdrawn partly from the occupations in which women are superior, and partly from the other occupations, while, on the other hand, the men kept out of the formerly reserved occupations would, by their competition in other occupations, tend to lower men's earnings, so that men's and women's earnings would tend to be more equal.

This enlargement of the field of women's employment is probably the most important of the means by which women's earnings could be raised in comparison with men's. It is obstructed not so much by law as by the inertia of employers and their fear of inconvenience from the active resistance of the men employed at present. It is hindered too by the cry for equal wages for men and women, as the most powerful lever for increasing the opportunities of women is taken away if they are not to do the work cheaper. It has been assisted by the invention of new machinery, such as the telephone and the typewriter. If such things had been invented long ago, and owing to the conditions of that time the occupations connected with them had been made men's employments, women would probably have still been shut out from them.

Besides enlargement of the field in which women can be

employed, there are two other important ways in which their earnings might be raised. Firstly, the opinion of the consumer about the comparative quality of things produced by men and things produced by women might be modified in a direction favourable to women. At present, for example, many 'consumers' of the service of waiting at table appear to regard the service as superior when performed by a waiter, even if the waitress handles an equal number of dishes with equal dexterity and dispatch. Opinions – or prejudices – such as these are clearly as capable of being changed as opinions about the beauty of tight or loose skirts, or tall hats and bowlers. A change of opinion or taste might have quite an appreciable effect in increasing the demand for women's labour and raising their earnings. Secondly, women's capacity as compared with that of men might easily be raised, with the effect of increasing their output in the occupations in which they compete with men, as measured not only by taste but by pounds avoir-dupois or cubic yards. Girls as a rule do not have so much spent upon them as boys. If they were better fed and trained, their output would be bigger than it now is in occupations in which they compete with men: their average earnings in such occupations would rise more nearly to that of men, and their improved prospects here would relieve the pressure on the special fields in which women only are employed beause they are superior to men. These special fields might even be somewhat increased in area, as the rise in the capacity of women might add to the list. In some occupations women may be just a little inferior to men at present, and a small rise in capacity might make them more than equal. It should be noticed, however, that an increase of women's output, if it was confined to the employments in which women alone are at present employed, might very probably reduce their earnings by cheapening the unit of output more than the amount per head increased.

The disparity of incomes between the sexes is one of the two most prominent features in the inequality of the distribution of income. The other is the hereditary character of the inequality. Anyone can see that the distribution of income depends largely on the unequal inheritance of those natural qualities which enable one person to get more than another either by ordinary

labour or by better judgment in the management of his property. Careful analysis shows that acquired qualities which have the same effects are also in great measure hereditary, owing to the fact that the children of well-to-do parents have much better opportunities of acquiring them than the children of poor parents. On the top of this comes the fact that property is mostly acquired by way of inheritance, and that it is easier for a person to acquire more by saving when he has already acquired a great deal by inheritance. The result is that when persons are arranged in a scale of incomes from the highest to the lowest, the receivers of the high incomes are easily seen to be chiefly the children of those of the last generation who received in their time the high incomes of that time, and the receivers of the small incomes to be chiefly the children of those of the last generation who received small incomes. There are no clear-cut classes, no definite boundaries over which no man may step. The able members of the poorest class are constantly rising to the top, and the particularly incompetent members of the richest class are constantly falling to the bottom; but all the same, among the bulk of mankind there is a continuous hereditary transmission of inequality of income the importance of which it is foolish to ignore.

Acknowledgments

The Editor and Publishers acknowledge the following copyright owners:

For permission to reproduce Hugh Dalton, The Measurement of the Inequality of Incomes, from the Economic Journal 30 (1920), pp 348–63, and Blackwell Publishers.

For permission to reproduce Hugh Dalton, Some Aspects of the Inequality of Incomes in Modern Communities, Routledge.

For permission to reproduce William Letwin, The Case Against Equality, from Chapter 1 in William Letwin (Ed.), *Against Equality*, The Macmillan Press Ltd, pp 1–70, and the Foundation for Education in Economics.

For permission to reproduce Peter Bauer, *The Grail of Equality*, from Chapter 17 in William Letwin (Ed.), *Against Equality*, The Macmillan Press Ltd, pp 360–82, and the Foundation for Education in Economics.

For permission to reproduce R.H. Tawney, two chapters from *Equality*, Harper Collins Publishers.

For permission to reproduce Edward Cannan, *Wealth: A Brief Explanation of the Causes of Economic Welfare*, Harper Collins Publishers.

For permission to reproduce Lionel Robbins, 'An Essay on the Nature and Significance of Economic Science', The Macmillan Press Ltd.

For permission to reproduce William Charvet, 'The Idea of Equality as a Substantive Principle of Society', from *Political Studies* 17 (1969), pp 1–13, Political Studies Association and Blackwell Publishers.

For permission to reproduce James Woodburn, 'Egalitarian Societies', (Malinowski Lecture 1981) *MAN* (N.S.) 17, 1982, pp 431–51, Royal Anthropological Institute of Great Britain and Ireland.

For permission to reproduce Sidney and Beatrice Webb, extracts from The Decay of Capitalist Civilisation, The Fabian Society.

Index

For permission to reproduce Sidney and Beatrice Webb, extracts from The Decay of Capitalist Civilisation, The Fabian Society.

Index